Looking for Laura

Public Criminology and Hot News

David Wilson

Looking for Laura
Public Criminology and Hot News
David Wilson

Published 2011 by
Waterside Press Ltd.
Sherfield Gables
Sherfield on Loddon
Hook
Hampshire
United Kingdon RG27 0JG

Telephone +44(0)1256 882250
Low cost UK landline calls
0845 2300 733
E-mail enquiries@watersidepress.co.uk
Online catalogue WatersidePress.co.uk

ISBN 9781904380 702 (Paperback)
ISBN 9781908162 007 (e-book)

Cataloguing-In-Publication Data A catalogue record for this book can be obtained from the British Library.

Cover Designed by www.gibgob.com © 2011 Waterside Press. Original image of David Wilson courtesy of Sky TV.

UK distributor Gardners Books 1 Whittle Drive, Eastbourne, East Sussex, BN23 6QH. Tel: +44 (0)1323 521777; sales@gardners.com; www.gardners.com

North American distributor International Specialized Book Services (ISBS) 920 NE 58th Ave, Suite 300, Portland, Oregon, 97213-3786, USA
Tel: 1 800 944 6190 Fax 1 503 280 8832; orders@isbs.com; www.isbs.com

Printed by MPG Group, Kings Lynn.

e-book *Looking for Laura: Public Criminology and Hot News* is available as an ebook (for ISBN, see above) and also to subscribers to Myilibrary and Dawsonera.

Looking for Laura

Public Criminology and Hot News

David Wilson

Foreword Donal MacIntyre

WATERSIDE PRESS

Serial Killers

Hunting Britons and Their Victims 1960-2006

We are not all at-risk everyday from what he terms 'hunting Britons', rather it is people from a variety of vulnerable groups: the elderly, women involved in prostitution, gay men, runaways, 'throwaways' and children and kids moving from place to place.

- Looks at all serial murders in Britain from the 'gay murders' of Michael Copeland in 1960 to the Ipswich murders of 2006

- Throughout, the work follows events from a social and victim-related perspective

'This book is a stunning success, managing to both advance academic debate whilst at the same time, making the reformist agenda more accessible and attractive to a wider audience': *Prison Service Journal*

'A timely—and because of its quality—a significant contribution to the field': *Homicide Studies*

192 pages
Paperback
August 2007
ISBN 9781904380337

Visit WatersidePress.co.uk

Contents

About the author . . . .*viii*

Acknowledgements . . . .*ix*

Foreword . . . .*xi*

Introduction . . . .*xiii*

    Public Criminology! . . . .*xiii*

1. Children, the Internet and the Crime Figures *25*

    Academics on the Telly *31*

    Joining Us Live *34*

    Damned Lies. *36*

    Laura, Shannon and "Pure Evil" *39*

    But What Now? *43*

2. Serial Killer Thrillers *45*

    Deoxyribonucleic Acid *47*

    Forensic Science and Cross-Examination. *49*

    "No Comment" *52*

    Some Further Thoughts on Serial Killers *53*

    Labelling Serial Killers. *56*

    Catching Serial Killers. *60*

    "Breaking News" in Ipswich *62*

3. The Chief Constable

    — The Tale of a Criminal Justice Professional *67*

    Michael Todd QPM *68*

    Cop Culture *72*

    Alison Halford, a Swimming Pool and Mike Todd *75*

    Reform: A New Force? *79*

4. Celebrity Cons
      — Bronson, Banged Up and Bad Girls *87*
Prison Film — Prison Reform?. *91*
Banged Up *97*
"David Blunkett's Banged Up is a Sham". *102*
The Royal Television Society Awards *106*

5. Serial Killers
      — Now You See Them, Now You Don't. *109*
The Academy and the Serial Killer. *110*
Trevor Joseph Hardy *114*
Newsworthy?. *118*
So, Which Serial Killer Becomes the Celebrity? *123*
The Serial Killer in the Academy *126*

6. The Righteous Slaughter of Some Shootings. *131*
And then Another One *136*
A Paranoid Narcissist with a Gun *139*
Similarities and Differences. *142*
Big Bang Lessons? *147*

7. The Offender Profiler *149*
Profiling the Profiler: His Working Methods *151*
Originating Offender Profiles *153*
Talking with Serial Killers *155*
Killers Who Will Not Talk *158*
Organized and Disorganized *159*
Bind, Torture and Kill. *161*
At the End of it All *163*

8. Explaining "Ordinary" Murder and Murder Investigations *167*
Defining Murder. *168*
How Much Murder? *169*
Theories and Explanations. *171*
Psychoanalytical Psychology *174*

Evolutionary Psychology *176*
Social Learning and Cognitive Psychology. *178*
Police-Media Relations During a Murder Investigation *180*
Servicing Needs at Arm's Length *182*
Keeping the Media Onside in a Murder Investigation *190*

Postscript *193*
Still Looking for Laura? *193*

A Guide to Further Reading and Other References *196*
Introduction *196*
Chapter 1. . . . . *196*
Chapter 2 . . . . *197*
Chapter 3 . . . . *198*
Chapter 4 . . . . *199*
Chapter 5 . . . . *199*
Chapter 6 . . . . *201*
Chapter 7 . . . . *202*
Chapter 8 . . . . *203*

Index *205*

About the author

David Wilson is professor of criminology at Birmingham City University where he is Director of the Centre for Applied Criminology. A former prison governor, he is the editor of the *Howard Journal* and well-known as an author, broadcaster and presenter for TV and radio, including the BBC, Channel 4 and Sky. He has written a number of books for Waterside Press, including *Prison(er) Education: Stories of Change and Transformation* (with Ann Reuss), *Images of Incarceration: Representations of Prison in Film and Television Drama* (with Sean O'Sullivan)and *Serial Killers: Hunting Britains and their Victims 1960-2006.*

The Foreword

Donal MacIntyre is one of Europe's best-known and acclaimed investigative journalists, specialising in often high-risk undercover operations and hard-hitting exposés leading to prestigious awards in several countries. He has presented programmes for the BBC, ITV and Channel Five. In 2007, he directed the feature film 'A Very British Gangster: The Rise and Fall of a Crime Boss' set in the Manchester Underworld.

Acknowledgements

There are a number of people that I would like to thank who have helped immeasurably with the completion of this book. At Birmingham City University, Barbara McCalla, Naomi Faulkener, Judith Timms and Charlotte Wasilewski have answered the calls of and written letters to many members of the public who want to discuss public criminology with me, and so too I would like to thank my colleagues at the Centre for Applied Criminology—especially Michael Brookes, Laura Caulfield, Jane Hill, Nick Howe, Craig Jackson, Edward Johnson and Di Kemp. I am also very grateful for the unflagging efforts of BCU's Press Office, especially Sarah Archer, James Tallentire and Vicky Price. Before leaving acknowledgements at the University I would also like to thank my Masters and PhD students, especially Martin Glynn, Harriet Tolputt, Rachel Ashworth, John Lamb and Dean Wilkinson. Outside of Birmingham City University I would like to thank Jamie Bennett, Rob Mawby, James Treadwell and Emma Hughes—the latter two who were once my PhD students.

Jacquie Drewe, Fran Linke, Hannah Clarke and Gordon Wise at Curtis Brown are always a pleasure to work with, and I would especially like to thank Dr Nic Groombridge and Brenda McWilliams for their editorial help and encouragement. I am also grateful to my co-authors of a number of academic articles who have similarly encouraged me to re-work those pieces for this book.

At the Howard League for Penal Reform Frances Crook, Anita Dockley and Andrew Neilson have always been encouraging of my engagement with the media and have often supported me with the necessary "facts and figures" to make me appear sensible in what it is that I am arguing.

In the print and broadcast media I would like to thank Donal MacIntyre for writing the *Foreword* as well as Maureen O'Donnell, Jon Clements, Libby Brooks, Matt Seaton and the various producers and researchers on 'The Jeremy Vine Show'—Thursday wouldn't be the same without you! Special mention must also go to Paul Harrison of Sky News. Leo McKinstry is also always a pleasure to work with — even when he is in France.

Bryan Gibson at Waterside Press has long championed my work and I am very grateful to him for his continued support.

Finally, no book of mine would ever be completed but for the encouragement of Anne, Hugo and Fleur.

Foreword

In journalistic parlance, Professor David Wilson is an accredited source. He is a default repository for an intelligent quote, in-depth analysis and rounded perspectives on crime and the world which it inhabits. The road to this unofficial accreditation is built on excellence, availability and willingness to bring his expertise to a wider audience with all the risks that entails.

And make no mistake, there are huge risks in opening yourself up to media and sharing your vision and views with the great 'unwashed public' through the 'dirty hands of the media'. Inevitably, engaging with the public means diluting and simplifying whereas some academics recoil against such compromises.

They see themselves as above such low art and refuse to engage but to what purpose? David Wilson is a man on a mission and this book is the story of that odyssey. In the words of Lord Reith, the founding father of the BBC, a broadcaster which has nearly become David Wilson's second home, David has taken as his mission the task to 'inform, educate and entertain'.

And by entertaining I mean engaging, because if you don't engage then you cannot educate and inform. Wilson has taken on this mission fully aware of the risks, but has selflessly created a public footprint for criminologists as well as his vision for justice and fairness in our society.

He has helped mould public opinion and public debate in an often volatile and combustible arena and move it towards a more moderate and intelligent space. This is an honest and timely book written by a man not afraid of labels, nor afraid to speak the truth. It is an inspiring and intelligent read. For journalists, the police and citizens alike, there is so much to take from David's work.

The joy of the book is its accessibility. There is meat and weight in these pages and for me the chapter dealing with the Raul Moat case—'The Righteous Slaughter of Some Shootings'—shows David Wilson at his best: open, truthful and wise. In a time of frenzied observation there is always room for smart analysis that transcends the limitations of the intelligentsia and permeates the lives and minds of ordinary people.

There is never a better time to write a book like this and never a better and more appropriate writer to do the job.

Donal MacIntyre

February 2011

Introduction

Public Criminology!

Thursday is my teaching day. In other words it is a day devoted to students, both undergraduate and postgraduate, in all their various shapes and sizes and aimed at — as much as passing on to them academic information — trying to resolve their problems. These can range from the small, to the frankly gargantuan.

"Can you just have a look at this essay, before I hand it in?"

"Professor Wilson, my mother's been shot".

Sometimes teaching merges rather seamlessly into social work. Even so, Thursday is for teaching and therefore Thursday is also the day that I never do interviews for the media. Anyway, that at least is the theory.

In practice, rather than in theory, the university has cunningly positioned a broadcast quality ISDN line just 40 yards away from my office and so, if the poor researcher who phones up is especially pleading (or, indeed, is one of my former students), I'll agree to say something about the latest moral panic or *crime du jour.*

Usually it is the 'Jeremy Vine Show' on BBC Radio 2 that calls because, over the last four years, they've clearly worked out that I've got access to an ISDN line over my lunch break on a Thursday and so, perhaps more often than is good for me, I'll offer an opinion about various crimes and punishments and assorted groups of offenders. I've become such a regular that I now know most of the researchers and producers by name and on one programme they even congratulated my son on air for getting three 'A's in his A levels. I was rather touched, even if my son was somewhat less thrilled — I think that he hated the fuss. I thought that I had better not let him know that a well-known serial killer—on hearing the announcement—also sent his congratulations to him via a letter that he wrote to me at the university.

Because Thursdays are for teaching, the rest of the week is taken up with research, writing and, increasingly, administration. Anyway, that again is the theory. I try and keep this last chore to only one day per week, but as the Director of the Centre for Applied Criminology, one of Birmingham City University's "Centres of Research Excellence", I've started to feel the pressure about making certain that we are all on track for the Research Excellence Framework and that grant proposals are written and articles published. Professor John Rouse, one of the ex-Deans of my Faculty, used to joke that managing academics was like "herding cats" and I'm now beginning to understand the truth behind the humour. Talented academic people don't like to be tied down to deadlines—to actual work in fact—and less-talented academic people like to pretend that they are more talented and academic than they are, so as to claim the same rights. Frankly, administration is beginning to take over Wednesdays and Fridays, leaving time for research and writing on Mondays and Tuesdays. I'm writing this introduction on a Monday.

As I write, the telephone rings. It's a journalist from a Scottish paper called *The Sunday Mail*—which serialised my last book—and he wants to ask me questions about HM Prison Peterhead. I try to steer him as best as I can towards talking about the possibilities of treating sex offenders and how prison regimes, even overcrowded ones, can be places—often against all the odds—where good work can be done.

I'm not certain that he was convinced and, given that I spoke to him on the day that it was reported that there had been a murder in HM Prison Grendon—the only prison in Europe that operates exclusivley as a therapeutic community—neither was I. There are just too many people in prison at the moment and if we want to see real penal reform those numbers have to fall. How can I help to make that goal a reality? It was thinking about this issue several years ago that led me to consciously experiment with various ways to influence the public debate about imprisonment and who gets locked up, which, in turn, has led to my experiment in public criminology.

I have long been associated with the Howard League for Penal Reform and I am now vice-chair of that wonderful charity, which is, incidentally, the oldest penal reform organization in the world and enjoys United Nations consultative status. I am also vice-chair of New Bridge—set up in 1956 to create links between prisoners and the community; chair of the Grendon Friends Trust; and a trustee of the Prisons Video Trust. I am a co-editor of *The Howard Journal of Criminal Justice*, one of the premier academic criminology journals in the country. I mention these roles and positions because they are just some of the formal—and established ways—by which, over the course of my career, I have tried to influence public policy about prisons, offenders and what should happen to them. They are the running thread behind the academic work that I do, but they are not what this experiment in public criminology has been about.

Rather, for the past few years, I have very deliberately and consciously adopted a strategy whereby I talk to the print and broadcast media. By this I don't just mean talking to a few old friends from my undergraduate days who now work as producers, or as editors in the broadsheet media, or on "respectable" radio and TV programmes—as many criminologists surely have done and still do. Instead I have been engaging with journalists who want to ask some toe-curlingly specific and not at all respectable questions. These can often be about issues that are, for want of a better description, "tabloid staples". You know the sort of thing—sex offenders, serial killers, naming and shaming, child killers, "holiday camp prisons" (have I mentioned sex offenders?), bringing back hanging, yobs, slobs and ASBOs. However, I have wanted to see if I could answer these questions by putting them into the broader context that recognises the complexity of what it is I'm being asked about. A complexity that introduces the "grey" about these issues that are usually reported upon as if they were simply black and white. So, in one sense this strategy has had two dimensions: one that involves my own behaviour and also the behaviour of the media, and a second which has a much wider target.

Clearly, as far as my own behaviour is concerned, this has not only been about my engagement with the media, but also about my attempts through that engagement to get the media to understand and then report upon the bigger criminological picture. This, in turn, has also involved trying to get other criminologists to behave in a similar way, and thus to take seriously what the media and their readers and viewers are interested in discussing. For, whether we like it or not, there is a public debate going on about crime and punishment that transcends the broadsheet press and "respectable" news programmes and, dare I say it, what academic criminologists discuss. And, all too often, it is that public debate that seems to dictate the policies that successive governments have taken towards crime and punishment. Unfortunately, because that public debate doesn't usually hear from criminologists it cannot take too seriously criminological theory, because for most of the time that criminological theory never gets expressed. That's a pity, for I believe that, by engaging with this debate, it is possible to inject some reason into what is understood about crime and punishment and which serves to cool the often red-hot nature of the public discourse about these matters. Anyway, that's the theory.

Along the way, as this loose strategy has taken more shape, I have come to believe that criminologists have a choice. We can either isolate ourselves in our "ivory towers" and have nothing to do with the media, or we can engage and deal with what they care about and try to shape those concerns accordingly. In various ways I have very deliberately pursued this latter course and this book can be read as part of the product of those labours. It can also be read as a plea for other criminologists to do the same.

Has this strategy been successful? How should I measure success? There are some immediate things that I could point to. For example, for the last two years, I have topped a poll of the "most quoted criminologists" in the country, compiled by Dr Nic Groombridge and published in *Times Higher Education*. I have made documentary series for the BBC and Channel 5 and one-off documentaries for Channel 4 and Sky. Some of my proudest moments as a criminologist have come through writing and presenting documentaries such as "Too Young to Die?" on BBC1, about the plight of children on America's death rows (access to which I would never have secured as a mere "Professor"), and "No More Victims" on BBC4 about the work of Circles of Support and Accountability in Canada. I have written and presented "specials" for BBC2's "Newsnight", about the increasing numbers of elderly prisoners in our penal system and about fire-starting for BBC1's flagship children's strand "Newsround". I have made programmes about forensic science and serial killers; documentaries about historical figures; appeared on every major news programme; and written and presented series about the development of our criminal justice system both on radio and TV.

A series that I helped to make was even nominated for a Royal Television Society Award. I describe some of these — and other programmes — in the pages which follow, and especially in *Chapter 4*.

I've even managed to encourage a number of other criminologists to speak to the media, in part through formally press-releasing the lead article from *The Howard Journal of Criminal Justice* and developing a column in that journal called "Counterblast". Admittedly, many of those who I have encouraged have been former students of mine — such as James Treadwell at Leicester University and the child protection expert, Mark Williams-Thomas — or colleagues at the university such as Professors Doug Sharp, Craig Jackson, and Nick Howe. There is still more work to be done. However, I am not trying to take credit for their media efforts, or indeed to ignore several other criminologists who have also been prepared to share their work with a wider and non-academic audience. Indeed, I have already drawn attention to Dr Nic Groombridge who has been heroically experimenting with "new media" through his criminology blog and Twitter and of course, the criminologist, Professor Laurie Taylor who continues to present "Thinking Allowed" on BBC Radio 4. So too, Dr Martina Feilzer, now of Bangor University, wrote a column in *The Oxford Times* about crime and punishment. However, I do think that my very deliberate and sustained approach to engage with the "old media" and their public debates about crime and punishment is worth thinking about more carefully.

As for the print media, the period covered within the book charts another very conscious decision to stop writing so often for *The Guardian* (although I quote from several articles that were published there) and to start writing in the *Daily Mail* and *Tribune*. These two papers are not natural bed-fellows, but the move to the *Daily Mail* was made because I felt that my views and opinions were naturally accepted by most of the readers of *The Guardian* and if I wanted to see real change then getting the readers of the *Daily Mail* onside seemed to me to be more important. I'm still debating with myself if that part of the strategy has worked, although I have thoroughly enjoyed learning to write about issues that are important to me in a different style and aimed at a different readership. The move to *Tribune* was meant to reinforce the fact that in deciding to write for the *Daily Mail* I hadn't lost my left-leaning principles.

Towards the end of the period covered by this book, Professors Ian Loader and Richard Sparks — two of the UK's most eminent criminologists — published a book, which they entitled *Public Criminology?* Please note, there's a clue in the title (as there is in the title to this *Introduction*). Unlike this work, theirs was not a book about "Public Criminology" at all, but rather about "Public Criminology?" The question mark revealed that they were not advocating for — or indeed against — public criminology (a phrase borrowed from Public Sociology), but rather that they had used this merely as a "convenient and available shorthand for, and a space within which to think about, a set of issues that have long held our interest and which form the backdrop to, and explicit focus of, this book". So even though they have both previously occupied positions that caught the public eye — for example, Loader as a Commissioner on the independent Commission on English Prisons Today and Sparks as a defender of the Barlinnie Special Unit — they claim to have "no hotline to success" about how to write reports to persuade government or assist an NGO, or how to survive in a television studio. In other words their book was not a manual of how to *do* public criminology, even if they then argue that criminology has to "cultivate the will and necessary tools to make sense of the place and functions of the debate around crime and punishment in contemporary political culture".

On the other hand, this book can, in part, be read as a manual about how public criminology can be *done*, or at least how it has by me. As such, some of the tools that I have used have been the different writing styles that I have had to develop to reach the audiences that I want to reach and my growing familiarity with how to communicate effectively during a radio or TV interview. I still sometimes find these tools difficult to work with, even if I have had some advantages in honing my skills. For example, I was given presenting training by the BBC in 1999, prior to co-presenting the BBC1 series "Crime Squad" and I was commissioned to write a weekly column for the *Birmingham Post* almost from the month that I took up my appointment at the university. This latter experience allowed me to begin the process of cultivating a different writing style. It would probably now be more accurate to say "styles", given that how I write is dictated by a number of factors such as whether the piece is for a journal or a book, a particular newspaper, or commissioned as a TV or radio documentary, and the intended audience.

So, too, my work with the various charities and Non-Governmental Organizations (NGOs) that I have mentioned, has given me great insight into how policy related to crime and punishment is developed and how the political process listens to a number of competing voices. Over time I have learned that the voice that gets listened to is not necessarily the one which shouts the loudest, or even the one that has the best "evidence" to support its argument. Making things happen in the world of public policy is often more complex and decidedly more idiosyncratic.

However, the book is meant to be more than just a "how to" manual. Given that I have been using this strategy of media engagement for several years, I hope it also charts the threats and opportunities that using such a strategy entails. There are, for example, a number of threats that I have had to carefully negotiate. Above all it has been important to remember that I am an academic and that I am not part of the media, even if the temptations to simply become a presenter, or a commentator—filling space on the airwaves—have become more real as I have grown in confidence about how to work with the media. If this was a book about ethnography, I'd probably label this temptation as "going native".

Frankly, over time many of the journalists who have interviewed me have become friends and so I understand all too well the pressures that they are under to get the story, or to be the first at the scene of a crime or some other tragedy. I have watched money being exchanged for information and the door of a victim's family being knocked on in the hope of an interview. None of these techniques would have been approved by my university's ethics committee. I understand how pressured they are about deadlines, or how they are sometimes desperate to get someone—anyone—to say something about what has caught the editor's attention on that particular day.

These various pressures have to be resisted, or you are quickly reduced to becoming what one journalist described as "the rent a quote" and another as a "media tart". In fact, at a rough estimate, I will now turn down nine out of ten requests that I get to comment or to be interviewed. There is also the associated threat that you simply become used as an unpaid researcher by the media; a sort of "one-stop" criminological shop who becomes their first port of call about any criminal matter. Indeed, this becomes cumulative. Once your name is associated with a story it exists there forever in the cuttings — made all the more accessible through Google — until another similar story emerges, or someone with whom you have previously worked recommends you to one of their friends. And so it goes on. In short, engaging with the media takes time and you have to be able to develop the skill of saying "No", or as I have had to do, hire an agent.

There are other threats too. Sometimes some journalists can become involved in what Dr Rob Mawby of Leicester University has described as "supermarket journalism". In other words, the journalists simply "buy" their stories off the shelf from the press offices of the organizations that are responsible for "managing the media" about a particular crime or event. In my experience, police force press offices are particularly adept at spinning what they want to get reported (and not reported) and the threats here for me have been that I am often used to counter this spin — which has the potential to damage my own relations with the police — and that true investigative journalism gets left behind. In this respect I have become fascinated by the process whereby some serial killing episodes get reported and how others all but disappear — a theme I investigate in *Chapter 5*. Of course, there are different issues when journalists begin to investigate, for example, a series of murders for themselves and this is something that I discuss in *Chapter 8*.

But I should not ignore the opportunities that this strategy has created. Indeed, I have already mentioned how the media have an enviable knack of creating access to people and organizations to which academics would simply not get access — certainly whilst events are unfolding, or even later on their own terms when things have quietened down. It has been through the media that I have been able to secure access to, for example, everything from crime scenes, courtrooms and specialist units within prisons in this country, to the death rows of the United States of America. I have also been able to use my own knowledge of people and organizations, or developments that need wider publicity to get them the attention that they deserve. In this respect it was my research for an academic book called *Innocence Betrayed: Paedophilia, the Media and Society* which first drew public attention to the pioneering work of Circles of Support and Accountability in Ontario, Canada with warrant-expired paedophiles, and I was subsequently able to ensure that their work was filmed as a documentary for the BBC. Of note, a charity called Circles UK has now been set up in this country.[1]

This is, of course, another opportunity—the reach that the media has in relation to audience numbers. Quite simply many more people are going to read an article that you have written in a newspaper, or watch a programme that you have made for broadcast, than will read a peer-reviewed paper in a specialist journal, or attend a criminology conference.

Of course, the greatest opportunity that I have witnessed emanating from this strategy is that people respond to what the media are interested in discussing; they react to what is being discussed; and, just occasionally as a result of that reaction, things change, or action gets taken. My use of the word "people" of course hides a multitude of "peoples". My postbag at Birmingham City University has grown enormously and, because it is obvious where I work, I also find that many members of the public think nothing of calling me up and offering me their opinions about what might be in the news. In short, they see me as part of the public discourse about crime and punishment. Sometimes this can be heart-warming; on other occasions rather annoying, to say the least. But so, too, think tanks, elected politicians and other policy-makers also want to discuss with me what I have been describing or commenting upon and the opportunities that flow from these contacts are limitless. Perhaps if this was a book about the Research Excellence Framework I would call this "impact".

The temptation here is to name some changes—some impact—but I want to resist that temptation for a number of reasons, although it should also be obvious from what I go on to describe in the book what I am thinking about. First, most of the policy-makers and politicians who I have encountered don't like to admit where the pressures have come from that have influenced what they have done. Identifying that I may have contributed to that pressure seems to me to offer up a hostage to fortune for any changes that have taken place. Second, how in reality would I measure that I actually did influence a policy development through engaging with the media? There doesn't seem to me to be any direct way that I could do so, although perhaps I might suggest that the change in government during the period

---

1. www.circles-uk.org.uk

that this book covers has resulted in some very different messages about the use of prison being expressed by the new Coalition government than by those who previously held power. Did I play a small part in these messages being used, as opposed to others that might have been communicated? Frankly, I don't know, (and, of course, we have had a banking crisis which has led to financial pressures being exerted to stop using prison as much as we do) although I did yell with delight when I heard one politician use an exact sentence in a speech that he was giving that I had written in an earlier article—"It is perfectly possible to have less crime, safer communities and fewer people in prison". We still have to wait and see if that sentence can be turned into the reality of public policy.

So far I have introduced the idea of the "public" within this strategy but not really described anything of the criminology. Here I will use a very specific example of how the strategy that I have outlined has come together in relation to one public "hotspot" about a specific type of offender—the serial killer—and on how this gets reported.

Criminologists have rarely discussed serial killing as a phenomenon—it seemed almost to be beneath them—or when they did, they concentrated on issues relating to definition. During the period that this book covers, serial killers have struck on a number of occasions—most obviously in Ipswich in 2006 and more recently in Bradford in 2010. There has also been the case of Peter Tobin. I have commented on, and written about, all of these cases, and much of that comment was based on academic work that I wrote up in *Serial Killers: Hunting Britons and Their Victims, 1960–2006*, which is also published by Waterside Press. I have made these comments not just because serial killing is a media and entertainment staple, but because criminologically there was something that I felt could be done to harness this public fascination to a greater public policy agenda. Specifically, by pointing out that British serial killers overwhelmingly target just five groups of people—the elderly, prostitutes, gay men, runaways and throwaways, and babies and infants—I have very consciously tried to move the debate about serial killing away from the individual serial killer and his motivation, and focus more directly on why these five groups are so vulnerable to attack. Such an approach brings us directly into the sphere of criminology through, for example, the need to discuss how prostitution gets policed, or homophobia, or the various pressures that exist on young people to leave home.

Throughout the book I use two distinct sources. The first is my reflexive diary. I have kept such a diary for over 20 years and my bookshelves now groan with the strain of accommodating hundreds of leather-bound volumes of Paperchase's finest. Sometimes I have simply transferred whole sections from these diaries into the text, which I hope gives a sense of the immediacy of doing public criminology for the broadcast media as well as the various tensions and conflicts that I have been under at the time. I also use several newspaper articles that I have been commissioned to write to illustrate the themes of several of the chapters, and include some of the public reaction to those articles. These are but a fraction of the material that I have written for various newspapers and magazines over the last few years.

The second source has been the various academic books and articles that I have written. These are not simply reproduced verbatim but have been re-written to suit the style of the book and the messages that I want it to convey. Most obviously they are almost totally devoid of references. One of the first lessons that I learned from a "trade" publisher of "true crime" is that no reader wants to wade through references. In no uncertain terms she let me know that the reader has bought your book because they want to know your opinion — even if that opinion has been built on the ideas, theories and writings of others. My compromise with this approach has always been that I try to name those by whom I have been influenced, and more formally also produce a *Guide to Further Reading* when I write in the true crime genre. I am also using such a guide in this book, even if I regard what I have produced here as more formally academic than true crime.

Does this distinction matter? Is it really important to badge and label our work as criminologists in this way? What I care about is influence and trying to use all of the means that I have available to me to make a difference about issues that I have long felt passionately about. Frankly I don't care if this is labelled as true crime or as academic criminology. Indeed, I am more or less certain that most of the students who come on to our university courses have applied because they have been introduced to criminology through true crime. Nor do I mind that for some I am seen as a "Left Idealist", or that others might view me as a populist. I'm not particularly keen to be seen as a "Cultural Criminologist" or even as a "Public Criminologist", even if these two labels might, in fact, actually apply to me. Rather, what I care about is making things "better"—from communities being safer and large corporations and governments being held to account, to fewer people being used, abused, hurt or killed. I'm not certain that I know what label best applies to these concerns.

Anyway, that's the theory and I would be delighted to discuss all of this with you further. Read and enjoy what follows and by all means call me up to talk and debate about the ideas or opinions that this book contains.

But please, remember, Thursdays are my teaching days!

CHAPTER ONE

Children, the Internet and the Crime Figures

The news in January 2009 was temporarily dominated by 15-year-old Laura Stainforth, who had gone missing from her home town of Cleethorpes, in Lincolnshire. Well, actually, she wasn't "missing" at all because she had in fact "disappeared" with 49-year-old Robert Andrew Williams, who is also known as David Ingram, and who was already on police bail for an alleged rape of a 16-year-old girl in December 2008, in West Sussex. Far from having disappeared, Laura's CCTV image seemed to be everywhere in, and on, the media, and so everywhere that Laura had gone prior to running away with Williams—and especially at Grimsby railway station where the pair had probably first met up, and then in Dover where they had been seen trying to sell two mobile phones—had been captured on screen for us to view. Dover seemed to me to be the most important clue. No doubt they were already in Europe, and most likely in France by the time that these rather desperate images were being consumed with breakfast.

Laura is white and has dark brown, shoulder-length hair, which was tied in a ponytail in the images that we saw. She also seemed to be a little overweight, and was wearing a cream-coloured zip-up jacket, light blue jeans and a pair of black trainers.

According to an increasingly eager number of newspaper and online reports, Laura had met Williams through an internet chatroom. I doubted that he had presented himself online to her as a 49-year-old man on police bail for an alleged rape, and he had probably implied that he was younger—much younger—than he actually was, and more than likely good-looking. Very early on, Williams, in the various press reports, came across as someone who liked to play with his identity (why else would he call himself David Ingram?) and so he had no doubt carefully constructed an online profile that he thought would attract the attention of young girls. Perhaps that's also how he had gained access to the 16-year-old who he is alleged to have raped. Even so, his description of himself would have been the easiest part of the "grooming" to which he would have subjected Laura, and by the time that they met — when she could clearly see that Williams was no Brad Pitt — he would have convinced her that he knew her better than anyone else, and that he was the right person to deal with all of her problems and worries. By then they would, together, and in secret, have had fantastic dreams to make their lives less ordinary, and in the process Williams would have become Laura's best friend, her confidante, the perfect antidote to the problems that she felt that she had at home, at school or in Cleethorpes. So the fact that he wasn't physically as she might have wanted — or as he had presented — would be something that she could forgive, or at least temporarily overlook.

I've written about this process before, in June 2007 in a column in *The Guardian*. I called that particular column "Radio Ga Ga" given that it related to the Jo Whiley Programme on Radio 1, but what really interested me was how people reacted to what I wrote.

Radio Ga Ga

On the day that CEOP[1] were rightly celebrating smashing a British-based paedophile ring that worked through peer-to-peer networks on the internet, I happened to be driving in my car with my 15-year-old son who had just finished his GCSEs, and who seemingly as a result had to be ferried everywhere to celebrate this rite of passage. So instead of listening to Radio 4 or Radio 3, I found myself bullied into tuning into Radio 1 and the Jo Whiley show.

There is — seemingly — a regular feature called "Changing Tracks" on the programme, whereby listeners are encouraged to phone or email the show to nominate a song that has particular memories for them, and which frankly was

---

1. The Child Exploitation and Online Protection Centre works across the UK tackling sexual abuse and provides advice and guidance to young people and their parents. See http://www.ceop.gov.uk

a concept not unfamiliar to me, or I imagine, to those of you who remember Simon Bates.

On the day that I was driving, an unnamed girl contacted the programme to say that she wanted to nominate a song which had helped her to overcome the memories of being sexually abused by her stepfather. As the friendly, "big sister" Jo explained, this listener had been abused and as a result had found solace in food. In doing so she had tried to make herself unattractive to boys — and men — by being overweight, and then over time, through an online friendship, she had found love.

I listened, worried about where all of this might be heading, and lo and behold Jo informed us that the "Changing Tacks" listener wanted to nominate a song that reminded her of meeting up with her online friend. She had lied to her mother about how they had met — she said that they had met at work—and she had travelled to some undisclosed destination to see him. The song that she nominated was the one that was playing in his car when they met. Cue big ballad, and the "happy ending".

I was incandescent with anger and immediately phoned (and subsequently emailed too) the show, to point out that here was a child — she was 15, meeting up with a man (after all the title is justified by the fact that he was driving his own car) that she had met online, travelling to see him unaccompanied, and having lied to her mother about where she was going. The happy ending that the segment in the show seemed to endorse was at best misjudged and at worse a crass dereliction of everyone's duty to protect children from those paedophiles who prey on a child's loneliness, and often themselves masquerade as children on the internet to groom their victims into a meeting.

I never heard anything from the Jo Whiley programme, and I probably didn't expect to. However, for what it's worth, no one should encourage a child — in whatever fashion — to meet up with an "online friend" without being accompanied by an adult, and to do so is merely undermining the work done by CEOP and all the other organizations who fight the good fight against paedophiles and what they are trying to do.

And, by the way, my son now thinks I am completely "uncool".

The Guardian has one of the biggest online communities in the world and what I write usually attracts its fair share of very right-wing and critical comment, which is maybe surprising given the ideological stance of the paper. This column was no exception. Typical comments in relation to "Radio Ga Ga" came from "Pinkgum" who thought that "a 15-year-old has every right to go out unaccompanied and every right to meet people online … meeting people you have never met before is a completely natural thing to do"; "HerrEMott" thought that the article was simply "hysteria, hysteria, hysteria"; and, "MrPikeBishop" questioned, "aren't people allowed older or younger friends these days? Even older or younger lovers?"

It is impossible to know the true identity of those who comment in this way, so I do not know the most basic information about the writers' genders, ages, race, or even the part of the World that they might be writing from, although it is sometimes possible to make a reasonable guess. Might it be fair to suggest, for example, that "MrPikeBishop" has himself (and I am also presuming that he is a "he") a younger lover, or has had a younger lover, or at least that he does not find it morally offensive for a 15-year-old to have sexual relations with an older man? Of course the fact that this is illegal does not seem to have featured in his argument, but his, and indeed the other comments that were made in response to this column, did seem to reveal a widespread ambivalence about children and childhood. After all, for all the claims that this was "hysteria" and that meeting strangers was "natural", the simple facts remain that the 15-year-old featured on "Changing Tracks" was a child, who, like Laura Stainforth, deserved to have our protection from potentially adult abusers who might take advantage of her loneliness or unhappiness, and that there are far better ways to deal with the problems that young people have than encouraging them to run away from home to meet up with strangers who they might have met in chatrooms.

Our ambivalent attitude towards childhood or children results in many different things but, above all, children—especially other people's children—have to be older earlier in their lives, so that, paradoxically, we adults can inhabit the space that we call childhood for much longer. As a result, childhood has become a fiercely contested space and some children resolve that conflict by simply opting out of the competition altogether and running away. In fact children running away from home—and the associated phenomenon of "throwaways" (children being thrown out of their homes) — is all too common in England and Wales, even if it is rarely commented upon; in other words, even if it hardly ever becomes "news".

The British charity, The Children's Society, has conducted extensive research with young people aged 16 years or under who leave home for one reason or another, and they were the driving force behind the very first refuge for child runaways — the Central London Teenage Project — which opened in 1985. They draw distinctions between those young people who make a decision to leave — or "run away" from home — and those who were forced, or who felt that they were forced, to leave home — the "throwaways". Some young people do not see themselves as having run away from home at all, and would prefer to describe themselves as "staying away" from home. There are also important distinctions to be made between running away and young people being reported to the police as missing, by their carers, as not all young runaways are reported as missing. Research in the late 1980s — based on missing person reports — estimated that there were some 100,000 incidents of young people under the age of 18 years being reported as missing in Britain annually, which gives some idea of the scale of the problem.

The Children's Society research — conducted first in 1999 and more recently in 2005 — with 10,772 young people in 70 mainstream schools, 11 pupil referral units and 13 special schools — paints a depressing picture of the numbers of young people who leave, or are forced out of their homes, and the circumstances in which they find themselves as a consequence. In 2005 there were at least 66,000 first-time runaways who stayed away from home for at least a night in England and Wales, and the majority of young runaways are, just like Laura Stainforth, in the 13- to 15-year-old age group. Some 7.5% of young people in England aged 14 or 15 years run away for at least a night. Perhaps even worse, ten per cent of their sample who had run away were under 11 years old. Girls were more likely to run away than were boys, as were those children with moderate learning difficulties, or who characterised themselves as gay or lesbian. Most runaways were white, or young people of mixed race.

In looking beyond these basic categorisations The Children's Society tried to determine if there was a link between the structure of the family within which young people lived as teenagers, and the likelihood of them running away. They discovered that young people living in lone parent families were around twice as likely to run away as those living with both parents, and young people living in stepfamilies were almost three times as likely. In each of the above cases, young people who ran away were more likely to have a negative view of their relationship with their parent or carer—a finding which suggests a general unhappiness at home, or at school. For example, a third of young runaways said that they had problems connected with attending school, and those young people who had been excluded from school were three times more likely to run away compared with young people who did not have issues at school. Poverty was also a factor, and The Children's Society's research was specifically designed to identify young people living in low-income families through asking questions about the number of adults in the household with a paid job, and whether the young person was entitled to free school meals. Of the young people who indicated that they were entitled to free school meals, 13.4 per cent had run away overnight, compared to just under ten per cent of those who said that they were not entitled. So, too, 15.6 per cent of those young people who ran away lived in families with no adults in paid employment, compared with just under ten per cent of those young people in families where there was at least one adult in paid employment.

Most young people reported problems at home as being the primary reason for their running away. In particular, they described conflict with parents and other family members, physical, sexual and emotional abuse and neglect. Throughout their research the voices of young people being "slapped", "beaten up", "hurt" and "hit" are heard time and again. Quite simply it is clear from The Children's Society's research that many of the young people who run away do not find home a safe environment, and as a consequence many suffered from depression, which led to many wanting to self-harm or take their own lives.

All of this is not to imply that Laura Stainforth met up with Williams for all, or indeed any, of these reasons—especially given that her family was quick to report her as missing to the police, and then made increasingly frantic appeals to the local and national media for her to come home—but rather is presented here to show how widespread this problem is, what it is that drives many young people to run away, and who are usually never reported as having done so. What is it that makes Laura's story news, but not the stories of the 66,000 young people who ran away in 2005? Might it be that we are simply interested in the vicarious pleasures of "the chase", but that there is no audience for the circumstances that create that chase in the first place? After all, chases can often end in crashes — a prospect which serves to heighten the pleasure of the audience — and I worried that some of the interest in Laura might also be because people wanted to see what her "crash" might look like.

Academics on the Telly

BBC's "Look North" phoned and asked if I would agree to be interviewed "down the line" on their 6.30pm news slot about Laura's disappearance. I weighed things up. I had still the school run to do, as my wife was abroad for a short break with her sister, and I had promised to help my son prepare for the psychology exam which he would be sitting the following day.

Siobhan — the programme's researcher — was persuasive, and flattered me that she had read some of the things that I had written about the subject. So I agreed, and I let her know that the closest studio to my home is BBC Oxford. This usually confuses most people in the media, as they think that because I teach at Birmingham City University I must live in Birmingham, rather than in leafy north Buckinghamshire. Even worse, I used to use a studio in Milton Keynes which was close to where we live, but that closed down a couple of years ago, so now I am forced to drive into Oxford, which is some 40 minutes away. On a good day, that's a round trip of just under two hours, depending on the state of the traffic on the A34. Only "Sky News" regularly interviews me at my house, and my neighbours have now got used to the huge, intimidating "Sky News" truck pulling up in the drive, spewing out cables and wires, and then feeding them in through the window of my study before the interview goes "live". I like giving live interviews best of all, as I always feel that I can say what it is that I want to say without being edited, and having my comments twisted and re-fashioned to suit the narrative of the story that the news programme wants to create.

I asked Siobhan for my travelling expenses, as I wanted to drive into Oxford rather than accept the taxi that had been offered to me. This seemed to cause a problem. In fact, money always causes a problem when I am asked to do interviews. News and Current Affairs never seem to have any budget whatsoever, and so I get out of most interview requests simply by asking for a fee. So over the years, asking for a fee has become a way of rationing my appearances on TV and radio because I know that as there is no budget, that asking for payment is simply another way of saying "I'm not doing it". If the person making the request is not to be deflected, then I direct them towards my redoubtable agent, who has got bags of experience in dealing with various producers who think that academics should be bending over backwards just to appear on the telly. "He's one of the country's leading criminologists", she'll say, "why should he appear on your show to give his expert opinion, based on years of research— for nothing?"

Siobhan quickly got permission to pay my travelling expenses (I was subsequently sent a BBC cheque for £21.74), and then asked me some further questions about Laura and Williams. I suggested that they'd be caught quite quickly, and then mused whether or not to mention that I doubted that Laura would be harmed. By that I didn't mean sexually assaulted, but rather attacked, or even murdered by Williams. That would be rare—even for a man on the run—but I reasoned that it was probably better not to raise it at all, as it might, nonetheless, worry Laura's family. Thankfully, Siobhan didn't ask me anything about this, but rather sketched out the two areas around which they wanted to construct the interview. In a nutshell, they wanted to ask "what type of man" makes contact on the internet with young girls, and "what sorts of girls" tend to agree to meet up with people who they have met online. We talked for about five minutes, and I then made my apologies as I had to get over to my children's school, bring them home, give them something to eat and then get ready to drive to Oxford. My 17-year-old son is now old enough to look after his younger sister.

BBC Oxford is never very welcoming and they positively hate people parking in their cramped lot. I usually have to go on bended knee to some "job'sworth" for daring to bring my car to their studio, and asking for a parking space. It's easier later in the day, when presumably the journalists working on the day shift have gone home and the smaller numbers working the late shift have taken their place. Thankfully no "job'sworth" blocked my entry. I was supposed to meet my "fixer" or "greeter"—someone called Chris—who was to get me sorted out in a studio, but the traffic to get to Oxford that night had been light and so I sat in the car park listening to Obama's inauguration speech on PM. The cadences and many of the phrases were familiar from the speeches that he had given on the campaign trail, but I cried nonetheless, so I was rather pleased that my mobile phone rang. It was Siobhan asking me how I "wanted to be introduced". I would have thought that she would have worked that out already, but I said "Professor of Criminology at Birmingham City University" and, on reflection, concluded that it was just as well that she had checked.

Birmingham City University (BCU) used to be called The University of Central England, but no-one knew where that was, so we have only recently been "re-branded" as BCU. Worse still, people kept getting the old name wrong, and on one memorable occasion I was introduced on BBC Radio Scotland as "Professor of Criminology at the University of Middle England". Perhaps they thought that Tolkien was the Vice-Chancellor.

I asked Siobhan who would be interviewing me and she let me know that it was their regular newscaster, Peter Levy. That was helpful to know. Using the name of the person conducting the interview is a trick that was taught to me some time ago, as it seems to suggest intimacy, and at times even complicity. It certainly makes me feel—if not appear—more professional when I am being interviewed, and for an academic (and anyone else for that matter) that's important.

Most of my academic peers would rather do a year's marking than sit in front of a camera. I have never been able to work out if that's because they tend to be rather snooty about the media. From what many have told me, they often regard it as "cheap and nasty" and not at all as valuable as a peer-reviewed article in an academic journal—that will nonetheless, in all likelihood, be read by approximately 15 people. Or, if they are not snooty, perhaps they are simply scared by the whole process of being interviewed in a studio? In fact, tonight's interview—"down the line"—is for me the hardest type of interview that I ever do, given that I have to sit in a studio with an ear-piece precariously shoved into my head, looking directly at camera but unable to see the interviewer, with a fraction of a second time-delay between their speaking and me hearing what is being asked, all set against the backdrop of various BBC Oxford journalists walking about, talking and drinking tea. Whatever the cause, it does seem to me that if academics ever want to reach an audience outside of academia then they will have to engage with the media and learn the skills that they need to use to make themselves comfortable in presenting themselves to a wider audience.

After coverage of the Presidential inauguration ended, the next three news stories were all crime-related, including the appalling tale of a 70-year-old man convicted at Kilmarnock Crown Court in Scotland for sexually abusing his daughters and impregnating two of them. His name wasn't revealed so as to protect the identity of his victims, who presumably had to think very carefully about bringing charges against their father. I wondered if they had in the past also tried to run away from their home, or if they had simply felt unable to escape the abuse that he had meted out to them? Justice for them came only when they were adults — when they had a "voice" that was denied to them in childhood, and when their abuser was an elderly man.

Joining Us Live

I rang the bell of the back door at BBC Oxford, and a glamorous young blonde woman let me in. Another, heavily-pregnant woman, asked me who I was and I gave my name and explained what I was supposed to be doing, and also told her that my "greeter's" name was "Chris". For whatever reason, the heavily-pregnant woman tried to repeat my name but called me "David Waddesdon". I smiled and corrected her, and she apologised and said that she had got a lot on her mind.

Chris duly appeared. He was in his mid-twenties, with a small media goatee, which are now beyond passé, but have become almost mandatory for anyone who works in such a position. We walked up a couple of flights of stairs to get to the studio. Chris had a badge on his lapel and I asked him what it represented. It was a student radio station that he had worked on at Edinburgh University, and I asked him if he had read media studies. He laughed and said, "No". It is one of my favourite ironies that despite all the media work that I have done and continue to do I rarely meet anyone working in the media who has read media studies. By far the most popular degree that I encounter when I ask about the subject that the researchers, producers or interviewers read at university is English. It also strikes me that I meet lots of historians, geographers and former language students but I have yet to meet a scientist, a mathematician or medic. Chris was a geographer.

Chris asked to "sit in", by which he meant that he'd like me to sit on the high chair in front of the camera. I did as asked, and he attached a microphone to my lapel, and gave me an earpiece. For the next five minutes he played around with the camera, and tried to get my head in the centre of the picture. I looked at myself on the monitor by my feet and thought that I looked like an academic. I was wearing a cord jacket, white shirt and a striped tie, and for some unknown reason there was a green handkerchief in my top jacket pocket. As Chris played around with the picture a disembodied voice entered my head, and asked me to confirm that I was indeed David Wilson. I was then handed over to Peter Levy who asked me to keep my answers "short" so that he could ask as much as possible in the two minutes allocated to the interview. Two minutes!

And with that, off we went. I heard the "Look North" reporter bringing Levy up-to-date with the latest developments about the case, and it did indeed now appear that Laura and Williams were in France. There were some other pre-recorded interviews played — most notably a further appeal from Laura's mother — and then Levy came to me, introducing me as "Professor of Criminology from Birmingham University". Urghh! I didn't correct him, but inwardly sighed.

"So, Professor Wilson, what sort of man makes contact with young girls on the internet?"

As best I could, and remembering to keep the answer short, I described how men use the internet as this affords them a degree of anonymity, so they are able to be someone they would like to be, as opposed to the person they are. I also pointed out that Williams had already played with his identity by taking the name Ingram, and that in all likelihood he had presented himself in a very appealing way to Laura on the internet. Common sense. Levy asked about the "type of girl" that would run away with a stranger who she had met in a chatroom, and I tried as best as I could to bring into my answer The Children's Society's research, and to place what was happening to Laura in a broader context. Actually that makes it all sound far too grand, for in reality it was all over in seconds — 120 seconds to be precise — even if, at the end of the interview, Levy thanked me by saying "fascinating".

Chris let me out of the studio and I made my back to the car, and the return journey home.

Damned Lies

Laura's story was still high on the news agenda the following day when the latest police crime statistics were published, which had been collected some months earlier, for the period July to September 2008. There are two main ways of "measuring crime". The first is the police, or the "recorded crime statistics", which involves a member of the public who has been offended against — or who has witnessed an offence — coming forward to the police and reporting that a crime has been committed. The police usually, but not necessarily, record this allegation and then add these crimes to any that they themselves have been able to detect.

Of course these figures only measure crimes that are detected or reported, and do not, therefore, measure those crimes which go undetected or unreported. Members of the public do not necessarily want to report that a crime has been committed against them, or one that they have witnessed. They might think, for example, that the crime is too trivial, or that it is too much of a hassle to report it, or, if they did, that they won't be listened to and treated fairly when they go to a police station. When I interviewed a number of young women working as prostitutes in Ipswich in 2006, for example, when a serial killer was active in the town, they often told me about being beaten up, raped or having things stolen from them, but they would rarely report any of this to the police. "They think that we are all just slags and deserve what we get", was the typical justification for not reporting most of these crimes, and of course some of the women concerned also had outstanding warrants, and so didn't want to draw attention to themselves. At best the recorded crime statistics can be seen as a snapshot of the bigger crime picture that is bubbling away beneath the surface, and might also help reveal new crime-trends.

The second way of measuring crime is through an annual survey of householders undertaken by the Home Office called the *British Crime Survey* (BCS). The BCS is one of the largest social surveys conducted in Britain, and is in reality a victimisation survey. Conducted first in 1982, and thereafter every two years, the BCS became an annual survey in 2001, in which respondents are asked about their experiences of crime over the previous year. Interviewees do not need to have reported these experiences of crime to the police, so the BCS is often seen as revealing a more accurate picture of the amount of crime that has been committed in any one year. Even so, there are problems, and of course an interviewee might not want to reveal to a researcher any issues related to, for example, domestic violence, especially if the person who has committed that violence is listening to the interview.

BBC Online's headline captured the gist of the narrative that greeted the publication of the new figures — "Burglaries and Knife Robberies Up" — based on the fact that domestic burglaries had risen by four per cent during this period, and that "robberies with knives or sharp instruments also rose, going up by 18 per cent", according to the report written by their Home Affairs correspondent, Dominic Casciani. A little way down the story it was also reported that recorded crime overall had actually fallen by three per cent, but this didn't make the headline. Nor did the rather more interesting statistic that recorded firearms offences had actually fallen by 29 per cent during this period make any headlines, or dominate the reporting of the story in any paper or broadcast. Unsurprisingly, Jacqui Smith, at the time the Home Secretary, wanted to talk about the overall drop in recorded crime, while various Opposition spokesmen wanted to seize on the increases in domestic burglary and knife crime.

Frankly, there is always something that a politician from any party can claim as "fact" about the recorded crime figures to make the point that they want to make, so criminologists tend to stay out of the debate. This always strikes me as ironic, given that "crime" is what criminologists study, but, by and large, we usually say nothing at all about the crime figures, beyond the rather dismissive observation that they are "meaningless". That doesn't seem to make good copy, and so it is rare for criminologists to be reported in the press, or appear on the radio or TV talking about this subject.

A good example of how this works in practice came on the day that the figures were actually published. It was a Thursday, so I was in my office at the university. As Thursdays are my major teaching day, by and large I will not speak about anything in the media as I simply don't have the time. However, on this particular Thursday I only had my postgraduate students to teach, so had free time in the morning, which was when a researcher on the BBC Radio 4 programme "The World at One" telephoned. I went through my usual spiel of explaining how meaningless most of these figures were, and also drew attention to the fact that overall recorded crime had fallen—which was quite different from the spin of the questions which were being asked of me, and which were all related to crime increasing. In other words the "news" that day was to be about crime rising.

The researcher also asked me some questions regarding whether we should expect crime to increase "even further" (interesting phrase given that the figures actually supported a fall in crime) during the economic downturn—a concern which had become something of an issue when leaked documents from the Home Office suggested that this would be the case. I replied that certain types of crime would inevitably rise, although we had to remember that the period over which these figures were recorded was a few months before the recession had actually taken hold. However, my main point to the researcher was, in effect, "a plague on both their houses", which I said to reflect my belief that each political party would spin the figures to suit the narrative that they wanted to present. But what was the narrative that The World at One wanted to tell? The researcher sounded pleased with what I had said, and indicated that she was going to discuss everything we had covered with her producer. But that was that. I never heard anything further, and I did not appear that day on "The World at One".

Now I have no way of knowing if what I would have said, had I been invited onto the programme, was actually said by someone else—by one o'clock I was in the lecture theatre—or if my sceptical attitude towards the angle that was suggested by the questions posed by the researcher was simply not what the BBC wanted to hear. The line being taken seemed to me to be all about crime increasing, whereas the figures—for good or for bad (and there were issues relating to the collection of these particular figures)—seemed to suggest otherwise.

In any event, when I had a chance to read the full report about the recorded crime figures I happened to notice that, while recorded firearms offences had fallen by 29 per cent, there were some other rather troubling statistics which hadn't been noted, or commented upon. More than 350 under-11s had fallen victim to gun crime. 350! Now this did seem to me to be worrying, and if the recorded crime figures can be seen as providing a snapshot about crime-trends bubbling beneath the surface, here was a trend that might be indicative of the daily violence that children experience and have to deal with, and might also suggest that gangs are becoming a more common feature of our towns and cities. David Barrett—a journalist on *The Daily Telegraph* for whom I have a great deal of time—picked up on this too, so I duly appeared in that newspaper commenting that:

> We must always remember that young people make up a disproportionate number of the victims of crime, and that children are often the victims of violent crime. I believe that the issue of gun culture will increase over the next five to ten years, and that we are living at a time when American-style gangs are taking hold in our towns and cities. Part of that gang culture is proving one's worth by showing that you are prepared to carry a weapon.

Laura, Shannon and "Pure Evil"

By the end of a day that had been dominated by the recorded crime figures, Laura had been found in Lille, France. In fact "found" doesn't seem to be a fair description, as she seemed to have gone to the British consulate in the city with Williams, where he was subsequently arrested. Laura's mother, Debra Stainforth, read out a tearful statement to the media, thanking them and the police for their support. Mrs Stainforth said: "I am pleased to inform everybody that my daughter, Laura, is safe and well. I am grateful for all the support from the papers and all the publicity that has brought Laura back home to us. We are grateful for all the support my family and myself have been given from the police. Thank you".

It was hard not to think of other families who had had daughters disappear when Mrs Stainforth read out her statement. I wondered how Kate and Gerry McCann would greet the news that Laura had been "found", in part thanks to the publicity that surrounded the case, or knowing that Humberside Police had been working with Interpol, the National Missing Persons Bureau, the Serious Organized Crime Agency and other UK police and border forces in their search for Laura from the moment that she had been reported as missing; how this might have made them reflect on the different approaches taken towards child disappearances in Britain compared with what had happened when their daughter Madeleine had gone missing in Portugal. Most of all I found it hard not to think about Karen Matthews, who was due to be sentenced the following day with her accomplice Michael Donovan at Leeds Crown Court.

The disappearance of nine-year-old Shannon Matthews on 19 February 2008 — her hazy image caught on CCTV as she left Dewsbury Sports Centre where her school had been on a trip — dominated the public's imagination in the same way that Laura's disappearance would 11 months later. But there were differences too. In Shannon's case it was the Moorside Estate, in Dewsbury, West Yorkshire, rather than Cleethorpes that provided the setting for the disappearance, and the context of her going missing wasn't the internet — even though Shannon's stepfather, Craig Meehan, would eventually be convicted in September 2008 for downloading pornographic images of children — but the the apparent deprivation and disadvantage of the Moorside Estate.

Karen Matthews had seven children by five different fathers, and it was soon abundantly clear that she and some people in her circle—who set up a support group to help find Shannon — rarely worked, and survived on state benefits. A class element soon emerged in the narrative of how Shannon's disappearance was discussed, and so, for example, the backgrounds of Matthews and her partner Meehan — "a former supermarket fishmonger" we were reminded — were compared unfavourably with the professional, middle-class and medical backgrounds of the McCanns. For the 24 days that Shannon was missing the Matthews family were consistently pathologised and stigmatised — in other words they were seen as the architects of their own misfortune — and while rewards to help find Madeleine McCann totalled £2.6m within a fortnight of her disappearance, rewards to help find Shannon in the same time-scale amounted to £25,500 and never exceeded £50,000. Karen Matthews wasn't afraid to mention the class angle herself.

She also claimed that she was being unfairly judged when she attempted to get financial assistance from the Madeleine Fund that had been set up to support the McCanns and help other families who had had children abducted.

Shannon was eventually discovered in her step-uncle's flat, where she had been drugged, and in all likelihood tethered, so as to keep her away from the windows where she might be recognised. Mr Justice McCombe described all of this as a "despicable and inconceivable" kidnapping plot that had been dreamed up by Matthews and Donovan to extract money, although Matthews' QC also suggested, during mitigation pleas, that the plot had been an elaborate ruse to help Matthews leave her abusive partner. Whatever might have inspired or triggered these events, Matthews allowed her friends and neighbours to sacrifice time and energy in extensive searches for Shannon, and by mid-March there were also 250 officers and 60 detectives working on the case, which amounted to ten per cent of West Yorkshire Police's operational strength. Detective Superintendent Andy Brennan, who was in overall charge of the investigation, put the cost of the inquiry at £3.2m, and described Karen Matthews when she was convicted as "pure evil".

In fact in the week of her conviction, D S Brennan wasn't the only person to use the description "evil", which was applied by the press, or by those quoted in the press in a number of diverse circumstances, including—although not in any particular order—in relation to an analysis of the failings of Lapland New Forest, to describe a breed of dangerous dog and also the British National Party. Presumably the description of Karen Matthews as "pure evil" was meant to convey an even deeper evil than that possessed by the BNP or Lapland New Forest. Yet if "evil" can be used in these cavalier ways—from references to a political party, or fraudsters, to a woman convicted of kidnapping her own daughter, does the term actually have any meaning at all, and perhaps more importantly is "evil" ever a suitable description for the wicked and depraved?

I have worked with a number of people who would—and are—considered to be evil. People who have murdered—sometimes many times, as well as those who have raped, sodomised, abused and caused untold damage to their fellow human beings, often members of their own families. I have spoken at length with scores of these offenders and have often noticed in one group the deadness in their eyes—the lights being on, but no-one actually being home; their inability to empathise or to see the world other than from their own perspective. With others I noted their callousness, and their arrogance and self-serving charm, which could be turned on like a tap when the occasion demanded and when they thought that there was an advantage to be gained by doing so.

But was any or all of this "evil"? I never felt so and with the first group of offenders it was often mental illness that I was viewing—and the effects of the drugs that they were taking to keep that mental illness at bay, and with the second, simply the evidence of the character traits of the psychopath. Of course—at a common-sense level—we would want to see all psychopaths as "evil", but many of the traits that would define psychopathy can, and do, appear in individuals who would not only never come into trouble with the law, but are also regarded as being successful in business and the community.

I have other issues with the label "evil", especially as it has come to be used in our essentially secular society. First and foremost even when "evil" is reconnected with its Biblical origins, it is often used in a dynamic way, as in "the Devil has all the best tunes". "Evil" in short becomes something which is aggressive and challenging of "good", and at times almost seductive. "Evil" people can thus also become seductive, and I am all too aware that when people ask me to talk about serial killers, for example, they are expecting the Bach-loving, Renaissance-man Hannibal Lector to be described, rather than the pathetic and weedy and needy folk who become serial killers in our culture, preying as they do on kids, the elderly and prostitutes.

More than this, "evil" disconnected from these Biblical roots seems at best simply to have become a synonym for "inexplicable", even if the failings of Lapland New Forest, the BNP or Karen Matthews's behaviour can ultimately be explained, even if we could and should be appalled by that explanation. At worst, it is deployed by those who would rather not try to understand or to explain and is thus simply used to imply condemnation. This might provide consolation for some—most obviously D S Brennan—but it hardly helps to advance our understanding of what "evil" is and how we should think of it as a concept. If "evil" is to have any meaning, and I believe that that remains a moot point, it has to reflect absences rather than anything which is tangible and positive. "Evil" operates in the shadows rather than in those places which are filled with the light of reason. Sadly, the reasoning of

Karen Matthews was all too obvious and even if she was cruel—and frankly stupid, she was not "pure evil".

Mr Justice McCombe sentenced both Matthews and Donovan to eight years' imprisonment, and also went out of his way to criticise D S Brennan's description of Matthews as unhelpful, given that it contributed to her being demonised—a demonisation, I imagine, that was also attached to other members of the underclass and therefore used to confirm how different "they" were from the rest of "us".

But What Now?

With Matthews and Donovan behind bars, and Laura safely at home in Cleethorpes, there is a danger that some of the deeper lessons about these cases will be allowed to disappear, and eventually forgotten. Perhaps mindful of this, Mr Justice McCombe allowed the press to publish extracts from a social worker's report that Shannon was "disturbed, traumatised and frightened", when taken into care after her release, and that she "appeared to relive her experiences and often complains of having nightmares where she is tied up". (We also know that the four other children who were living with Matthews at the time of her arrest have also been taken into care.) This depressing report is now all that we know of Shannon, who will have to rebuild her life in the knowledge that her mother drugged and used and abused her to further her own ends. For Karen Matthews, Shannon was simply a piece of property, rather than a child with rights, hopes and dreams; a child who should have been filled with possibilities and love, rather than the adult sedative temazepam to keep her quiet—not just during her 24-day kidnapping, but also for the previous two years.

Just a week after Karen Matthews was sentenced, the Good Childhood Inquiry, which had taken evidence for three years, and was commissioned and organized by The Children's Society, concluded that the aggressive pursuit of personal success by adults is now "the greatest threat" to all British children. In other words, selfish adults destroy children's lives—a sentiment that might serve as the most insightful conclusion to the tragedy of the events that surrounded the saga of Shannon Matthews.

And will we hear anything further from Laura? Will whatever it was that led to her running away from home be put right? Will she find solace back in Cleethorpes with her family and friends? Maybe we'll discover a little more when Laura becomes an adult, and if she chooses to talk about her experience. Even if she does, what of the other 66,000 children who The Children's Society discovered ran away for at least a night in 2005 — many of whom complained about being slapped, beaten up, hit and hurt? Will we hear about them, and their stories, or will the news continue to concentrate on the chase to find that one lucky child who goes missing and is deemed "newsworthy" enough to warrant our attention?

CHAPTER TWO

Serial Killer Thrillers

The family of the serial killer, Steve Wright, announced that he had dropped his bid to appeal against his conviction for the murders of Gemma Adams, Tania Nicol, Anneli Alderton, Paula Clennell and Annette Nicholls in Ipswich in 2006. Wright's brother, David, stated that the hearing which had been planned at the Royal Courts of Justice on 24 February 2009 would not now take place, and that they were, instead, planning to have the Criminal Cases Review Commission (CCRC), which deals with miscarriages of justice, take up the case. This seemed a bit odd to me—not just because I think that Wright is as guilty as sin—but because the CCRC usually advises prospective applicants that they have to exhaust the appeals process prior to making an application to them. Perhaps the Wright family had been badly advised, but, even so, there was David popping up on BBC Online claiming that "the CCRC will pay for things like DNA tests", and suggesting that the DNA evidence that was used to convict Wright had been "flawed".

David Wright had emailed me the previous weekend prior to making his announcement:

Dear Professor Wilson,

We are looking to get a psychometric evaluation of Steve which we are hoping will help us with the appeal, could you recommend someone who would be recognised by the court or is this something you do or would consider doing?

Your advice in this matter would be greatly appreciated.

Yours sincerely

David Wright

This was the second time that David had emailed asking me for advice, and I had tried to be helpful on the previous occasion, but I found this particular request quite troubling. I couldn't quite understand, for example, why he thought that I would be willing—or even suitable—to undertake a "psychometric evaluation" of his brother, given what I had publicly said and written about the case, and I worried that even advising him about colleagues who might be willing to talk to his brother could be seen as unethical on my part. After all, I had co-written a book called *Hunting Evil: Inside the Ipswich Serial Murders* which had very clearly detailed not only why I believed Wright to be guilty of the five Ipswich murders, but also went as far as to name other women who I thought he had killed. Being charitable, perhaps all that this revealed was just how desperate the Wrights were for advice, but even so, I found it hard to understand why they were contacting me, given that I had made no secret of my belief in Wright's guilt.

I thought about my reply quite carefully—a reply which I also sent to Gordon Wise, my literary agent, and Paul Harrison, my co-author on *Hunting Evil* and the "Sky News" journalist:

Dear David

Many thanks for your e mail. You say "psychometric evaluation", but are you in fact looking for a psychological or indeed psychiatric assessment? The former tends to measure specific variables—such as sexual arousal—whereas the latter try and provide a deeper analysis of the individual. If it is the former, I imagine—but do not know—that such an evaluation would have already been done in prison (if Steve agreed to allow this to happen) by the psychology department. If the latter, was one completed for his trial? The key issue here is participation—Steve would need to talk openly about his life, behaviour and offending (although I believe he is still denying any involvement in the five murders). In other words, is he appealing against conviction? If he is, I would have thought that I would be ethically compromised from conducting such an evaluation for you, given what I co-wrote with Paul Harrison. However, there are a number of forensic psychologists/psychiatrists (often attached to universities or hospitals) who would be able to help, and Steve's barrister will be able to advise.

Yours Sincerely

David

Cheekily—in the copy that I sent to Paul—I queried in a "PS" if perhaps David should read our book!

Looking now at my reply I'm conscious of it containing a number of what I think of as "serial killer specifics". Above all, I was clear about the need for Steve's "participation" in any evaluation that was to be undertaken. In the email that I sent to David, for example, I described how his brother would need to talk "openly about his life, behaviour and offending". Serial killers with whom I have worked by and large have fallen into two distinct groups. In my experience and opinion, the first group—such as Dennis Nilsen—talk endlessly about their lives, although often not to any great purpose. By this I mean that they construct a narrative about their life that allows them to emerge from any discussion as if they were the victim, rather those people they killed. Or, they carefully paint a version of events that they think is acceptable to the listener, whom, at some later stage, they will hope to manipulate for their own advantage. On the other hand, the second group never talk at all, and some—such as Fred West and Harold Shipman—take their own lives, rather than discuss what it was that led them down the path of serial murder. From everything that I had read and heard about Wright since his conviction, it seemed to me that he fitted into the second group—he was never going to say anything, other than, "I didn't do it".

However, one thing that David had got right was the importance of the DNA evidence that had convicted his brother. I attended every day of the trial in Ipswich and it was very clear to me that DNA specifically, and forensic science more generally, were the "star witnesses".

Deoxyribonucleic Acid

Deoxyribonucleic Acid is more commonly known as DNA, the genetic material of a cell. Since an overall DNA sequence is unique within any species, and to any individual within that species, it can be used as a form of identification. This process is sometimes called "DNA profiling" or "DNA fingerprinting", and it was first used to catch a killer in 1987. At the time Leicestershire Police were trying to catch the killer of 15-year-old Lynda Mann who had been found raped and strangled in the village of Narborough in

1983, and also the person responsible for the murder of another 15-year-old, Dawn Ashworth, discovered strangled and sexually assaulted in a village close to Narborough three years later. Having exhausted most of their leads, the police contacted Professor Alec Jeffreys, a geneticist at Leicester University, who claimed to have identified a technique (called restriction fragment length polymorphism, or RFLP) that could reveal an individual's genetic fingerprint from an adequate sample of that person's DNA, such as from blood, saliva, hair or semen.

Semen had been found on the bodies of Lynda and Dawn and this was used to create the DNA profile of their killer. The police then asked all the men in the local area between the ages of 16 and 34 years to provide a DNA sample—drawn from their blood—which could then be compared with the killer's. In August 1987 the police received information from a woman working in a local bakery that one of her co-workers, Ian Kelly, had taken the blood test for another employee called Colin Pitchfork. Apparently Pitchfork had convinced Kelly that he had already taken the blood test to help out another friend who had a criminal record, and that he didn't want to take another for fear of being arrested for deception. In any event the police acted on this information and tracked Pitchfork down. Pitchfork—who had a criminal record for exposing himself—readily confessed to the double murders when questioned by the police. He was sentenced to life imprisonment in January 1988.

Since Colin Pitchfork's conviction, the science of DNA profiling has advanced greatly, and has become a standard weapon in the police's armoury to fight crime. And while in 1987 a considerable quantity of cellular material was needed for the RFLP technique to create an individual's profile, today only the smallest traces of saliva, blood, hair, sweat or semen are necessary. These would include allele-specific testing, and short tandem repeats (STRs), which, allied with the process of polymerase chain reaction (PCR), can identify an individual from a very small amount of cellular material. The latest technique is called low copy number (LCN) DNA evidence. This has been in development only since 1999, but allows forensic scientists to link DNA to a person even if only minute amounts of cellular evidence are present. However, this technique has to be used with some care, especially as such small samples can often become adulterated.

While scientific techniques have been developing quickly since Pitchfork's conviction in 1988, so, too, has the national database of DNA samples. Established in 1995, Britain has the oldest national DNA database in the world with some five million people registered on it. When it was first established only those with a criminal record were added to the database, but now anyone who is arrested for an offence which might lead to imprisonment is subject to a mouth swab, the results of which will then be added to the database. In Steve Wright's case, his DNA was on the national database as a result of his having been arrested and convicted of stealing £80 from a former employer, when he was working as a barman at the Brook Hotel in Felixstowe. Little did he realise then just how important that theft would become, and how it would later help convict him of murder.

Forensic Science and Cross-Examination

Forensic science dominated the course of Wright's trial from the opening day until the close. Hardly a day passed without evidence from one scientific expert being offered, and I almost began to feel some sympathy for the jury who had to get their heads round just what was being objected to, explained or argued about without the benefit of a chemistry degree. In retrospect my sympathy was misplaced. If the jury had been even remotely interested in popular culture, forensic science and forensic scientists would have become very familiar to them through television, cinema, newspapers and magazines. DNA and forensic science seemed to be everywhere, and there was a danger here for Wright's defence.

In popular culture, forensic science suggests glamour, certainty, self-discipline, objectivity, truth and justice all rolled into one, although whether or not anyone has ever bothered to question what it really is, or looked too deeply at how and when scientific principles come to be applied within the criminal justice and legal systems, is rather doubtful. The key word here is "science", which has recently had rather a bad press. On the one hand it is criticised for being too hard for the new schools curriculum; on the other the principles under which science operates may be perceived as less rigorous than scientists had previously led us to believe, and are just as likely to be the result of conjecture, prejudice, omission and error as anything else. There is a clue in all of this as to how Timothy Langdale QC—Wright's barrister—eventually ran the defence at the trial and which was hinted at in his opening statement:

> … it is not the case that the defence suggests the scientific findings are wrong … The defence challenge the assertion that these findings illustrate that [Wright] was responsible for their deaths as opposed to someone who had sex with them …You will have noted more than once in the case of the opening speech, the prosecution counsel suggested that another person or others may, they say, in addition have been involved in the deaths and disposals. This is a matter to which you will no doubt pay close attention. You will have to consider the evidence, for example, from the scientists as to the real possibility of someone being able to kill the victims without leaving any trace on the bodies of the victims.

Mr Langdale was not so much implying that the scientists had got things wrong, rather that the prosecution had placed too much emphasis on certain findings, and had not paid enough attention to other possibilities. He was less concerned with prejudice, conjecture and error, but much more with omission. Specifically, that the police, prosecution and forensic analysts had not paid enough attention to the possibility that Tania, Gemma, Anneli, Annette and Paula had been killed by someone else—which seemed to chime with what David Wright was saying on BBC Online.

At Wright's trial, one of the key exchanges which revealed Mr Langdale's defence strategy in operation came when he challenged the prosecution's forensic expert, Dr Peter Lau, about DNA that had been found in blood and semen stains on Wright's reflective jacket and which belonged to Wright and Paula Clennell. Mr Langdale asked an increasingly hesitant Dr Lau if he had conducted further tests on other, low-level DNA that had been found on the same jacket. Dr Lau answered that he had not and was promptly asked by Mr Langdale if he could rule out that DNA from "unknown contributors" was also present, to which Dr Lau replied "Maybe, maybe not", hardly a ringing endorsement of his scientific conclusions. So, too, in turning to DNA found on a pair of Wright's gloves, Mr Langdale suggested to Dr Lau that his results indicated another possible component—apart from Wright and Paula—and which "could indicate a third contributor". Dr Lau was asked why this wasn't investigated further, to which he replied: "It hasn't been ignored, it has been considered. In this instance it was just so low-level. In my opinion it was not worth scientifically doing".

What Mr Langdale had been trying to do was to create doubt — reasonable doubt — in the jury's minds that there might have been another person involved; someone who had escaped detection because they had taken more care than Wright, and who had thus been able to evade scientific discovery. At all times Mr Langdale reassured the jury that what he was doing was "not a criticism from me", but in truth that is exactly what it was and it seemed to me at the time that Dr Lau looked mightily relieved when he eventually left the witness box.

Roy Palmer, the prosecution's expert on fibre analysis, was more robust in the witness box than Dr Lau, and his evidence was just as significant. Specifically, he suggested that a single black nylon fibre found in the hair of Tania Nicol implied that she had been in "forceful or sustained" contact with the car owned by Wright, for the fibre that he found matched the carpet in the front passenger footwell of Wright's Mondeo. Mr Palmer went on to say that nylon carpets found in cars were designed to be "tough and durable" and therefore did not shed their fibres easily, all of which suggested that "some force" was needed to break the fibres before they could be transferred to another surface.

Mr Peter Wright QC, who put the case for the prosecution at the trial asked: "What are you able to conclude in respect of this single carpet fibre in her hair?", to which Mr Palmer replied: "The findings in my opinion represent a more forceful or sustained contact with the carpet of the car or items in Steve Wright's home environment at or around the time of her disappearance rather than a brief contact". Quite apart from fibres found in Tania's hair, Mr Palmer was able to demonstrate links between fibres found on the bodies of all five women and the home, car or clothing of Wright, and that these findings would "not occur by chance".

This was devastating evidence in favour of the prosecution, and Mr Langdale had to work hard to put up a defence. He stuck to the procedure that he had adopted when cross-examining Dr Lau, which was not so much to dispute the scientific findings themselves but to ask about omissions. So he asked Mr Palmer how many other Ford cars had similar carpets to

Wright's and Mr Palmer was forced to concede that he did not know. This prompted him to put to Mr Palmer: "so there is nothing to say, bearing in mind these girls' lifestyles, that she did not pick up a carpet fibre from a vehicle other than this?", to which Mr Palmer replied: "I cannot rule that out". Here was the familiar tactic of trying to plant doubt in the jury's mind that someone other than Wright was guilty of the murders. Even so, when re-examined by the prosecution, Mr Palmer concluded that the chances of finding fibres linked to Wright on just one of the bodies of the five women were "very small", and of finding fibres that linked Wright to them all were "even smaller".

"No Comment"

We also have some evidence from his trial to support my claim that Wright falls into the second group of serial killers—those who never talk. For example, we learned that Wright had been interviewed on ten different occasions between 19 and 21 December 2006 and that these interviews had lasted just over eight hours altogether. Prior to being charged by DC Richard Ford of Suffolk Constabulary for murder "at 2150 hours on Thursday 21 December 2006 at Stowmarket Police Station" it was revealed that Wright had been asked a series of questions, among them: Did he know any of the five girls? Had they ever been to his house, or in his car? Did he use any of these girls as prostitutes? Had he ever been to Nacton, Copdock or Hintlesham? Did he suffer from insomnia? How could he account for the fact that his DNA was found on the bodies of Annette Nicholls, Paula Clennell and Anneli Alderton? And did Pam know that he used prostitutes?

To all these questions Wright had replied: "No comment", and the prosecution reminded the jury of the police caution: "You do not have to say anything, but it may harm your defence if you do not mention when questioned something which you later rely on at court. Anything you do say may be given in evidence". Wright was duly convicted in February 2008, and sentenced to a "whole life sentence", which means that—unless the CCRC discover something to suggest that his conviction is unsafe—Wright will die in prison.

Some Further Thoughts on Serial Killers

Academics and practitioners have developed a very precise definition of what it means to be a serial killer. To be labelled in this way a killer needs to have murdered at least three victims in a period greater than 30 days, typically murdering one person in each killing episode. So, there is an element of time—the killings have to go on beyond a period of 30 days, and there is a numeric threshold in terms of the number of victims who the killer must kill. Using this definition allows us to differentiate between serial killers and other types of murderers. For example, take the case of Thomas Hamilton, who murdered 16 school children and their teacher at Dunblane Primary School, Scotland in March 1996 (and who then committed suicide), but all in the one episode. Thus, Hamilton qualifies in relation to the number of victims, but not with regard to the period of time, and is best described as a "spree" or a "mass" murderer, rather than a serial killer.

Of course this definition gives the impression of certainty, although there are still ambiguities. How are we to label the killer who murders two people in one episode, and then another many years later? In fact I worked with one such killer quite closely, when I was a prison governor at HMP Grendon, which was where, and how, I got to know Paul Brumfitt very well. He had been convicted of murdering two men in 1980, and then served 15 years of a life sentence before being released in 1995—partly as a result of the psychotherapeutic work that he had completed at Grendon. Four years after his release he murdered 19-year-old Marcella Ann Davis in Wolverhampton, where she worked as a prostitute. Is Brumfitt a serial killer? I have always taken the view that he is not, given that the gap between killing episodes is so great, although others may form a different impression.

However, what is of interest to academics—and it would seem to also interest the public—is how serial killers can inhabit our world, where they present themselves as perfectly normal, but all the time this mask of normality hides the secret that they are inhabiting another universe too; one in which it is acceptable to routinely maim and kill. Dennis Nilsen, for example, was a former soldier, police officer and, at the time of his arrest, was working as a civil servant. These respectable careers went hand-in-glove with murdering at least 15 young men and boys in London between 1978 and 1983. Peter Moore was a respectable businessman in North Wales, who appeared on the local BBC News talking about the most recent addition to his chain of cinemas, before going out that evening to kill the first of his four victims. The UK's most prolific serial killer—Harold Shipman—was a trusted GP in Hyde, Greater Manchester, who used his position in the community (and his easy access to drugs) to murder at least 215 elderly people, and possibly another 45. A more recent serial killer—Colin Norris—who was convicted in 2008, had a medical background too, and while working as a nurse in Leeds, killed four of his elderly patients by injecting them with insulin.

The serial killer Ian Brady—one half of the notorious "Moors Murderers"—captured this dichotomy rather nicely when he described serial killers as a "house divided". In his self-serving, part-autobiography/part treatise on the nature of serial killing, called *The Gates of Janus*, he observed that:

> It is yet once more paradoxical that, on the one hand, the serial killer often wishes to demonstrate his contempt for society, yet still feels compelled to maintain his good name ... the inner knowledge that he is a house divided slowly corrodes the artificial boundary the killer has tried to build within to separate his two selves, his dual personality.

Brady wrote this after speaking in prison with Peter Sutcliffe—the so-called "Yorkshire Ripper"—and no doubt he intended his analysis to be applied to Sutcliffe. However, it could equally be applied to Brady himself, and indeed to Steve Wright.

Looking over the reflexive diaries that I kept throughout Wright's trial, which started at Ipswich Crown Court in January 2008, I came across the note displayed here that I had scribbled to myself after having studied the case for several months.

Steve Wright is socially conservative, which is why he's so determined to "look the part" in his suit, tie and neatly polished shoes. He's embraced a culture that rewards hard work with upward mobility, and yet he can't find his place in that World—he can't move upwards. He's denied power through his class, his lack of education and skills—power that he feels is rightly his. He plays golf, sometimes it is claimed with the Chief Constable of the local police force; he's worked as a steward on the QE2. He's travelled the World, but ended up back where he started from and things seem to him to have gone from bad to worse. The pub that he ran in Norwich failed, and he thinks that the life that he wants — deserves — is slowly melting before his eyes. He has nothing to show for his efforts except failed marriages and a failed business. He has failed within a culture that he has wholeheartedly embraced.

Only one thing now gives him power; gives him a sense of his rightful place in the World — the place that he truly believes is his anyway. He's powerful when he pays for sex and is in the company of prostitutes. He pays them; they have to respect him; he befriends them. They accept (or at least he thinks that they accept) all of his lies, his stories, his bragging about where he has been and what he has done.

So, why does he kill? There are several inter-linked layers going on here it seems to me. Obviously killing is the ultimate expression of his power; he has the power to decide who will live and who will die. He's also good at it — after all, he's escaped being caught in the past, and so he also has some power over the police (whom he is alleged to play golf with). There's sex too, and he'll experience a climax in these deaths that is better than anything he experiences with his partner. Finally, there's revenge. Not revenge on these women, but on a culture that has failed to reward him — to give him his due; a culture that has failed to recognise his worth. At least in his own mind, killing Gemma, Tania, Anneli, Paula and Annette (and others too I suspect) makes him believe that he's not dull, unimaginative, self-absorbed, self-pitying, but he is, in fact, Superman.

Re-reading these diaries makes me doubly certain of Wright's guilt, and how unethical it would have been to have tried to help his family in their attempts to clear his name.

Labelling Serial Killers

In the same week that Wright dropped his appeal, there were numerous other stories in the press and on television related to "serial killers". I use inverted commas for that description here because — remembering the academic definition that I have outlined — some of those being described as serial killers should not have been labelled in this way. For example, Matt Rudge's documentary for Channel 4 called "My Dad the Serial Killer", followed the eldest daughter of Levi Bellfield as she approached her 18th birthday. Bellfield was convicted in February 2008 for the murder of Marsha McDonnell in February 2003, the attempted murder of Kate Sheedy in May 2004, and the murder of Amelie Delagrange in August 2004. Thus Bellfield — through luck, rather than design — should not be called a serial killer, although, had Kate died, that description would have been accurate. It is also worth noting that, in common with many "serial killers", Bellfield is suspected of having been involved in a number of other murders, including the disappearance of Milly Dowler in March 2002.

The *Guardian* also covered this story. Their journalist — Sarfraz Manzoor — accurately entitled his article "The Murderer in Our Midst", and asked, "How do you come to terms with the revelation that your father was responsible for two brutal murders?" However, even he couldn't quite resist the temptation to take this a little further by asking in the body of his article, "How does a family come to terms with discovering a serial killer in its midst?"

Of course it is interesting to note the power of the description "serial killer" — it clearly sells newspapers, and generates an audience. Serial killers titillate; they send shivers down the proverbial spine; so serial killers also make money. As such our culture has used serial killing as a commodity and in the process serial killers become celebrities. Simply typing "serial killers" into Google produced over nine million sites that I could have browsed, and uncovered over 800 specialist books on Amazon. Number One on the Amazon list was Harold Schechter's *The Serial Killer Files: The Who, What, Where, How, and Why of the World's Most Terrifying Murderers*, and one of my own books was placed at number 14. I always find this commercialisation of serial murder interesting, although this is clearly not a new phenomenon and was a feature of the events that surrounded Jack the Ripper in 1888. However, the commercialisation of serial murder does seem to have become more pronounced and marked with the publication of Thomas Harris's *Red Dragon* in 1981 and *The Silence of the Lambs* in 1988, and then the subsequent movies of the same names. In the process, these books and films intensified the interest in the phenomenon of serial killing, but specifically from the perspective of the serial killer. In other words, what makes Hannibal Lector — the protagonist of both stories — tick? Why does he enjoy eating the liver of his victims with a "nice Chianti and some 'fava beans'"?

This relentless focus on the serial killer and his motivation has been overplayed, and has obscured what the phenomenon of serial killing can actually tell us about our culture. In particular it also seems to me to be ironic that there are no documentaries about the families of the victims of these killers, and I do not know why Matt Rudge chose to follow Bellfield's family, as opposed to following the family of, for example, Amelie Delagrange. Would there have been the same audience for that documentary? Would it even have been commissioned? I have no way of answering these questions, but I do know that until my academic book *Serial Killers: Hunting Britons and Their Victims, 1960–2006* was published, no book dealing with this subject put the names of victims on their dust jacket, nor did their pictures appear on the front cover until *Hunting Evil: Inside the Ipswich Serial Murders*. In fact, even though *Serial Killers: Hunting Britons and Their Victims, 1960–2006* is aimed at an academic audience, and was published by Waterside Press — a small, highly respected academic publishing house — the publisher still wanted the phrase "serial killers" to come first in the title.

Why should "serial killers" have this power? How are we to make sense of this popularity of serial killing, a popularity which seems to deny the personal and social suffering that serial killing produces? How are people able to gain pleasure and satisfaction from the awfulness that is the reality of those who repeatedly kill?

For me, Peter Morrall of Leeds University has come closest to providing an answer. Using the "mythical werewolf" as a "suitable metaphor for personal and social ambivalence regarding murder", Morrall has argued:

Just as the werewolf metamorphoses drastically from benign normality in the daytime to nighttime savage abnormality so "normal" humans and "ethical" societies on the one hand pledge disgust at and instate penalties for violence, but on the other hand requisition and exhibit malevolence and murder.

This suggests that there are two ways to understand the disjunction between the suffering that murder produces and the satisfaction that it seems to be able to generate in those who buy all the serial killer books, or watch documentaries about them on television. The first of Morrall's propositions is that globalisation has driven all of human life into the market place, so all of human life—including murder—has become a commodity, which can be bought and sold. Murder thus becomes simply another product that can be consumed, although this hardly explains why this product—as opposed to any other—is consumed in such large quantities. Here Morrall employs Freud's observation that violence and sex drive human behaviour to buttress his second proposition. In other words, that there is something sensual and erotic about murder, and that images of pain, torture and suffering can be both intolerable and tolerated because of their erotic quality.

But how can we find pleasure in the pain of others? I think that the much overused German word *schadenfreude* (Lisa in the cartoon series *The Simpsons* explains what this means to her father, Homer) is still the most obvious way to explain how the "werewolf culture" allows pleasure to be derived from pain. In German "schaden" means "damage" and "freude" means "joy", and when joined together we can employ *schadenfreude* to explain why it is that we take such a malicious interest in the agony of our fellow human beings. Of course, this explanation—while as likely to get near to the truth in understanding a collective fascination with murder and serial killing as any other—does not excuse, or celebrate that fascination. For, at the end of the day, if this fascination is not allied to any greater purpose than the chronicling of ever more gruesome, spine-tingling and fetishistic detail about the killer and his victims then nothing is being done to challenge the "werewolf". We will have looked in vain for a silver bullet to challenge our fascination with the pain and suffering of others. In this respect my silver bullet has been to write from the perspective of the victims of serial killers, rather than the serial killers themselves, to see if that might allow us to think more clearly about how we can reduce the numbers of people who will fall victim in the future.

When I first drafted this chapter a new, three-part, drama series about a serial killer had just started on ITV—one of the main British terrestrial channels. The series is called "Whitechapel", and as the press pack that accompanies the series explains:

> London 2008. A series of bloody, tragic and impossible crimes suggest that someone is carrying out copycat Jack the Ripper murders 120 years after the killer first struck. The clock is ticking as the case turns into a hunt for an old adversary, with three unlikely heroes at the centre of it all. Mondays 9pm, ITV1.

The series is filmed almost entirely in Whitechapel itself—the scene of the Jack the Ripper murders—but there are also echoes of other "serial killer thrillers" within the feel and look of the programme. For example, how the titles are filmed reminded me of the David Fincher serial killer movie "Se7en", which was made in 1995, and as if to bring things up to date, at the end of the first instalment of "Whitechapel" the continuity announcer let viewers know that they could switch over to ITV4 to watch the hit American series 'Dexter'—based on the novel *Darkly Dreaming Dexter* by Jeff Lindsay, which has as its central character the eponymous "reformed" serial killer who now only murders so as to mete out justice. In this respect Dexter has become the latest of a long line of fictitious serial killers with whom the reader or viewer is now expected to identify—in much they same way that we are expected to empathise in some small way with Patricia Highsmith's Tom Ripley, or even Hannibal Lector.

One of the three "Whitechapel" "heroes" described in the press pack is a "Ripperologist", played by Steve Pemberton. Pemberton explained that: "this is a word I had never heard before I did this job. Then I realised there is still a thriving industry in Ripper books, tours and memorabilia". In fact, as preparation for his role, Pemberton went on one of a number of "Ripper walks", although he claims to have read very little about Jack the Ripper. Even so, Jack the Ripper is by far the most "popular" subject of the 100 best-selling books in Amazon's criminology list. Some of the best-known titles—which amply describe what the books contain—include *The Complete History of*

Jack the Ripper; Uncovering Jack the Ripper's London; Jack the Ripper: The Facts; and *Portrait of a Killer: Jack the Ripper: Case Closed*. And Jack's influence is not just confined to books. Amazon also listed 34 DVDs, 20 Music CDs, a video game, and an assortment of toys and games. In the latter category, for example, it was possible to purchase a Jack the Ripper "action figure", with the promise that "this faceless villain comes alive with MEZCO TOYZ 9-inch Jack the Ripper roto-cast figure. Jack is fully articulated and comes complete with appropriate accessories including five knives, satchel, hat, and cloth cloak".

As if to confirm all of this ambiguous interest, Jack the Ripper was voted the "worst Briton over the last 1,000 years" in a poll conducted for BBC "History Magazine's" February 2006 issue, beating historical figures such as Thomas à Becket, Titus Oates, King John, Eadric Streona and, from more recent times, Oswald Mosley, for the title. Given this notoriety, entering "Jack the Ripper" in Google produced 2,840,000 mentions devoted to the serial killer, with the most comprehensive site being http://www.casebook.org

Catching Serial Killers

I haven't yet seen the final instalment of "Whitechapel" to discover if Jack the Ripper is eventually unmasked — or, as Patricia Cornwell has put it in her best-selling book, that we should now regard this as "case closed" (she wrongly claims that the killer was the artist Walter Sickert) — but I am intrigued that, as ever, the police come out of the series with a "good press" in their ability to bring serial killers to justice. In fact our police are, at best, barely adequate in tracking down serial killers, especially if the serial killer for whom they are searching is organized and mobile. These latter two words are again "serial killer specifics". By "organized" I mean that the killer leaves few clues by way of forensic evidence, and will also often hide the body of their victim which again helps to hamper detection. "Mobile" simply means that the killer might pick up a victim in one part of the country, but kill and then dump the body of that victim somewhere else. In doing so the killer crosses police force boundaries, and in this way delays investigators from seeing a pattern emerging which might help to link one murder to another.

And, of course, there are also police rivalries between different sections of the police—which "Whitechapel" uses to generate tension, and especially between different police force areas.

In practice these rivalries led to Peter Sutcliffe—the so-called "Yorkshire Ripper"—who attacked and murdered women in the north of England between 1975 and 1981, being interviewed eleven times during the ongoing police investigation, but not once arrested as a result of those interviews, as few of the interviewing officers seemed to be aware of any of the previous interviews. Sutcliffe was interviewed on average once every four months over the course of the investigation. Even the serial killer, Ian Brady—who befriended Sutcliffe in prison and discussed these police interviews with him—thought that it "defied comprehension" that Sutcliffe was not arrested, and offered the opinion that these interviews showed an "astonishing lack of intelligence" on the part of the police. Sutcliffe's eventual capture, on 2 January 1981, was as much a matter of luck as judgment, as Sutcliffe was arrested with a prostitute in his car in Sheffield, and police became suspicious after they realised that his car had false number plates. Even so, before being taken back to the police station, Sutcliffe was able to convince the arresting officers that he needed to urinate, and when doing so was able to hide the hammer that he would have used to kill his next victim. The hammer was not recovered until the following day.

The failings of the Sutcliffe investigation were so great that they led to a major review conducted by Sir Lawrence Byford, which was presented to Parliament in January 1982, but then suppressed by successive governments and only released under the Freedom of Information Act in June 2006. Sutcliffe's murders form the background to Channel 4's three-part drama series which began in March 2009 called "Red Riding".

There have also been criticisms of the police in their handling of the investigation into the murders committed by Dennis Nilsen (who was in reality caught simply because the body parts that he flushed down the toilet blocked the drains), and of the investigations of the murders committed by Robert Black—a geographically-mobile serial killer who targeted very young girls—and Colin Ireland, who ultimately had to telephone the police querying when they were going to arrest him!

"Breaking News" in Ipswich

Hard on the heels of Channel 4's "My Dad the Serial Killer", the channel's new season of Cutting Edge documentaries started with "Killer in a Small Town", about the Ipswich murders and was directed by Louise Osmond. Cutting Edge is sponsored by the "beautifully engineered Passat", and the channel must have been thankful that Steve Wright drove a Ford Mondeo when picking up the women he was about to murder. On the whole, Osmond's documentary seemed to me to get the tone right, and tried to tell the story through the eyes of the victims of Wright and their families, rather than from the perspective of Wright and his motivation. I watched the documentary quietly counting the people that I had myself interviewed for *Hunting Evil*. There was an awful familiarity about the streets, cafes and underpasses in which Osmond's participants were interviewed, although it was wonderful to see how some of the women to whom I had spoken looked healthier, and now claimed to have "come off the game". I hoped for their sakes that it was true.

I even caught a glimpse of myself sitting in one of the press conferences given by Detective Chief Superintendent Stewart Gull—on the day that the final two bodies were discovered, and when an increasingly emotional Gull announced that, "This is breaking news and we're giving it to you as we get it". I still find that an odd statement for Gull to have made—and found it odd again when I watched him deliver it within the documentary, given that this is the language of the broadcast media, rather than how we expect the police to describe events (and see *Chapter 8*). Perhaps by then Gull had simply become seduced by the wall-to-wall coverage of the case and had unconsciously allowed the words, tropes and metaphors of the hundreds of journalists reporting from Ipswich to seep into his psyche. I remembered, too, that in the very early days of the investigation, when the only national broadcaster present was "Sky News", we had even been allowed to use the police's canteen facilities, and would sit cheek by jowl drinking tea with detectives working on the case, occasionally glancing up at the canteen's television (which was tuned to "Sky News") only to see myself pontificating about an aspect of their investigation. This only caused problems for me once, when I was unable to fathom how a new coffee machine worked. "*Oh, you can solve murders, can you, but can't pour yourself a cup of coffee!"* said an, admittedly smiling, WPC standing behind me in the queue, but I was embarrassed nonetheless. Two days later we had to make our own feeding arrangements.

Osmond largely told her story from the perspective of the families of Wright's victims, or used former, Ipswich-based, prostitutes to describe events. Even so the police — in the shape of Detective Superintendent Andy Henwood and DCS Stewart Gull — did prompt the narrative of the documentary at several key moments, and I wondered if their inclusion had been the price that Osmond had paid for access to various interviewees and bits of historic footage. I also wondered how the documentary would editorialise about the conduct of the police investigation itself, given that Wright had repeatedly struck under the noses of the police, and was even living in the red light district of the town. Indeed, throughout the investigation there had been a number of commentators querying whether a small, county police force was up to the job of catching a serial killer, and others who questioned the advice that the police had, at one stage, given the warning to the public that "no woman was safe" in Ipswich, even though the killer was clearly and specifically targeting prostitutes.

The documentary glossed over these issues and the voiceover (VO), narrated by Janet McTeer, was overwhelmingly sympathetic towards the police. We were assured, for example, that after Gemma Adams had gone missing, "the police investigation was already escalating", and that the police "stepped up their patrols" and "re-doubled their efforts". At no stage did the documentary question why, if all of this was so, three further women who worked in the red light district of the town were subsequently murdered. More worryingly, the VO suggested that the true source of the police's difficulties had been the simple reality of "the killing of five women in ten days". This is completely inaccurate. Tania Nicol — who was the first of the five women to have disappeared — was undoubtedly murdered at the end of October, even if her body wasn't found until December 8. So, too, Gull sought to convince the audience at the conclusion of the documentary that Wright was "on our radar; he was in our system; we'd have got him", although there is no way of proving this, and ultimately Wright was caught because his DNA was on the national database.

These criticisms excepted, "Killer in a Small Town" was a worthy piece of broadcast journalism, and had the great advantage of attempting to see the phenomenon of serial killing from the perspective of who it is that gets murdered by serial killers, rather than a seemingly endless number of programmes that want to delve into the psychology of the serial killer. For, by and large, serial killers in this country have only been able to concentrate their efforts on five groups of people—the elderly, babies and infants, young people leaving home, gay men, and as in Ipswich, prostitutes. And while the documentary didn't attempt to place the Ipswich murders in any broader context, these five groups that are victimised by serial killers tell us something about the adequacy of our social arrangements and reveal something about our culture, our values and our civic society.

Serial killing emerges as the elephant in the sitting-room of public policies that create a culture of "them" and "us", and which sees our society developing a widening gap between the "haves" and the "have nots". In such societies it is presumed that some people—people like Tania, Gemma, Anneli, Paula and Annette—simply don't have value for the development of that society, and can, therefore, be cast adrift as unrepresentative, or as a burden on the state's resources. It is these circumstances and those groups that are characterised in this way that serial killers use, target and kill. After all, surely it can come as no surprise that no heart surgeons, TV producers, journalists, bankers and accountants, lawyers, or academics fell victim in Ipswich, and that Wright could only gain access to, and murder, vulnerable young women who sold sexual services so as to be able to buy their next fix.

I finally got round to watching the last episode of "Whitechapel" and the killer who had been copying Jack the Ripper was eventually stopped before he managed to kill his fifth victim—the police broke into his intended victim's apartment just in time to save her. Unfortunately, the killer might have been stopped but he was also able to avoid capture, and so we viewers were left with only a number of clues as to his identity. Specifically, that he might have used the name "Dr David Cohen" and that after coming so close to being apprehended, he had committed suicide. In other words, the writers played on some of the perennial Jack the Ripper clichés: he was Jewish, a doctor, and that he took his own life. The series ended with our brave and gallant police officers walking off into the night to begin their next case—and thus resorted to another cliché which, in effect, presents our police as a "thin blue line" that keeps us all safe in our beds and on the streets, even if "safety" as far as serial killing is concerned might be better created through changes in our public policy, rather than more and more resources being devoted to our police. In any event, as far as the "Whitechapel" police were concerned, they would have to solve their next case without the benefit of a Ripperologist.

A few days later, and despite what his brother had been saying, Steve Wright's application for leave to appeal went ahead, but this was rejected by three judges who ruled that his trial had been fair, and that his conviction was safe.

CHAPTER THREE

The Chief Constable
— The Tale of a Criminal Justice Professional

One of the oldest areas of enquiry within the discipline of criminology is trying to understand to what extent an individual is personally responsible for his or her criminal behaviour, or alternatively how that personal responsibility might be constrained and limited by the reality of the social, cultural and economic circumstances that the individual finds himself or herself inhabiting. This question is often posed in a number of ways. Are "criminals born or made"; is the cause of crime "nurture or nature"; and, does the offender have "free will" or are his or her actions "determined" by external forces? Of course, as befits an essentially philosophical question, there is never an easy way of answering and perhaps the best that we might conclude is that there is always going to be a subtle, or sometimes even a messy relationship between individual motivation, and how that individual responds—in whatever way—to the circumstances that he or she faces.

In other words, this is not a question of either/or. Allowing room for free will, and also for "determinism", helps us to explain how individuals in essentially the same set of circumstances might behave differently, but also how those circumstances might more generally create, for example, more ill health in some communities than in others, or more poverty, unemployment, school truancy or crime.

I usually think about this question in relation to how it applies to crime and criminals, but the tragic end to the life of a senior criminal justice professional made me think about whether an individual can exercise free will to change the culture of a criminal justice agency, or if the individual's behaviour working within that agency is in fact constrained by pressures such as the culture of that organization, and which will impact on how he is

67

thought of by his colleagues and superiors, and so how he will gain reward, advancement and promotion.

In fact this question is very dear to me, given that in 1997 I resigned from HM Prison Service, for which I worked as a prison governor (at the time of my resignation I was in charge of Prison Officer and Operational Training for England and Wales), because I no longer believed that I could challenge some of the appalling culture of the prison system that, as a senior member of staff, I was increasingly expected to defend, and indeed on occasions represent. In short, I answered the question that I pose by saying that I could not change the culture in which I worked through individual free will — or if you prefer, by me changing the prison system from "within" — and so had to leave and, as best I could, challenge that culture from "without".

But how do other criminal justice professionals make sense of this question for themselves, and to what extent should we judge them as having, or not having, free will in relation to how they conduct themselves in the course of their duties?

Michael Todd QPM

On 1 October 2002 Mike Todd became the Chief Constable of Greater Manchester Police (GMP). He had joined Essex Police in 1976 and over the next 18 years rose to the rank of Chief Superintendent. While serving with Essex Police he received a scholarship to attend Essex University and in 1989 graduated with a degree in Government. In 1994 he was also awarded an MPhil from Essex University. The previous year Todd had attended the police's Senior Command Course, and in the words of the official enquiry that was held after his death, his "performance placed him in the top quartile of the highest graded officers and he was subsequently assessed as having potential for the highest ranks in the Police Service". As such, before joining GMP, Todd had held senior positions within Nottinghamshire Police and the Metropolitan Police, and so great was his standing with the police that at the time of his death he was Vice-Chair of the national Association of Chief Police Officers (ACPO).

Todd died in March 2008 on Mount Snowdon in Wales, and an inquest held seven months later in October 2008 concluded that "Todd died of exposure when the state of his mind was affected by alcohol and drugs and confusion, namely his personal life". In other words, this was suicide in all but name. The reference to Todd's personal life was at the nub of the circumstances that had led him to leave his wife and three children and head for the mountains, for it is widely believed that Todd feared that his three-year affair with the head of Manchester Chamber of Commerce was going to be exposed by a Sunday newspaper. More than this, the Chief Constable was known within GMP as "Hot Toddy" or "Shagger Todd" and it is also believed that Todd had had affairs with five female police officers or staff within his force, and "liaisons" with 38 other women.

Unsurprisingly, the media covered Todd's death extensively, as well as the inquest into his death, and then reported on the official enquiry that had been set up to "conduct an examination of the circumstances to ensure that nothing in the conduct of Michael Todd's personal life had adversely impacted on the professional discharge of his duties as Chief Constable". This latter enquiry was headed by Sir Paul Scott-Lee—at the time, the Chief Constable of West Midlands Police—although it should be noted that potential witnesses could not be compelled to give evidence to this enquiry and several chose not to do so. In any event, the enquiry cleared Todd of any professional wrongdoing, and found that his private life had not affected his duties. Whilst acknowledging that Todd's personal life was "complicated" and that there was "significant potential for compromise to him as Chief Constable", Sir Paul could find no evidence to support the view that Todd had, in fact, been compromised. The enquiry concluded by stating that:

> It is clear that throughout his career Michael Todd was an exceptional Police Officer and the professional qualities that he brought to Greater Manchester Police must not be underestimated. Michael Todd used his rare talents to the benefit of the people of Greater Manchester and in doing so led the Police Force to a new level of public service.

Todd, in other words, not only represented the best that the police had to offer—and hence his promotion to one of the most senior positions within the police — but had come to symbolise a "new level" of public service. His was a career to celebrate, not to denigrate and so he was in effect through the enquiry being "reclaimed" by the police as "one of us". Not unreasonably we might also look at Mike Todd's career to learn something about the culture of our police, and the skills and qualities that it takes to reach the highest levels of policing.

Sir Paul Scott-Lee's conclusion seems to have contributed to a silencing effect about Todd and his personal life. In other words, by reclaiming Todd, those who might want to criticise or question his behaviour were by implication also criticising the police more generally — that "thin blue line" that we most recently met walking off to solve their next case in "Whitechapel". And, of course, culturally we have difficulties when we "speak ill of the dead", or "trample on their grave", especially if that dead person has also left behind a widow and three children and has used his "rare talents" to take policing to "a new level of public service". It is also worh reflecting on the fact that Sir Paul used "QPM" after Todd's name.

I found all of this troubling and said so publicly, as well as criticising the conduct of the enquiry. In one of my regular columns in *The Guardian* — which is reproduced opposite — I suggested that Todd did, indeed, represent police culture, and that we should therefore reflect very carefully on what that culture meant. After all, despite what Sir Paul might have concluded, Mike Todd's lifestyle was clearly less than one might have hoped for, or expected, in a senior police officer. Might we also question the wisdom of having a senior police officer conduct an enquiry on another senior police officer? Did they know each other? Perhaps they had socialised or attended the same training courses together? Had they gone on holiday together? Were they friends? Sir Paul was silent about these questions but they seem legitimate ones to ask given that they go to the heart of the independence — or otherwise — of the enquiry and what it sought to discover and make conclusions about.

The broader point here is, of course, to continue to question the extent to which Todd represented police culture. In other words, was he a successful example of the values, skills and sound judgment that the police expected of its personnel — and which had taken policing to a new level of public service, or was he, instead, an aberration? And, if he was the latter, how had he been able to have gained such status and advancement? Thinking about how to answer these questions takes us into the territory of "cop culture".

Copper Toxicity

The enquiry into the suicide in March last year of Michael Todd, the former Chief Constable of Greater Manchester Police (GMP), by the West Midlands Chief Constable, Sir Paul Scott-Lee, concluded that Mr Todd's numerous affairs and colourful lifestyle had not had an "impact on his ability to do the job," and that there was "no evidence that these relationships adversely affected the day to day discharge of his duties as Chief Constable."

Frankly, did we really expect Sir Paul to have come to a different conclusion? After all, throughout Mr Todd's career — a police officer since 1976 — we could see the very essence of what Professor Robert Reiner of the London School of Economics has described as "cop culture". In other words a culture that is dominated by mission, action, cynicism, suspicion, isolation, solidarity, conservatism, prejudice, pragmatism and machismo.

I first became aware of Mr Todd when he volunteered to have fellow officers fire a 50,000 volt taser gun at him, in an effort to convince the Home Office to make tasers more widely available. In all of this we might also see the pragmatism and the machismo that Reiner is alluding to, and former officers in GMP who have commented publicly about Mr Todd since his death have also praised his "old fashioned approach". By this they seem to have meant that Mr Todd was known to "get out from behind his desk" and walk the beat, thus showing solidarity with his fellow and more junior officers.

A measure of the prejudice within the culture of the force that Mr Todd led can perhaps be gained from re-watching the BBC documentary that was broadcast in October 2003 — more than a year after Mr Todd had taken charge at GMP — called *The Secret Policeman*, and which saw an undercover reporter secretly film his police training at Bruche National Training Centre in Warrington, Cheshire and his first forays on the self same beat that Mr Todd walked with his junior officers. In the documentary one police officer is seen wearing a Ku Klux Klan hood, talking openly about wanting to kill Asians if he "could get away with it," while others regularly describe black people as "niggers" and "Pakis".

There were also well documented cases of Mr Todd having a number of sexual liaisons — some with junior officers — and in this we can see both the machismo and the conservatism of police culture, and it is reported that what drove Mr Todd to suicide was the threat that one of his affairs was about to be made public. Indeed when conducting research with the police for one of my own books I became aware that female police officers were called "whoopsies" or "slits", and that Detective Inspectors — "DIs"– were known as "divorce impendings".

Of course every profession has its own culture, and those who work within that profession have to judge how far they have to assimilate to the norms of that culture to be able to succeed in their career. Frankly, Mr Todd was at the very height of his career, and as such he symbolised what police culture was all about. As such, for Sir Paul to have concluded that Mr Todd's lifestyle and approach to his job might have had an impact on how he had performed as Chief Constable of GMP would have been tantamount to saying that there is something wrong with the values and standards of our police, and that they tend to promote and reward the wrong type of person. Well, we couldn't have that could we?

Cop Culture

Professor Robert Reiner of The London School of Economics has been at the forefront of academic attempts in this country to try to understand if there is a distinct and identifiable set of beliefs and assumptions that determines how the police will behave operationally in the streets, or whilst conducting investigations. He suggests that "an understanding of how police officers see the social world and their role in it — 'cop culture' — is crucial to an analysis of what they do, and their broader political function". In other words, "cop culture" shapes police practice. Whilst some academics are reluctant to accept that what one says and what one actually does is directly related, others are more "appreciative" of "cop culture" — which is usually seen as a "bad thing". We have to remember that given the great discretionary powers that the police have over individuals, or in shaping investigations, it is not unreasonable to presume that what police officers say, and how they socialise, would mould their responses to what they find in the streets, or how they attempt to solve problems. Nor is it unreasonable to assume that successful exponents of "cop culture" would get promotion and advancement.

Based on extensive interviews with various police officers of different ranks, and in different police force areas, Reiner suggested that the main characteristics of "cop culture" are:

- mission-action-cynicism-pessimism
- suspicion
- isolation/solidarity
- conservatism
- machismo
- prejudice
- pragmatism.

Reiner suggests that the central characteristic of "cop culture" is a sense of "mission". In other words that being a police officer is not simply just another job, but one that has a worthwhile purpose of protecting the weak from the predatory. The police exist to protect society, and this inevitably means that they have, on occasions, to take action. Indeed, some police officers might want to take rather more action than is often necessary, and will pursue exciting and thrill-seeking activities, rather than repetitive, mundane or boring police tasks — such as paperwork or 'form-filling'. Over time, Reiner suggests, police officers will become more cynical and pessimistic — they have "seen it all before", with each new development in society seen in almost apocalyptic terms, with the potential to destroy the moral world that has shaped the sense of mission that the police have developed.

So, too, they are trained to be suspicious, but the worry here is that this suspicion can lead to stereotyping potential offenders, which, in turn, means that this stereotyping becomes a self-fulfilling prophecy. For example, a disproportionate number of young black men get stopped and searched in the streets, leading to more young black men being arrested, which, in turn, "confirms" the stereotype that more young black men are offenders than are young white men. Indeed, given that police officers are often socially isolated, there is little likelihood that they will encounter young black men who play the piano, read books, or who might wish to become police officers themselves. Similarly, the need to rely on one's colleagues in a "tight spot" means that a great deal of internal solidarity exists, which does little to erode their sense of isolation from other members of society that they might encounter.

Of note, Reiner also suggests that police officers tend to be conservative both politically and morally, and thus culturally would distrust those groups—such as gay men and prostitutes, which might be seen as challenging conventional morality. However, this does not mean that "cop culture" is puritanical. Rather, it is dominated by what Reiner describes as "old fashioned machismo", where there are high levels of stress, drinking and divorce. Based on his own research from Bristol in the early 1970s, Reiner also suggests that the police were hostile to and suspicious of black people, and this issue was again to come to the fore with the Macpherson Inquiry into the murder of the black teenager Stephen Lawrence in April 1993. The last aspect of "cop culture" to which Reiner draws attention is pragmatism. By this he means the simple desire that a police officer has to get through the day as easily as possible. A police officer does not want fuss—especially paperwork—and would rather stress the practical, "no-nonsense" aspects of the job. Reiner describes this as "conceptual conservatism", given that this pragmatism often masks a common-sense culture that dislikes research, innovation and change.

How might we interpret Todd's career and his tragic and untimely death from this perspective? Todd first became a national figure when he allowed some fellow officers from GMP's Tactical Firearms Unit to fire a 50,000 volt Taser-gun at him in July 2005, so as to demonstrate that conventional Tasers were safe and therefore could be made more widely available by the Home Office.[1] A video of the event—usefully supplied by GMP—is available on 'You Tube', so you can still watch Todd falling to the ground after being "Tasered". Less than a minute later, he's up on his feet again, smiling, and saying that the Taser hurt and that for a few seconds he couldn't do

---

1. Yet following the Raoul Moat case discussed in *Chapter 6*, a different and unauthorised form of Taser was withdrawn from use and the company that supplied the ones used by police in that "standoff" stripped by the Home Secretary of the right to supply the such weapons..

anything—which would have allowed officers in a real incident to have handcuffed their suspect—and that he wouldn't want to do it again.

In just this one incident there are a number of the components of cop culture on display. Most obviously machismo, pragmatism and action. Todd didn't want to commission research to look at the safety of Tasers, or spend time sitting in committees organized to consider this question based on research that already existed. No, for him that would have been a waste of time, especially if that research might have come to the "wrong" conclusion! So, instead, he metaphorically rolls up his sleeves, gets out of his office and has a Taser fired at him, all of which has been carefully filmed so as to have the maximum impact. In all of this he is also displaying solidarity with his officers, who would have to fire these tasers if they were made more widely available, and his sense of being at one with his staff who were on the "front line" of policing is underscored by Todd's willingness to walk the beat with his junior officers.

Of course the most marked aspect of cop culture in Todd's career was his willingness to have numerous sexual affairs, as his nick-names "Shagger Todd" and "Hot Toddy" would seem to imply (there are a number of photographs of him with various women with whom he is alleged to have been having an affair on the internet). We do not know if these names were ever used in his presence, or if he was aware of them, but the fact that they were quickly leaked to the press surely reveals that they were in common usage. Does it matter that the Chief Constable of GMP had numerous affairs, some of which were with junior members of his staff?

We have evidence from an unusual source who came forward in the days after Sir Paul reported which helps to throw light on how to answer this question.

Alison Halford, a Swimming Pool and Mike Todd

Alison Halford joined the Metropolitan Police Service in 1962 when she was aged 22, and over the next 30 years eventually rose to the rank of Assistant Chief Constable (ACC) in the Merseyside Police. When she was appointed ACC in 1983 she was the most senior female police officer in the United

Kingdom. However, Halford was thereafter passed over for promotion to even higher office—Deputy Chief Constable and Chief Constable—on nine other occasions, and claimed that her failure to advance further within the police was as a result of sex discrimination. She took her employers to an Industrial Tribunal in 1990, but her employers, in turn, claimed that Halford should face disciplinary charges over an incident in which she was alleged to have swum in her underwear at the home of a local businessman. An out of court settlement was eventually reached in July 1992, and Halford then retired and went on to write her autobiography—*No Way Up the Greasy Pole: A Fight Against Male Domination in the British Police Force*. Five years later she won a landmark case in the European Court of Human Rights, as a result of her former employers bugging her office phone when she had worked in Merseyside. That was not the end of her public life, for Halford was then elected as a Labour Assembly Member for Delyn in the National Assembly of Wales (1999–2003), and—having changed political parties—is now a Conservative Councillor for Ewloe.

Halford writes regularly on her website to bring her constituents up-to-date with various events, and keep them in touch with what she has been doing on their behalf (see http//www.alisonhalford.co.uk). In a section entitled "Musings" she sometimes moves beyond these essentially local horizons and in the aftermath of the publication of Sir Paul's report she considered the case of Michael Todd. In particular she asked "what went wrong with the promotion process?" In short Halford suggests that Todd—who because of his rank would have been given automatic entry to COBRA, the Cabinet Office's security high command, which takes charge during a terrorist attack, or in a security incident—should not have been given this level of trust as a result of his "Achilles Heel", as she puts it. She claims that it "beggars belief" that "Mr Todd's tortuous love affairs" were not known to those who promoted him. Halford also claims that she had never heard of Todd until, "a Flintshire councillor sought my help when I was the Assembly member for Delyn". She continues:

> Deeply upset, she poured out a nasty little tale of how her police constable son in the Met. Police had fallen foul of Michael Todd who had taken a shine to his partner. It ended in tears when Jonathon was sacked for drunk driving, a serious

but not an automatic dismissal offence. Despite Jonathon and his partner sharing a house and producing a child, my Cllr. Friend firmly believed that Todd had bust up the relationship in a ménage a trios. It was suggested that he had authorised the sacking and, with the Opposition out of the way, then moved into Jonathon's bed. Karin produced compelling documents to support her case and I appealed to the Metropolitan Police Authority for help. Even the Merseyside Police Federation fought Jonathon's case and felt that he had been poorly served by his bosses. Despite the Federation's best efforts his re-instatement was refused. Shortly after, Mr T took command of GMP in a blaze of glory and congratulations.

What should we make of this? Are these just the bitter and unfair comments of a woman who failed to achieve the same level of promotion and command as Todd, and who seems to have retained a measure of animosity towards the police? Indeed, in the same section of her "musings" about Todd, she complains that she had never been awarded the QPM, and lets us know that: "I wrote to Buck House in a moment of mischief and asked why not and why was this prestigious award being given to rogues and knaves in the police?" Seemingly, Buckingham Palace replied explaining that they had nothing to do with identifying those people who should be given the award, and that it was a matter for the Government. Clearly, awards of this kind matter in police culture, and her failure to be given this honour obviously still rankles. But does this affect her judgment about other matters, and how are we to interpret the story of Jonathon, his partner, and Michael Todd QPM? She ends her musings suggesting that: "I can't blame Mike Todd; he put himself up and fools accepted him despite his weaknesses. I blame the promotion system that throws up maverick appointments. No more floral bouquets are needed for the dropped commander. Just an honest assessment on why the appointment was so wrong".

If Halford was expecting Sir Paul's report to provide that "honest assessment" she will have been disappointed. As far as Sir Paul is concerned Mike Todd should have been promoted, especially as that promotion brought with it advantages both for the police and for the public. Was Halford really expecting one male Chief Constable and the recipient of the QPM to criticise another male Chief Constable who had received the QPM too? Or, was she really using Todd's career to draw attention to the unfairness about her own relative lack of promotion "up the greasy pole" within the police?

If it was this latter issue then she seems on safer ground, especially as we like to think that the police—and police culture—have developed since the bad, old days of the racism and sexism that used to characterise how they went about their business. Indeed TV programmes such as 'Life on Mars' with its iconic, unreconstructed male, Detective Chief Inspector Gene Hunt and more recently "Red Riding", the Channel 4 adaptations of David Peace's novels which are set in West Yorkshire at the time of the hunt for the Yorkshire Ripper, encourage the viewer to believe that the police corruption, sexism, racism and ineptitude that are the backdrop and context to these programmes are what characterise the past rather than the present. They let the viewer imagine that our police have been reformed and rehabilitated in the years after those in which these programmes have been set, and that no police officer today would dream of "fitting up" a suspect, accept bribes, or speak or behave in ways that would be at odds with the responsibilities of their office. This is why Mike Todd's career—remember he joined the police in 1976—and his tenure as Chief Constable matter, for they reveal that the reforms that we might have hoped for in the police since the "bad old days" of the policing culture of Gene Hunt have not gone away at all, but are, in fact, still the basis for how to gain advancement and promotion.

Did Mike Todd ensure that a police rival for the affection of one of his officers got sacked while he was working in the Metropolitan Police? Who can tell, despite the insistence of Alison Halford and her friend's story about her son Jonathon? After all, even what Halford reveals tells us that Jonathon had in fact been arrested for drunk driving, and it was this serious offence which must have been the basis for his dismissal. If Todd did indeed use this opportunity to gain access to Jonathon's partner's bed this was without doubt unethical, and it would also be hard to imagine that this was not known to large numbers of people working for the Metropolitan Police. What is significant is that behaviour of this kind did not stop Todd gaining advancement and promotion for, in all likelihood, behaviour of this kind was accepted and perhaps even expected. It was normal within the culture of policing, and therefore didn't require explanation or excuse. So the answer to Halford's question is that "nothing went wrong with the promotion process". No one questioned Mike Todd about his "Achilles Heel" because to have done so would have required them to have questioned everyone else about similar behaviour, and perhaps also to look more closely at their own that had resulted in their being in a position in which they were able to decide who was to be appointed and promoted and who was not.

Reform: A New Force?

These issues about the promotion of one man dance around another serious and more general question. Are our police any good, or, if you prefer, are they effective in fighting crime? Of course we like to imagine that our police are "the best in the world", and it was cosy, unquestioning, blinkered sentiments such as this that encouraged Mrs Thatcher at the 1985 Conservative Party Conference to declare that "if they [the police] need more men, more equipment, they shall have them". So they did. Between 1979 and the early 1990s police budgets rose in real terms by almost 90 per cent and, by the time that New Labour came to power, total expenditure on the police stood at just over £7 billion. This spending has continued to rise, and as a result our police are now the most expensive in the developed world, costing a fifth higher as a share of GDP than policing in the United States of America. But is this money which is well spent?

One way of measuring whether or not we get value for money is to look at detection rates, which in their broadest terms refer to crimes that are "cleared up" by the police. Detection rates are, of course, only one measure of police effectiveness and we should also remember that detection will vary considerably depending on the type of crime that is being reported, and the manner in which it is brought to police attention. But even so, let's consider some recent recorded crime statistics. In 2005–2006 the police in England and Wales recorded 5.6 million crimes, and in Scotland 0.4 million crimes were recorded. That year around 1.5 million crimes—or 24 per cent of the total—were detected in England and Wales, and just under 0.2 million crimes—or 46 per cent—were detected in Scotland. Put simply, as these overall figures reveal, the police would seem to have very little impact on crime detection given that only about one in four crimes is actually cleared up in England and Wales. Nonetheless, we should also acknowledge that detection rates did vary dramatically depending on the type of crimes that were reported and, thankfully, serious crimes of violence had high detection rates — the detection rate for murder is consistently around 90 per cent (largely because most murders have been committed by someone in the extended family of the victim), while crimes such as vandalism, car theft and burglary had low detection rates.

Let's take the example of domestic burglary. How effective are the police in catching burglars and, if they are not, would putting more "bobbies on the beat" — as opposed to having officers doing "paperwork" back at the police station — be a more effective policing strategy? The first thing to note is that the amount of domestic burglary has actually fallen since it hit a peak in 1995, although a 1998 report by the Audit Commission revealed that even if overall numbers had decreased, the police still failed to solve as many as 92 per cent of burglaries. While detection rates have improved of late, domestic burglary remains one of the crimes that the police consistently fail to clear up. The usual "common-sense" cry here is that more patrolling police officers would both prevent burglary and help the detection rate to rise. Yet a Home Office study into the effectiveness of patrolling, conducted in the early 1980s, discovered that a bobby on the beat in London was likely to pass within 100 yards of a burglary in progress once every eight years. The same study went on to acknowledge that the patrolling officer would not necessarily realise that the burglary was taking place, or have much chance of catching the culprit.

A policy paper published in the weeks after Sir Paul's report about Mike Todd, by a right-wing think-tank called Reform, suggested that: "without effective police reform, England and Wales will lose the fight against crime in the years to come". It went on to suggest that there were five "myths" that had prevented politicians achieving the reforms that were needed to tackle crime, and that "the police's extravagant spending increases over the last decade cannot be sustained". These myths are worth reproducing in full:

Overall, Reform suggested that these myths should be acknowledged as "reality" at both a local and national level, and that the Metropolitan Police Service be given a formal role to lead national serious crime policing, with much more local accountability through the creation of smaller policing units. These policing units would be held accountable by County or City Councils.

Myth 1

Policing should not be politicised. In fact the police should be accountable to elected politicians. Currently the Association of Chief Police Officers (ACPO) — a self-perpetuating oligarchy — is the key influence on police forces, in a textbook example of producer capture. It will gain more power in the new Policing and Crime Bill.

Myth 2

All policing is local. In fact England and Wales does have a national lead police force — the Metropolitan Police — which is already coordinating serious crime fighting across the country. In addition national politicians interfere in day-to-day policing, preventing local leaders from answering their democratic mandate to fight crime.

Myth 3

The 43 police forces work well together. In fact the 43 forces operate separately, in particular failing to share information, as the Bichard Inquiry found.

Myth 4

The 43 forces generate economies of scale. In fact waste occurs at two levels: unnecessary regional bureaucracies, and duplicated spending on serious crime at a national level.

Myth 5

The creation of the Serious Organized Crime Agency (SOCA) has solved the serious crime problem. In fact serious crime is rising, while SOCA is a white elephant.

Source: *A New Force*, London: Reform.

As someone with a different political outlook from Reform, what strikes me is that I have a measure of support for their conclusions, although I've also some problems. For example, the report does take it for granted that crime will rise, and that our police are in the best position to do something about that rise in their guise as "crime fighters". Yet the report has no sense of how the underlying economic situation in the country might be the catalyst for these rises, and therefore how inadequate a policing response is in these circumstances, rather than one that deals with, for example, employment. So, too, the presumption that our police are "crime fighters"—the report is even entitled *A New Force*—prioritises one particular role that we might like the police to play. Here we might also legitimately ask that if our police are cast in this light as a "force" which "fights crime", to what extent can we see them as a "police service", or as servants of the community. Some might argue that they can be both at the same time—after all, fighting crime does provide a community service—but this argument avoids the question. For "crime fighters" inevitably have to become armed and develop tactics which distance the police from the community and this leads to a culture of difference; a culture of "us and them" that feeds back into cop culture.

These objections notwithstanding, there is much to support in what Reform argues and in their contention that these five "myths" have helped to shape the policing debate so far. In particular, the need to have both a national and a more local police service that is accountable to publicly elected officials specifically attempts to deal with the current so-called "tripartite model" of policing, that sees power shared between the Home Secretary, Police Authorities and Chief Constables. For, as a result of this power sharing arrangement, the Government does not really have control at all over national policing priorities, and—to use Reform's phrase—"the 43 forces are run as fiefdoms by their Chief Constables". Look again at "Myth 1". Reform describes ACPO as a "self-perpetuating oligarchy", and a "textbook example of producer capture". This latter concept was at the heart of many New Labour public sector reforms, and describes the process whereby the goals of the organization reflect the interests and prejudices of its employees (the producers), rather than the interests of the people who it is supposed to serve—in the shape of the public. I do not necessarily find this concept useful more generally, but it does seem to describe the power that Chief Constables have to shape the debate about what policing is, how it should develop, and what resources should be made available to them to be able to do so.

This also brings us back to Mike Todd, and the report that was written about him by Sir Paul. Let's consider again Todd's willingness to be filmed whilst being shot by a Taser-gun We have previously analysed this from the perspective of cop culture, and specifically how it represented action, machismo, pragmatism — and also solidarity with the officers who served under him and who would have to carry Tasers if they were made more widely available. Can we also interpret this from the perspective of "producer capture"?

Todd first allowed himself to be shot with a Taser in July 2005 and two years later the Home Office announced that the deployment of Tasers would be trialled in ten police force areas — Avon and Somerset, Devon and Cornwall, Gwent, Lincolnshire, Merseyside, The Metropolitan Police, Northamptonshire, Northumbria, North Wales and North Yorkshire. This trial was declared a "success", and as of December 2008 all police force areas were allowed to extend taser use to specially-trained units in accordance with ACPO policy and guidance, and a fund for up to 10,000 additional Tasers was made available. Given all of this, it would seem fair to conclude that Todd was successful in his Taser strategy and had worked out precisely how to get his priorities accepted. To paraphrase Mrs Thatcher, he had wanted more equipment, and powerless to resist the pleas of a Chief Constable, the Government caved in.

Only a month after it was agreed that Taser use could be extended in England and Wales, The Braidwood Inquiry, which was established by the Provincial Government of British Columbia in Canada, began to take evidence into the death of Robert Dziekanski. Mr Dziekanski — a Polish immigrant — died after having been Tasered five times at Vancouver International Airport by four Royal Canadian Mounted Police (RCMP) in October 2007. Mr Dziekanski — who was travelling to Canada for the first time to join his mother — spoke very poor English and had never before left Poland, or even been on an aeroplane. He was supposed to meet his mother when he arrived in Vancouver, but for a number of reasons this did not happen, and there were also problems with Mr Dziekanski's visa which were compounded by his lack of English. Clearly confused, he began to shout and throw things about, and was obviously distressed. This, in turn, brought him to the attention of airport security. Thereafter four RCMP officers arrived and within 35 seconds they tasered Mr Dziekanski, and then Tasered him again after he had fallen to the ground. One officer placed his knee on Mr Dziekanski's neck, and he was also handcuffed. They needn't have bothered for by that stage Mr Dziekanski was dead. At no point did the RCMP officers attempt CPR after Mr Dziekanski had lost consciousness, and he was pronounced dead at the scene.

Again, and even though we are describing a Canadian incident, we might like to interpret this incident as indicative of cop culture—especially pragmatism, action and machismo. None of the four RCMP officers attempted to speak to Mr Dziekanski or calm the situation down, and, when the officers first arrived, Mr Dziekanski put his hands behind his head, which suggests that he perhaps thought that they could help him in his predicament. The first action of the RCMP was to use their Tasers, not once but several times. This was seen by them as the pragmatic way to deal with the problem of a distressed man who spoke no English; Taser him now and ask questions later. It was a show of force and a demonstration of machismo, and perhaps we might also like to reflect that this is how policing is done when we emphasise the role of the police as crime fighters, rather than as servants of the community. Thereafter, Seargent Pierre Lemaitre, a spokesman for the RCMP, gave an interview to the news media about what had happened, but this was less than accurate about the circumstances that I have outlined. For example, he suggested that the four RCMP officers had tried to "communicate" with Mr Dziekanski, but that they "didn't get through to him", and that when it was clear that Mr Dziekanski was in trouble they had rushed off to get medical assistance. None of this is true, but in everything that he said we can suspect solidarity between Sgt Lemaitre and his four fellow officers.

I know all of this and can describe these details with some certainty because the whole incident was captured on camera by Paul Pritchard, who had also been at the airport on the day that Mr Dziekanski died and who became aware of the incident. At first the RCMP tried to confiscate this photographic evidence, but eventually it was released and is now freely available on "You Tube" (as is Sgt Lemaitre's interview). Pritchard's film stands as a visual antidote to the Tasering of Mike Todd, and reminds us that people can die from this supposedly "non lethal force". Indeed, so worried were other Canadian police forces by this incident, and by the fact that more that 20 other people have also died after having been Tasered, that both the Toronto Police and the Royal Newfoundland Constabulary placed their large orders for new Tasers on hold.

And what about Sir Paul's report? It is hard not to escape the first policing "myth" to which Reform draws attention and put his report in that context. In other words, that ACPO is a "self-perpetuating oligarchy". Would one Chief Constable really criticise the behaviour of another Chief Constable, given that both belonged to the same small group of privileged people who effectively governed the police? I find it difficult to imagine this happening, for in effect, Sir Paul was behaving in exactly the same manner as Sgt Lemaitre did in response to the death of Mr Dziekanski—he was showing solidarity with a fellow officer.

CHAPTER FOUR

Celebrity Cons
— Bronson, Banged Up and Bad Girls

The cinema was half-empty, even though the film that I'd come to see had only gone on general release the day before, had been the subject of a number of high-profile reviews and a great deal of media comment. I was expecting the place to be packed. Clutching my popcorn and a diet coke I peered around at the audience. Everyone was male, and a significant number seemed to have half-shaved heads — just like the subject of the film. I found a seat, and took out some paper and a pen and waited for the film to begin, all the time thinking about the reviews that I've already read about "Bronson"— the film about Charles Bronson, dubbed "Britain's most famous prisoner" — and about the various debates that had taken place about the pros and, no pun intended, cons of the movie. However, I had yet to read a review or hear an opinion from anyone who actually knew Bronson, or who had worked with him during the period over which this film is set, so I hoped that my connection to him and to the events that the film suggests that it dramatises will add to a better understanding of the film, and, of course, to Bronson himself. Anyway, that was the rationale behind *The Guardian* sending me.

After all, the film is keen to claim that it is "based on a true story", and yet there had been no attempt to understand the film, based on what is true and what is imagined, in much the same way that few wish to question what is true about Bronson, the various myths that have grown up around him and to which he has contributed, and all of which have undoubtedly added to his celebrity status. The fact that I went to watch the film in Milton Keynes — in a cinema no more than ten minutes drive from HM Prison Woodhill, the prison in which I got to know Bronson — seemed to add a reality for me, even if what I would eventually watch on the screen was nearly always imagined and partial.

Mention of HMP Woodhill will make those who know something about the penal system immediately think about the two Special Units which are located there, which I helped to design and then manage. They were, and still are, used to house the 12 most disruptive prisoners in England and Wales, and here's the thing—Bronson was never located in those units at all. Instead he was housed in the Segregation Unit, and typical of him, he consistently resisted any attempt to work with him so that he might have been able to move out of the Segregation Unit and onto normal location, or, indeed, into a Special Unit at the jail. Only one person wanted Bronson to be in solitary confinement—Charles Bronson.

It didn't take me long to realise that Bronson didn't actually want to be on normal location probably because he couldn't survive there. By this I mean that being "normal" was exactly what Bronson didn't want—he wanted to be "extraordinary". His entire focus was centred on creating a sense of difference that normality would have stifled and killed. As his character would eventually say at the beginning of the movie: "My name is Charles Bronson and all my life I've wanted to be famous". Only one of those statements is true, and of course "famous" and "normal" do not make good bed fellows.

In trying to become famous—not just through this film but also through a number of books that he has written—Bronson is attempting to follow a long line of "celebrity cons". Most immediately I think of Jimmy Boyle, the former gangster who came to fame through his rehabilitation in Barlinnie's Special Unit in Glasgow, and as a result of his wonderful autobiography called *A Sense of Freedom*. Boyle is now a sculptor of some note, although Barlinnie's Special Unit has long gone. So, too, there is Norman Parker—also a noted author—Mark Leech, Frank Cook and Erwin James, the latter who works as a journalist on *The Guardian*. Perhaps the best recent example in this genre is Noel "Razor" Smith, who has not long been released from custody but has produced a fantastic autobiography called *A Few Kind Words and a Loaded Gun* and even has Will Self as his agent. Jeffrey Archer also produced three books about his time inside. It's harder to think of women who have gained this type of fame, but there have been a number of good prison autobiographies produced by women who have, for one reason or another, ended up inside. Ruth Wyner — the former Director of a Cambridge-based organisation for the homeless called Wintercomfort — wrote a marvellous book about her time in prison called *From the Inside*, and so, too, Audrey Peckham, who was a school teacher, described her time in prison in a rather moving account called *A Woman in Custody*. From an international perspective, Sandra Gregory produced *Forget You Had a Daughter: Doing Time in the Bangkok Hilton* in 2002, about her experiences in a Thai prison.

These "prisoner autobiographies" can be divided into two distinct types. The first — usually written by men — are known as "cons' accounts", in that their narrative is driven by the criminal lifestyle of the author, who has often been committing crime from a very early age. In these accounts the author usually accepts a prison sentence as an occupational hazard, and the focus of the narrative might be centred on how prison has, or has not, helped the author to rehabilitate. More often than not these books will have a picture of the muscled or tattooed author on the front cover staring out at the reader, almost threatening you with violence if you dared to walk on by without a purchase. The second type — usually written by women — are described as "straights' accounts", reflecting that the author did not come from a criminal background, and therefore found being sent to prison a shocking experience. In these accounts the author takes the reader on a tour of prison conditions, perhaps using the narrative to point out how what the penal system says that it wants to do is far removed from the reality of what happens inside, which is usually presented as bizarre and unhelpful. It is rare for the front covers of these books to have a photograph of the author, who all seem to want to distance themselves — to disappear — from the prison sentence and what has happened to them.

The cinema's lights dimmed, the auditorium grew quiet and very quickly it was apparent that "Bronson" was the quintessential "con's account".

My primary responsibilities at HMP Woodhill were to the prison's Special Units, although I saw Bronson regularly enough in the Segregation Unit. When I went there I'd ask if he was OK, and say that I was concerned that he was locked up by himself. On one memorable occasion he waited for me to visit, and when we opened his cell door he had stripped naked and covered his entire body with black shoe polish. He then threatened to "stab me" with his moustache, and told me to "fuck off". I did. Over time we would negotiate with each other about giving him a radio, having exercise in the yard, and about making certain that he had access to books in return for his good behaviour — in other words, not assaulting any of the staff. He did, indeed, take the librarian hostage when he came to deliver those books over which we had negotiated, and as "Bronson" names him so will I — the librarian is called Andy Love, although he was not, as the film suggests, a prison officer. Andy is a decent man, who believes passionately in helping prisoners to learn to read, and I occasionally still see him at the prison to which he moved after the hostage incident ended.

I was the Governor who acted as Hostage Commander during that incident, and I hope that I was nothing like the film's rather suave, detached, chain-smoking, balding, bespectacled and calculating character who, for example, refused to take one of Bronson's pictures when it was offered, although I have to say his drawings, unlike a great deal of prison art, are in my view infantile (though some people might regale them as "primitive") and hardly worthy of serious scrutiny. Of course, I might have been calculating — or appeared so to Bronson — but I am not bald, bespectacled and I have certainly never smoked.

There are a great number of other inaccuracies in the film—from the relentless misportrayal of what prisons actually look like (and at that time HM Prison Woodhill was had a "state of the art" design) and how a control and restraint team would operate, to the ease with which Bronson is given access to certain facilities and privileges. Of course, the most glaring inaccuracy is the rather gothic violence. I am not suggesting that prisons are not, at times, violent places — far from it, but the film revels in a type of interpersonal, brutal, "Hollywood-style" violence perpetrated by prison staff, which is at odds with the professionalised approach that staff would and did take when dealing with a prisoner such as Bronson. This might of course still be viewed as "violence", but it is a form of violence that is perfected through approved—and therefore legal—techniques that are taught to staff.

One aspect about Bronson — the man — which I think that "Bronson" — the film — did get right is how seemingly camp Bronson was. I was not the only person working in the prison who thought that there was something sexual about all that stripping off to show us his muscles and his genitals. He seemed to want to display his body and impress on everyone that he was a "real man". The idea that he was also in touch with his feminine side or suggestions of homoeroticism were not what the readers of "lads' mags" wanted to hear, especially as Bronson has become a poster boy for unregulated masculinity.

In a scene towards the end of the film, the suave, calculating, chain-smoking. bespectacled and balding Governor during a second hostage incident — set in the film in the same jail, but in reality in another prison entirely — tells Bronson that he fears he might die in prison. Actually, I did say that to Bronson during one of our conversations. I still think that that is probably true, for Bronson knows that in the same way that he can't survive on normal location nor can he survive in the community. Out here he would just be another sad old nutter that no-one would ever want to make a film about. Sadly, "Bronson" failed for me on virtually every level as a movie and as far as Bronson himself is concerned, I seriously doubt if anyone left the cinema wanting him to be released.

Prison Film — Prison Reform?

In my academic writing I have suggested that popular, mainstream TV and films about prisons and prisoners can serve a penal reform function through, for example, helping to set standards of decency for what is, and what is not, acceptable practice in prison, and by representing prisoners as people, with hopes and values, dreams and ambitions just like yours and mine, so helping to counter processes of dramatic depersonalisation and dehumanisation. Indeed, since first making this argument, other criminologists have also begun to argue that Public Criminology should be taken seriously and, in the words of the sociologist, Eamonn Carrabine, that: "the texts, audiences and industries involved in producing popular criminology ought to become targets for academic research".

Sandra Gregory, a British citizen working in Thailand as a teacher, fell ill and lost her job. Having no money to afford the plane fare home she unwisely agreed to act as a drug mule. She was arrested at the airport, charged with drug smuggling, convicted and sentenced to 25 years in the Lard Yao Prison, known as the "Bangkok Hilton". Later, writing about her experiences there in a "straight's account", she said:

> What I sensed immediately is that prison is not like the movies, or television dramas. It's far more insane, terrible, emotional and disgusting than any of those.

Gregory's comments do not appear to be aimed at the Thai penal system — she is simply saying that her impressions of prison gained from film and TV dramas did not prepare her for the reality. Prison was far more "insane, terrible, emotional and disgusting". But can drama educate us to the "reality of prison"? "Bronson" — with its emphasis on it's authenticity certainly would have us believe it could, but in the end took a lowest common denominator approach and acted very much like other movies or TV series, such as the American TV series "Oz" or Hollywood films like "Con Air" which, primarily for reasons of dramatic narrative, both resolutely presented prisoners as "alien others" — lacking decency and humanity, and who we viewers are asked to accept are certainly nothing like you or me. But what about ITV's "Bad Girls," or the iconic BBC situation comedy "Porridge"? Did they perform penal reform functions?

First aired in June 1999, ITV's prime-time, women's prison drama "Bad Girls" was, by the end of its second season, regularly gaining audiences of more than eight million viewers. In September 2003, as its fifth season came to a close — there were to be eight seasons of the drama in total before it ended in 2006 and then an opera — it was still achieving audiences of over six million viewers. The drama was set at the fictitious HM Prison Larkhall, a women's prison located somewhere in south London (although it was originally filmed at the old HM Prison Oxford before the prison was sold and became a luxury hotel), and in weekly episodes depicted the lives of prisoners and staff. The drama was set almost entirely within the prison, and eclectically combined aspects of soap opera, prime-time drama and cult-TV so as to deliver a variety of pleasures to its audience(s). However, over the duration of its existence the series maintained a consistent, critical and informative perspective on prisons and prisoners and combined a number of strategies to ensure viewer pleasure with authorial purpose. I would argue that "Bad Girls" is best understood as a more-or-less conscious attempt to "speak the truth about prison" and as such ranks as one of— if not the—best prison drama series ever made.

"Bad Girls" is very self-consciously a women's prison drama—in two senses. First, the structure of the programme and the choice of topics for inclusion make it quite clear that the drama is attempting to make some comment on real-life experiences of prison. But secondly, the producers and writers seem to be acutely aware that women's prison dramas have been done before, and that they are entering a field littered with the baggage of, most obviously, "Prisoner Cell Block H". So the series develops an original and novel approach to dramatising prison so as to achieve its aim of delivering a wide range of inclusive viewing pleasures to maintain the public's interest in a dramatic product that seeks to "speak the truth" about prison. After all, speaking the truth about prison does not necessarily make interesting television or films and so "Bad Girls" bribes its viewers to engage with that reality in return for viewing pleasure. In short it does a deal with its viewers—we provide you with viewing pleasures in return for which you accept that we have some things that we want to say about prisons and prisoners. As a result, at any one time the show ran storylines that were intended to primarily engage viewer interest and entertain, and at the same time included scenes and storylines which were intended to carry a message. This separation of "entertainment" and "message" was never total, and frankly one of the show's greatest achievements was its ability to make "message" elements as entertaining as those played for fun.

"Bad Girls" was a drama with a serious purpose, but its strategy for delivering that purpose was to produce an eclectic mix of the cartoonish, the camp and the serious. This is best understood when we consider the main characters within the series. Based on the first five seasons of the programme the show worked with four basic kinds of character types, although some characters inevitably fell between—or moved between—them. We could identify: "pantomime baddies" (such as Fenner and Shell) and "goodies" (the two Julies); "soap opera players" (such as Yvonne, Di Barker, Maxi); players in a "prime-time drama" (such as Helen Stewart, Nikki Wade); and finally "dramatic approximations" (such as Zandra).

Shell and Fenner are easily identifiable as "pantomime baddies", and their role within the series was as villains to motivate conflict. "Bad Girls" recognised that a women's prison drama needed a predatory "screw", and prisoner bully. So, Fenner's consistently over-the-top evilness is not intended as a comment on real-world prison officers and Shell's bullying of her peers is played mostly for dramatic entertainment, rather than as a comment on the violence within real-world prisons. Fenner also provides a foil for Helen Stewart — the idealistic Governor — although it could be argued that this relationship is also played for entertainment not "message", as Helen's real adversary within the jail is actually Sylvia Hollamby, whose constant carping and "old school" approach to her prison officer duties creates many of the problems that Helen has to deal with, and which undermine Helen's reformist intentions.

Hollamby is best thought of as a "soap opera player". Her character is played for fun, but not in the same way as Shell or Fenner. Sylvia's attitude towards her job is intended to carry more meaning than Fenner's deviousness or plotting. Sylvia's old-fashioned approach — which leads to the unsympathetic treatment of prisoners and causes problems within the prison (such as riots), is meant to reveal one approach to prison work and how this approach is not only outmoded but also problematic. Hollamby is also different from another "soap opera player" — Yvonne Atkins. Yvonne's main function is as a locus for storylines. She is the primary instigator of scams and schemes and is the "top dog" on the wing.

The characters of Helen Stewart and Nikki can be identified as players in a "prime-time drama". By appearance and behaviour they, and their story are therefore meant to be taken more seriously than the others that appear in the series — and in essence that story was built on the premise that they were in a relationship with each other. However, while it is clearly possible for prisoners and prison staff to enter into dubious relationships with one another, the love affair between Helen and Nikki was a device used to not only deliver viewer pleasure, but also to allow that relationship to carry a message. Through her on/off relationship with Helen, Nikki was able to act as an articulator of legitimate grievances about the management of the prison, and reform-minded Helen was able to respond to these within the constraints of the formal authority structure. By doing so the viewer is left in no doubt about what is fair and what is not, in relation to the running of a prison. In other words, Nikki articulates a standard of decency that should be encouraged and supported by Helen, and thus benchmarks what it is that all prisons should be striving to achieve.

The last character type might be termed "dramatic approximation". The best example of this type of character from the first three seasons of the series is Zandra, who carried a major storyline from season one, episode two through to season two, episode nine. Zandra entered Larkhall as a drug addict and briefly managed to kick her habit during the time of her pregnancy. After losing custody of her baby she returned for a short time to drugs before stopping using again, with the support and encouragement of her personal officer, Dominic McAlister. Just as she was beginning to get her life back in order it becomes apparent that she has a life-threatening illness, which eventually proves terminal. Zandra is portrayed as a minor offender who has taken the rap for her boyfriend, and for whom prison is not really an appropriate response for any of her problems. Thanks to some good work by Dominic she begins to sort out her life, although fate conspires to rob her of a happy ending. Zandra is intended to be a dramatic representation of the kind of person who can come to be inappropriately incarcerated in our penal system, and the viewer is asked to identify with her, and her ultimate tragic end.

Through these characters "Bad Girls" attempted to give a voice to prisons and prisoners. What did it have to say on their behalf? Is prison a necessary and useful part of the criminal justice system? Who gets sent to prison and why? Is prison necessary to protect society from dangerous criminals? What is the trajectory of people who experience prison—in other words, will prison make a difference to their offending behaviour? "Bad Girls" consistently made comment on these questions and generally concluded that, as far as women were concerned, for a surprising proportion of prisoners, prison was not a suitable response to their offending behaviour, or their underlying problems that had, in many instances, been the source of their offending behaviour in the first place.

"Bad Girls" had storylines devoted to suicide and self-harm, drug addiction, prison officer brutality and incompetence, racism, mental health, lesbianism, bullying, assault and murder—a storyline that brought its final season to an end. What about "Porridge"?—the BBC comedy which ran for three series between 1974 and 1977 and was set in the 1970s, when the penal system was known for corruption and unprofessional behaviour. "Por-ridge" — even if it was a situational comedy — used a number of aspects of real-world prisons, including a set featuring a prison landing, cells and an association area, plus other readily-identifiable prison features such as the Governor's office, the prison farm and a hospital wing. So, too, prisoners and prison staff wore uniforms, and the prisoners had to "slop out" and were "banged up" by the staff. The prison was shown as a hierarchy of authority, with a Governor, chief officer (a rank that would disappear in 1987), senior officers and rank-and-file prison officers. There was a clear division between prison staff and prisoners, with further divisions within these two groups arising from an overall culture of "us" and "them". Through its inclusion of these and other features, "Porridge" constructed a view of prisons and pris-oners which was intended to approximate in some way to an idea of what prison was actually like. But in constructing this approximation many issues related to the real-world prisons and prisoners were ignored, and various other issues modified in the process.

My criticism here is not that "Porridge" failed to show the "reality of prison" but rather that the approximation that it constructed was selective and sanitised. Even recognising that "what prison is really like" is problem-atic — which prisons are we considering and whose account of them are we taking to constitute the reality? — we can still identify a number of ways in which *Porridge* either excluded or reworked elements which we would agree are aspects of prison. We might note, for example, that throughout three series and two Christmas specials, the show never featured a suicide. The use of solitary confinement is alluded to but never actually shown, and the relationship between the "screws" and the inmates is portrayed as structured, mild antagonism. This is in marked contrast to the reality of the 1970s when British prisons were affected by a wave of roof-top demonstrations, riots and disorder, in protest against poor prison conditions, inflexible regimes and allegations of staff brutality. In "Porridge", inmate McLaren does, indeed, stage a roof-top protest and has to be talked down by the wily Fletcher, played by Ronnie Barker. But, as it turns out, the escapade is just a stunt worked up by the two of them to wangle Fletcher a job in the library, and McLaren one in the hospital. So, too, when there is a riot, Fletcher manages to convince the Governor that there is only one person who can end the disturbance—the hapless Officer Barraclough. "Now, you men, just stop all of this and get this mess cleaned up", Barraclough implores. Much to his surprise the riot subsides and his instructions are followed. The disturbance had been staged to make "soft screw" Mr Barraclough look good and prevent his transfer to another wing. Prison riots and "Porridge"riots are two very different things and that difference, it seems to me, contributed to a view of prison that still holds sway, that our prisons are too soft, and a bit of a laugh, or as the *Daily Mail* might put it, a "holiday camp".

Banged Up

The dual arguments that prison films and TV series can perform a penal reform function by setting benchmarking standards for what is acceptable and not acceptable in our prisons, and the idea that we should take seriously the texts, audiences and industries that produce prison dramas provide a context for considering the Channel 5 reality TV series "Banged Up". This four-part series was made by the independent production company Shine North and was shown on Channel 5 in the United Kingdom between 7 and 28 July 2008. And, while my comments about "Porridge", "Bad Girls" and "Bronson" are based on a textual analysis of what these products contained—and to a lesser extent how audiences responded to what was dramatised, discussing "Banged Up" allows me to also consider the industry that produced the series.

In brief, "Banged Up" saw the disused prison in Scarborough re-converted into a functioning jail—with suitably qualified prison personnel in attendance—and into which ten[1] young men aged between 16 and 17 years, all of whom had offended (one or two persistently) were received as "prisoners". Later on, adult former prisoners—who had been trained as mentors—were introduced into the jail as cellmates for the young prisoners. A specific device of having the young prisoners attend a "parole board" hearing was introduced by the TV production company, as a means of both telling the young prisoners' stories and measuring their progress within the series. The

---

1. In total—given that two young prisoners quickly withdrew from the programme and were then replaced—a total of 12 young people participated.

Rt. Hon. David Blunkett MP, the former Home Secretary (2001–2004) was recruited to chair the parole board hearings. Throughout, the programme makers not only wanted to entertain viewers with this piece of "reality TV", but also have the young prisoners experience what prison was like in the belief that this could change their future behaviour. In short, the programme was seen as performing a penal reform function.

As someone involved with the making of "Banged Up"—I advised the production company and appeared in front of the camera as the prison's "Governor"—I concentrate here on reaction to the series by way of newspaper reviews and discuss viewing figures—the "audience". However before discussing this audience reaction I want to describe the various groups of people who came together to make the series, and the various tensions and opportunities that arose during the filming of the show and which, in effect, created "Banged Up", or, if you prefer, the industry behind the series.

As might be inferred from the brief description of what "Banged Up" was about, it is possible to uncover a number of rough groupings of participants—prison staff, young prisoners, ex-offenders, other staff and staff from the TV production company. However, dividing the participants into these rough groupings does not capture the internal dynamics that were essential in creating the series, or reveal the overlapping and, at times, competing agendas which were to emerge. So, too, it is important to bear in mind that these groupings that I identify reflect only the filming process, and do not take into consideration other periods in the life of the series—either prior to the filming taking place, or afterwards during the editing of the series. However, as far as the filming process is concerned, I would suggest that all the participants could be fitted into three groups—irrespective of their established role—and that at any given time each of these groups fought for ascendancy within the series and demanded that their agenda should have priority.

I would describe those groups that emerged during the filming process as "Production", "Moral Guardians" and "Contributors". Those in the *Production* group were, in the main, from the production company, and this group largely prioritised the needs of filming. However, this group could also include a psychologist—who was regularly on camera—the Governor, parole board members, and prison staff. In short, the need to produce a product—a reality TV series—might involve those who saw their roles as outside of the production process, and who would have prioritised other issues but became subsumed within the need to appear on camera, say something to camera or to one of the producers. Thus, even though the prison and the filming schedule were agreed in advance, there could still be tensions. For example, on the second day one member of the production group reminded the prison staff that "I'm making a TV programme here!" as a very clear reminder that a "product" had to be produced.

The second group might be described as *Moral Guardians*. This group prioritised the needs of the young prisoners and ex-offenders, and was particularly keen to emphasise the voluntary nature of the series, and, therefore, the ability of the participants to withdraw. In short, this group prioritised the issue of informed consent and guarded the ethical dimension of the project and it is a measure of the concerns of the production company that they insisted on the appointment of *Moral Guardians*. This group monitored the day-to-day physical and psychological welfare of the young prisoners and ex-offenders, and raised concerns about that welfare if particular issues arose. While this group included the psychologist, the former Home Secretary, the Governor, and the on-site nurse, it also included members of the TV production company who, for example, were keen to stress the various formal and informal assurances that had been given to the participants, as well as more bureaucratic procedures related to Health and Safety.

So, too, this group could also include the ex-offenders who baulked at giving the young prisoners too much of a "hard time", especially after they had bonded as the series wore on. As one ex-offender suggested: "I wouldn't put up with bullying in a real nick and I won't put up with it in here either". However, it is important to acknowledge that everyone involved in the making of the series was keen to ensure that no bullying or unethical behaviour took place.

The final group might be called *Contributors*, and this group included all of those who appeared in front of the camera. As such it included the young prisoners, ex-offenders, prison staff, parole board members, works staff and so forth, as well as those members of the TV production company who had to take on front-of-camera, though not centre-stage, roles when the occasion demanded. For example, one of the female production team briefly became a prison officer, and it was common for the two main producers of the programme to wear prison uniforms too, so as to monitor proceedings. However, the key point to grasp here is that those who belonged within this group were often pulled in different directions as the occasion demanded, especially when either *Production* or the *Moral Guardians* were ascendant, which would often result in them abandoning their *Contributors* role. For example, the Governor and the psychologist were contributors to the making of the programme, and as such offered specialist advice and guidance as befitted that role. However, they also became part of *Production* when the need demanded them to do so in the furtherance of the making of the series.

Overall, it seemed to me that it was the tension between these three groups — which often had overlapping interests as much as interests which competed — that ultimately created the product that became "Banged Up". So as to illustrate this point and demonstrate how these groups operated in practice, I want to consider my own role in the first few hours of the series getting underway, and which involved two of the young prisoners withdrawing from the series (for different reasons).

Here it should also be said that the casting of the series and the various logistical difficulties of getting ten young prisoners, contributors and a film crew to Scarborough, as well as the many problems with setting up the prison itself, meant that the first few days of filming were always going to be stressful. However, stress was added to these administrative difficulties when it became clear that on the first night — some three hours into the filming of the series — one of the young prisoners wanted to withdraw. His withdrawal meant that those who saw themselves as *Moral Guardians* prioritised this young prisoner's physical and psychological welfare — as well as practical problems such as trying to find him a place to stay that night, and arrange for his journey home — and the needs of *Production* were consequently downgraded. Even so, these logistical and practical considerations — which clearly have a moral dimension — were organized by *Production*. Nonetheless, his withdrawal was also filmed and *Production* ensured that there was an appropriate narrative to explain this withdrawal. To that end I, as the Governor — who had until that point been keen to stress the need to look after the young prisoner who was leaving the series — nevertheless explained the situation to the young man by saying that, "You couldn't handle a pretend prison for three hours, how would you cope with a real prison for three days, three months, or even three years?" In this way I moved from *Moral Guardian* to *Contributor* due to the needs of *Production*.

In the example above — which came only hours after the experiment had started — the *Moral Guardians* could be viewed as being ascendant and the output of *Production* characterised as merely a by-product of the action that was prompted by the *Moral Guardians*. However, the withdrawal the following day by a second young prisoner saw a dramatic reversal of the relationship between *Production* and *Moral Guardians*. In short, a second withdrawal seriously undermined the ability of the series to continue, especially as it was feared that this second withdrawal might have been merely the prelude to other young prisoners withdrawing too. So while every effort was again taken to ensure the physical and psychological well-being of this second young prisoner, it was also clear that the needs of *Production* were becoming more pressing and would thereafter take priority. This became symbolised by the decision to allow the young prisoners to smoke in their cells.

The smoke-free legislation contained in the Health Act 2006 took effect in England on 1 July 2007, at which time smoking was also banned in all prisons (or as those holding prisoners under the age of 18 years are known, young offender institutions). This reality was enshrined in Prison Service Instruction 09/2007. As a result, the young prisoners within "Banged Up" should not have been allowed to smoke. Indeed, as this would have been the situation in which they would have found themselves had they entered a real jail, enforcing this regulation created a sense of reality about the experience that the young prisoners were undergoing. However, when it became clear that the second young prisoner may have withdrawn from the experiment as a result of not being allowed to smoke (among other issues), and recognising that all but one of the remaining prisoners smoked, a decision was taken by those within the *Production* group to allow them to do so. Of course I have no way of testing if more young prisoners would have withdrawn as a result of not being allowed to smoke in their cells, but as *Contributors*, the young prisoners, in effect, conspired to overcome any objections that those who saw themselves as *Moral Guardians* might have had to keep the prison smoke-free. These glimpses of the industry behind the making of the series are clearly not exhaustive, but they do illustrate the tensions and opportunities that arose during the filming process. But how did the audience react to "Banged Up"?

"David Blunkett's Banged Up is a Sham"

The quote above was the blogged response of Erwin James, *The Guardian* correspondent and ex-prisoner, and represents some of the more negative views on the series. Thus, more positive and occasionally tangential comments are presented below as a way of understanding how "Banged Up" may have positively contributed to public criminology through "benchmarking" what is acceptable and unacceptable practice in prison, and by humanising both the young offenders and their adult mentors.

Using LexisNexis a search was made of UK newspapers on 14 August 2008 for the term "banged up" in the previous three months. This yielded 42 stories over 24 newspapers in which the programme was mentioned. This mention might have been as brief as the programme being cited, with the return of "Superstars", as evidence of Channel 5's commitment to new programmes in the summer of 2008, to over two thousand words of interview with David Blunkett.

As might be expected, the majority of mentions were in TV previews (20) and reviews (8) and clearly the majority of other articles/profiles had been sparked by the series, or publicity for it. The setting of Scarborough's former jail ensured some coverage by local papers (four mentions in the *Scarborough Evening News*, ranking them second) as did the participation of ex-offenders (*Birmingham Evening News*), offenders (*Liverpool Daily Echo*) and prison officers (*Western Mail*) from around the country but it was the use of the former Home Secretary, David Blunkett, as the figurehead that created both coverage and criticism, as about half appeared to concentrate on him rather than the series.

The Guardian led with eight mentions (plus one in *The* Observer) with six different writers filing previews, reviews and a long profile. There was not a "party line" on this, and thus Gareth McLean (7 August 2008) concentrated on Blunkett and was scathing on the lack of reality: "without the random acts of violence, rape in the showers and being surrounded by people with mental illness. So nothing like prison, then". On the other hand, Andrew Mueller twice made it his "pick of the day" (19 and 26 July 2008) remarking: "It's astounding that, despite the uncountable permutations of reality television we've endured, nobody has done this before", "dazzlingly simple, and arguably meaningful" and "The drama is compelling, the insight into prison life fascinating".

On the other hand, Stuart Jeffries, reviewing the series, remarked: "Like Big Brother, this had sociological justification lost in the mists of production meetings and probably similarly disappointing viewing figures". So we have a "Marmite" product—people either loved it or loathed it, although the Glasgow *Evening Times* seemed to do both. For example, the paper made the programme its "pick of the day" while, nonetheless, being more critical and remarked,"Television, the nation's self-appointed problem solver, has the answer. A reality show" and "To give weight to the social experiment, the series is fronted by David Blunkett". The paper then selected this picaresque detail—"Ex-con Dave tells the guinea pigs: 'In prison, you could lose your life over a piece of toast or a bit of custard'".

Whilst much was made of the Blunkett connection (several stories in his local papers), the *Liverpool Daily Echo* (14 July 2008) merely noted in its preview: "David Blunkett's documentary series continues". On the other hand, Andrea Mullaney, writing in *The Scotsman* (29 July 2008) speaks of an "experiment in rehabilitating David Blunkett as a TV personality", and Alice Thomson in *The Times* (7 July 2008) allows Blunkett to insist that "he was not playing the role of Davina McCall. 'This was no Big Brother. It wasn't even 'The Apprentice'. We didn't seek to humiliate anyone'". The *Western Mail* (14 July 2008) is more respectful, and positive, in claiming it was "unquestionably this summer's toughest reality show, and what's more, it serves a very serious purpose—which is probably why it's presented by a former Home Secretary".

In addition to lengthy pieces (ranging from 585 to 2,450 words against an average wordage of 277) in *The Guardian* (7 August 2008), *Daily Telegraph* (5 July 2008), *The Times* (7 and 8 August 2008), focusing on Blunkett, the *New Statesman* magazine (17 July 2008) allowed him 1,400 words to justify himself and the programme. In this he sets out very fully much of the material mentioned above, name checks many of those involved front-of-camera and praises the ex-offender mentor, Bob Croxton, and the young offender who Bob helped and another who was to join the army. These mentions are by first name but some local papers did not give that level of anonymity. On 15 July 2008, the *Liverpool Daily Echo* focused on local "DC" who, "has gone from layabout to full time office worker since taking part in the programme", whose mother, "was starting to lose hope for her son, who always seemed angry and barely spoke to her".

Barb figures[2] for the week ending 13 July show that "Banged Up" had 0.99 million viewers and was ranked 28th for the channel; first was "Neighbours" with 1.73 million. The numbers had dropped slightly for week 2 at 0.96 million viewers but it was ranked 25th. It suffered a slight further decline for week 3 to 0.87 million viewers and 29th rank and, regrettably had dropped out of the top 30 in its final week, in which "Myra Hindley: the Prison Years" was ranked 16th with 1.07 million. For comparison, BBC1's 30th ranked programme that week, the "Six O'clock News", attracted 3.59 million; BBC2's "Eggheads", 1.36 million; ITV's "Trinny and Susannah Undress the Nation", 2.93 million and Channel 4's "Richard and Judy", 1.08 million. Whilst Channel 5 cannot boast the public service pretensions of the BBC or Channel 4, its schedulers/audience has a taste for crime dramas and documentaries, so that a reality TV format is particularly appropriate and will have reached more people than read this book.

In his discussion with Decca Aitkenhead (*Guardian*, 7 July 2008) David Blunkett explained:

> We spent a lot of time making these four one-hour episodes, actually looking at the problem and being able to talk it through. You don't get that space to be able to articulate it when you're in government. You just don't.

Elsewhere he mentions the difficulties of being Home Secretary and of finding funding for what he calls "experimental programmes". Here he is referring to "scared straight" and restorative justice or community interventions, and one of the most dramatic scenes within the series related

---

2. Available at: http://www.barb.co.uk/viewingsummary/weekreports.cfm?Requesttimeout=500& report=weeklyterrestrial

to a restorative justice initiative with two of the young offenders. In his autobiography, Blunkett complains of the "hand-wringing" at liberal dinner parties when enthusing about a community justice initiative he wanted to import from Brooklyn. Released from the shackles of office he could step back and consider other options. It is a shame that the late modern condition should render reality TV such power but it has to be recognised that the shortage of Habermasian civic spaces for communication means that criminologists, penal reformers and politicians alike may have to sup with this particular devil.

Even so, there are dangers, and James Rampton—writing in the *Daily Telegraph* (5 July 2008)—observed, "It's a serious social experiment. Parents, schools or youth offending teams might record these programmes and use them as a tool". And whilst hopeful about the outcomes for offenders, ex-offenders and "officers" alike we would stop short of Stephen Piles' suggestion—also in the *Telegraph* (12 July 2008)—that, "if all of them change their ways, the criminal justice system must be handed over to Channel 5 immediately".

"Banged Up" is a long way from the real life experiences of John Tulloch, Professor of Sociology at Brunel University, a victim of the 7/7 attack at Edgware Station (whose blood-spattered face became an iconic picture of that day despite the fact that his image was used by the *Sun* without his consent). He supported Tony Blair's call for 90 days' detention without charge and also argued:

> There is room for much more "public intellectual" engagement in the media than we might think. For academics, I believe there is no more important activity in the face of the growth of the criminal justice state.

Through benchmarking what should happen in our jails with those young people who are imprisoned there and by humanising them and their adult mentors, the cause of public criminology and penal reform was well-served by "Banged Up".

The Royal Television Society Awards

Some measure of support for this conclusion comes in the shape of the Royal Television Society (RTS) and their Programme Awards for 2008, when "Banged Up" was one of three nominees for Best Constructed Factual Series — the other two being "Britain's Missing Top Model", made by Love Productions for BBC3 and "The Choir: Boys Don't Sing", made by Twenty Twenty Television for BBC2. "Banged Up" was Channel 5's only nominee in any of the 25 categories. I went along on the night to the Grosvenor House Hotel in Park Lane as a guest of Channel 5 and Shine North, mentally preparing what I might say should we win, given that David Blunkett was unable to attend due to a vote in the House of Commons that demanded his attention.

It didn't take me too long to meet up with the two senior producers on the series — Andrew Nicholson and Robin Ashbrook — who, like me, both looked incredibly uncomfortable in their black ties. Robin was pretty certain that we would lose because we were up against two BBC shows, and Andrew — who was initially much more positive — gradually came to the same conclusion as Robin and thought that "The Choir" would win. I didn't know what to think — and I hadn't seen either that programme or "Britain's Missing Top Model" so just settled into my seat and took in the various familiar faces I saw around me. Gok Wan in particular floated by our table, smiled at me and said, "Hello gorgeous!".

My agent, Jacquie Drewe, had phoned me earlier in the day to tell me that she had been invited to attend too, and we loosely agreed that I should try to find her on the night. She had been invited to sit on the BBC table with one of her other clients — Gareth Malone, who fronted "The Choir", which, in hindsight, was probably an omen. I found Jacquie pretty much straight away, and she introduced me to Gareth. We wished each other good luck, and I said that everybody at my table thought that "The Choir" was going to win. Gareth laughed, and said that he thought that "Banged Up" would win, and I left thinking what a nice man he was. As it turned out, Gareth got it completely wrong, and he, rather than me, went up on stage to accept the RTS Award for Best Constructed Factual Series. He wasn't supposed to say anything — so as to keep the awards ceremony to time—but he slipped past Rory Bremner anyway, and announced, "Young people aren't so bad you know". I thought that that could have stood as an epitaph for "Banged Up" too.

My table slowly slipped into drunkenness, and then blamed and cursed the BBC's stranglehold on the RTS awards, congratulated each other on having been nominated, given that that stranglehold existed, and then pitched each other new ideas about future series that we would like to make which would definitely win next year's award! I went home in a taxi, rather depressed but still certain that "Banged Up"—like "Bad Girls"—had done something positive for penal reform. At the very least it presented to the viewer the chaos of the lives of young people who offend, and how—with the right support, including the support of ex-offender mentors—they can do something constructive with their lives, rather than believe that all they are fit for is a life behind bars. At the time of writing only one of the young offenders has reoffended. If only he'd been able to sing.

CHAPTER FIVE

Serial Killers
— Now You See Them, Now You Don't

It's Open Day at the university and so we are all on our best behaviour. Buildings look cleaner—and so do the staff. As part of the process of selling our academic wares, I'm always asked to deliver a "taster lecture" to the prospective students and, even more importantly, to their mums and dads. Mums and dads? Yes, parents now universally accompany their offspring to assess where they might be studying—and, no doubt, to influence their decision. When I was 17 I'd never have dreamed of asking my parents to come with me when I chose my university, but now its almost compulsory.

The mums and dads usually also ask all the questions at the end of the lecture as their increasingly sullen children look on, rather bored by proceedings. Perhaps it's the inevitable consequence of the costs involved. My student days were filled with the freedom that came with grants, but often now the graduate merely looks forward to significant debt—some of which gets financed by the mums and dads asking all about the course outline, the number of points that are needed to be accepted, the night life and sports facilities and even about accommodation. Last year someone asked me why there weren't heated towel rails in the halls of residence! I know I'm good, but plumbing has always been beyond me.

My lecture is basically a very easy introduction to the phenomenon of serial killing and, after providing a definition of what it means to be labelled a serial killer, I ask the audience to name some British serial killers since 1960. The list always goes something like this— "Myra Hindley ... The Yorkshire Ripper ... Rose West". At that point I usually say, "Isn't it interesting that of nearly 35 people whom we could label as a serial killer by the definition that I have provided there are only three women. Yet the first two names that you have given me are both female. Isn't it also interesting that these two women — Myra Hindley and Rose West — murdered in the company of a more dominant man in what is known as a *folie à deux*?". I always pause at this point and then ask, "Do you know the name of the only British female serial killer who murdered by herself, and not within a *folie à deux*?".

This question is rarely answered and I watch heads being scratched all round the room. However, this year a rather quiet woman in the back row stunned me by correctly answering, "Beverly Allitt". So unusual was it for anyone to identify Beverly Allitt that I asked the mother of the prospective student how she knew. "I'm a nurse at Grantham Hosptial", she replied, which was, of course, where Allitt murdered the four young babies in her care in 1993.

But why is it that some serial killers emerge into public consciousness — the Wests, Dennis Nilsen, Peter Sutcliffe, and Harold Shipman, to name the most recognisable — while others all but disappear? Why do these serial killers become iconic of the phenomenon, while others are rarely even discussed? Who, for example, has ever heard of Colin Ireland, who murdered five gay men in the same year that Allitt was murdering, or Peter Moore — the only Welsh serial killer I have encountered, who was active in 1996? Who, now, can even remember the case of Trevor Hardy? In part, it's the fault of academics and the media, but, more broadly, we all need to accept the blame.

The Academy and the Serial Killer

Until relatively recently serial killing was almost exclusively dominated by theorising that considered the biography of the individual serial killer and his or her motivation, or by questions of definition. Theorising that placed serial killers and the phenomenon of serial killing into a broader framework that accommodated social, economic and cultural factors was almost totally neglected, although a small group of scholars — largely inspired by, but not slavishly following, the work of Elliott Leyton — have begun to argue, for example, in the case of Britain, that: "The responsibility for serial killing does not lie so much with the individual serial killer, but can be better found within the social and economic structure of Britain since the 1960s, which ...

does not reward the efforts of all and in particular marginalised large sections of society". Kevin Haggerty—like Leyton, a Canadian academic—has also recently pushed this type of theorising further by suggesting that: "Serial killing is patterned in modernity's self-image" and that, as a result, modernity provides "the key institutional frameworks, motivations, and opportunity structures characteristic of contemporary forms of serial killing".

One of the key institutional frameworks to which Haggerty draws attention is the rise of the mass media, and while there have always been academics who have been interested in how serial killers are presented in the media, Haggerty goes further and suggests that "a symbiotic relationship exists between the media and serial killers. In the quest for audience share the media have become addicted to portrayals of serial killers". Part of this addiction stems from the fact that serial killers offer

> rich opportunities to capture public attention by capitalizing on deeply resonate themes of innocent victims, dangerous strangers, unsolved murders, all coalescing around a narrative of evasion and given moral force through implied personal threats to audience members. Serial killers were apparently ready-made for prime time.

In all of this, Haggerty would find much support from generations of criminologists who have looked more generally at crime reporting, and while crime—like sex—was a subject of popular fascination long before the rise of the mass media, there is little doubt that crime is a major feature of the contemporary news agenda. It is also clear that the media do not publish or broadcast every criminal act that is within the public domain, but are selective of the kinds of crimes, criminals and circumstances upon which they report. Some criminal acts are chosen over others because of their "newsworthiness"—in other words, those aspects of a crime that journalists argue make for a good news story, a judgment which is, in turn, a product of their "newsroom culture". As a result, it is also widely accepted that the most commonly-reported crimes—which would include serial killing—are those that happen less frequently. Robert Reiner, for example, has demonstrated in his study of British newspapers from 1945 that: "homicide was by far the most common type of crime reported, accounting for about one-third of all crime news stories throughout the period".

Yvonne Jewkes has expanded further on this notion of "newsworthiness" and has suggested a 12-point criteria of "news values for a new millennium". These news values, she argues, become the bases for the judgment that journalists and editors will make in gauging the level of public interest that a story will generate. Jewkes' news values include:

(i) Threshold: Asking whether a story is significant enough to be of interest to a national audience;

(ii) Predictability: Vital resources are often committed to pre-planned events ensuring their place on the running order;

(iii) Simplification: A crime story must be "reducible to a minimum number of parts or themes";

(iv) Individualism: Stories must have a "human interest" appeal and be easy to relate to;

(v) Risk: We could all be victims with little attention given to crime avoidance;

(vi) Sex: Sexual violence, "stranger-danger" and female offenders being portrayed as sexual predators;

(vii) Celebrity or high status persons: The media is attracted to all elements of celebrity and crime is no different;

(viii) Proximity: Both spatially and culturally;

(ix) Violence: As with sex, it fulfils the media's desire for drama;

(x) Spectacle and graphic imagery: Particularly for television news;

(xi) Children: Either as victims or offenders;

(xii) Conservative ideology and political diversion: Protecting the "British way of life".

This largely-theoretical territory hardly captures the depth or complexity of several of the arguments that have been merely alluded to here. However, when these news values that Jewkes identifies are applied to the circumstances surrounding the murders committed by Trevor Joseph Hardy it does nothing to explain why Hardy was largely ignored by the national media at the time of his murders, or why he has disappeared from subsequent popular and academic writing. After all, and as I will demonstrate, with the exception of celebrity, the crimes committed by Hardy fulfil all of Jewkes' news values. So, too, while Haggerty accepts that modernity is not a single, coherent movement which arrives fully formed in different locations all at the same time, it cannot reasonably be argued that Britain in the 1970s was not yet "modern".

Nor can it be suggested that the British mass media were disinterested in serial killers, although it should be noted that the Hardy case occurred before the Federal Bureau of Investigation (FBI) in the USA gave prominence to the phenomenon of serial murder and offender profiling as a means of apprehending this type of murderer. Even so, there was extensive coverage in Britain of the contemporaneous case of Peter Sutcliffe—dubbed by the press "The Yorkshire Ripper"—both at the time and subsequently, who committed his first murder in Leeds in October 1975. Indeed, given that Sutcliffe's first few victims were prostitutes it has been suggested that, "the fact that [they were] … good-time girls would be a major complication" in encouraging press interest or witnesses to come forward. As Michael Bilton, one of Sutcliffe's most perceptive biographers comments, "labelling a victim a prostitute in this situation was unhelpful. Experience showed the public were somehow not surprised at what happened to call girls".

None of Hardy's victims were prostitutes but were, in fact, teenage girls (aged 15, 18 and 17 years respectively), which might have implied that the news value of their deaths should have been that much higher, given that this series of murders had all the hallmarks of a "newsworthy" crime—a serial killer who preyed on young women. Nonetheless, coverage of these murders was negligible, as was reporting of his subsequent trial—where he was described by the judge as "utterly wicked". So, too, a search of *The Times* archive, for example, using the words "Trevor Hardy Manchester" produced just three, very short accounts. A search within the archives of the *Manchester Evening News* proved to be more fruitful—producing some 40 articles—but, even so, Hardy does not appear on, for example, the lists of British serial killers produced by Jenkins in 1988, Grover and Soothill in 1999, Fido in 2001 or Brookman in 2005. Nor was he included in my own original list compiled for *Serial Killers: Hunting Britons and Their Victims, 1960–2006*—although this has been rectified in my most recent book, with the observation that Hardy has been "consistently overlooked", and my admission that, until recently, "I had never heard of Trevor Hardy".

So why did Hardy "disappear" from public and academic scrutiny? Why was his case not "newsworthy" and what might this lack of attention suggest about Jewkes's "news values for a new millennium"? To answer this question I undertook research with Harriet Tolputt—one of my PhD students who also works as a producer for "Sky News"—with four journalists who worked on the case. Their insights allow us to examine why some serial killers emerge into popular and academic consciousness while others disappear, and thus to reconsider how "newsworthiness" and the symbiotic relationship between the serial killer and the media coexist. However, given that the Hardy case is so little-known, I start by describing this more fully and provide some background—largely culled from interviews, local newspaper accounts, or from the autobiography of Geoffrey Garrett the Home Office pathologist who worked on the case—about the murders that Hardy committed.

Trevor Joseph Hardy

Trevor Joseph Hardy was born on 11 June in 1945 in Manchester, England. He was 31 years old when he was sentenced to life imprisonment for three counts of murder on 2 May 1977, and is now one of Britain's longest serving prisoners. His criminal career began when he was just eight years old. At the age of 15 years he was sent to the adult prison, HM Prison Strangeways, for burglary—the judge telling him that despite his young age he would be jailed "for the public's protection". In 1963 Hardy was sentenced to one month in prison for indecent exposure, and Garrett and Nott describe Hardy as having an exterior "hard-as-nails" spirit, despite his slim 5ft 7in build. However, they say that in private he was "unusually close to his mother" having few "normal relationships with girlfriends", and that he "enjoyed dressing up in women's clothes".

Reports from the *Manchester Evening News* (1975–1977) build up a picture of Hardy's dysfunctional love life. In his early twenties he entered into a platonic relationship with an older woman, then after leaving prison at the age of 27 years he became besotted with a 15-year-old schoolgirl named Beverley Driver. Hardy almost immediately ended up in prison again—this time for assaulting a man named Stanley O'Brien with a pickaxe, during a row over a round of drinks. Hardy claimed he had been set up, and vowed to kill O'Brien. He also wanted to kill Beverley Driver, because she had, by then, ended contact with him at her parents' request.

On his release from prison Hardy discovered that O'Brien had already died, and all his anger was vented towards Beverley. On New Year's Eve 1974, just a month after having been released from prison on parole, he claimed his first victim — 15-year-old Janet Stewart — whom he mistook for Beverley. According to court records Janet had been walking to meet her boyfriend in a public house on New Year's Eve 1974, but she failed to turn up. It was not until Hardy confessed to her murder on 27 August 1975 that her family finally knew what had happened to her. In the presence of his solicitor, Hardy told police that he had seen Janet getting out of a car at around 10:40 pm and, mistaking her for his former girlfriend, he stabbed her in the throat, cut her neck and then dragged her body into a hollow and covered her. In March 1975 he returned to the shallow grave to bury her properly. Hardy then returned to the grave once more to remove her head, hands and feet, either to conceal her identity, or as "some very strange form of gratification". It later emerged that Hardy had, in fact, returned to the body to steal Janet's ring to give to his new girlfriend — Sheilagh Farrow — a divorcee ten years his senior. On 1 September 1976 he revisited the scene with his solicitor and showed police the waste ground where he had disposed of Janet's body. He later boasted in court that school children had seen him at the grave.

Hardy's second victim was barmaid, Wanda Skala. She was 18 years old when Hardy murdered her in the early hours of the morning on 19 July 1975. Wanda had been working at the Lightbowne Hotel in Moston, Manchester the previous evening and, after closing time, stayed on for a drink with some friends and some of the staff. Bill Stewart — the father of Hardy's first victim, Lesley, also worked at the hotel and may even have served his daughter's killer. Wanda left at around 2:15 am. At 10:00 am her body was found on a nearby building site, although she had been partially buried. The clothes on the upper part of her body had been torn open, her right breast had been bitten, and her trousers and underwear had been almost entirely removed. Her right sock had been tied around her neck. A post mortem examination revealed her cause of death to be severe head injures and strangulation and that:

The head injuries were consistent with having been caused by a large number of heavy blows possibly from a brick found at the scene. Part of the right nipple had been removed, possibly by biting and there was a lacerated wound and bruising near the upper part of the vulva which could have been caused by kicking or a blow from a blunt object.

In a police statement, Hardy said that he had read about a killer named Neville Heath in a book from Queen's Park Library, and had made the scene look like a sex attack. Heath—who bit off a nipple from one of his victims—was hanged in 1946 for the murders of two women, although police suspected that he had killed a third.

Hardy was immediately a suspect, but when the police visited his flat in Smedley Road, Newton Heath, Manchester, Farrow provided him with an alibi, and had already washed the blood from his clothes. She later told the jury that Hardy had confessed to killing Janet and had shown her where he had buried the body. It was also to emerge that she had helped Hardy hide behind an old fireplace in their flat when the police arrived. In the autumn of 1975, Hardy's brother, Colin, told police that his brother had confessed to the murder of Wanda while they were out drinking together, and as a result Hardy was taken in for questioning. Displaying some forensic awareness, Hardy realised that he had left clues on Wanda's body, so asked Farrow to smuggle in a file in order to rasp his teeth down so as to prevent the police linking him to the bite marks on his victim. The lack of dental evidence—and the fact that Farrow had given him an alibi—forced the police to release Hardy, which allowed him to kill again.

As with Hardy's previous victims, Sharon Mosoph was a young woman who was just 17-years-old when she died on 9 March 1976. Sharon—whose small stature earned her the nickname of "Titch"—had arrived in Manchester the previous evening and she had walked to the night bus stop with a friend. Some time later, screams were heard from the direction of the Rochdale Canal. At around 8:00 am on 9 March 1976 her naked body was found. Sharon's tights had been used to strangle her. When the frozen canal melted, a bundle of her clothes and her handbag came to the surface. Detectives believed she had been attacked whilst walking along the street, and then dragged on her back across a car park, and thrown into the canal. Again, one of her nipples was missing. Police suggested that Sharon may have confronted Hardy as he was trying to break into Marlborough Mill, where she worked as a cashier.

Once more Hardy realised that he may have left clues on his victim's body, so he returned to the scene. He found Sharon's body in the canal and mutilated it, erasing his teeth marks from her nipple. Hardy then appears to have left the area, and while living rough, he sexually and physically assaulted another woman in a public toilet. On 29 June 1976 Hardy appeared at Oldham Magistrates' Court charged with the murders of Sharon Mosoph and Wanda Skala, amid chaotic scenes from the victims' families. There was a second hearing on July 6 when Hardy's mother protested her son's innocence. He was driven from court to the screams of "monster" and "murdering bastard".

After the police charged Hardy with the murders of Wanda and Sharon he confessed to killing Lesley, who had, up until then, still been treated as a missing person. Despite his confession, Hardy pleaded not guilty to murder at his trial at Manchester Crown Court. Instead, he pleaded guilty to manslaughter on the grounds of diminished responsibility. On the fourth day of the trial, when Farrow was due to give evidence against him, Hardy sacked his counsel and began to conduct his own defence. The jury didn't believe him and convicted him of the three counts of murder, having retired for just 70 minutes. He was sentenced to life imprisonment. During sentencing the judge, Mr Justice Caulfield, described Hardy as "hopelessly evil" and praised the police for their hard work.

Sharon's father, Ralph, attempted to pursue Farrow in the civil courts, but due to the £15,000 needed for a private prosecution he was forced to give up. However, in 1981 he received a letter from Hardy in HM Prison Hull, spelling out further details about the murders. An enquiry was launched, but the Prison Service concluded that the letter was smuggled out with the help of a relative. On 16 December 1994, the then Home Secretary, Michael Howard, set the period to be served by Hardy, to satisfy the requirements of retribution and deterrence, at the whole of the applicant's life. Fourteen years later, on 12 June 2008, Hardy's appeal for a review of his sentence was rejected. Mr Justice Teare, sitting at London's Royal Courts of Justice said:

In my judgment this is a case where the starting point under Schedule 21 is a whole life order on the grounds that this was a murder of three very young women involving sexual or sadistic conduct. Each murder was of a young girl. Two were found naked or almost naked and had a nipple removed. These matters indicate sexual or sadistic conduct. This conclusion is consistent with the view of the trial judge who considered the applicant to be "utterly wicked" … Hardy "does not accept his guilt and therefore shows no remorse," however he is trusted to have access to sharp knives.

The judge concluded by saying that, "this is a case where the gravity of the applicant's offences justifies a whole life order. Even if this were a case where a 30-year starting point was appropriate the aggravating features would mean that a whole life order would be the appropriate minimum period".

Newsworthy?

As this background suggests, there should have been intense media interest in the case. After all, Hardy was a serial killer, preying on young women, and engaging in sadistic sexual practices with the bodies of his victims. There was also a female accomplice who provided Hardy with an alibi—which had echoes of the earlier "Moors Murderers" whose offences had also been committed in the Manchester area, or, to a more contemporary audience, similarities to the murders committed in Soham, Cambridgeshire in 2002, by Ian Huntley, who was also given an alibi by his girlfriend, Maxine Carr. There was also an element of police incompetence (given that they released Hardy from custody) and evidence of intense local hostility at the time of Hardy's trial, which was "predictable" in setting the media's agenda. Indeed, with the exception of celebrity, all of the news values identified by Jewkes would have been fulfilled by the Hardy case. Why, then, did it receive virtually no national media attention, and only a limited amount of local publicity? Why was this case not, to use Haggerty's conclusion, "ready-made for prime time"?

To answer this question, semi-structured interviews were conducted with four journalists who were based in Manchester at the time of the murders, and who reported on the case, either for northern editions of national newspapers, or for the *Manchester Evening News*. Given that all four have now retired, initial contact was made with them through our journalistic network and we also posted a question about Hardy on the website http://

www.gentlemenranters.com—a social networking site for retired journalists. This produced two volunteers who knew of the case, and they, in turn, suggested others who might also be willing to provide interviews. Each of the interviewees was interviewed at their home, and questioned about what they remembered about the Hardy case; why they thought that the case had attracted such little publicity; at what stage they had discovered that the three murders were linked; and, finally, what they knew about Hardy's female accomplice. All of our interviewees agreed to be indentified. They are: Alan Hart (AH), who was deputy news editor of the *News of the World* and based in Manchester at the time of the Hardy case; Andrew Leatham (AL), a reporter based in Manchester for the *Sunday People*; Brian Crowther (BC), who was a reporter in Manchester for the *Daily Mirror*; and Dave Goddard (DG), crime reporter for the *Manchester Evening News*, and whom Hardy contacted from prison after the trial.

All the interviews were documented using shorthand—in the hope that this would help to promote rapport with veteran news journalists—and thereafter transcribed to form a running narrative. And while the most striking feature from each of the interviews was the amount of information that they remembered from the case, several themes emerged which might help to explain why the Hardy case has all but disappeared. These are:

- the fact that there was no link between the murders before the trial;
- a north/south divide among newspaper publications;
- the social status of the victims and the area;
- the dilemma of "mad or bad";
- the fact that Hardy was not given a suitable nickname; and
- the role of Sheilagh Farrow.

Additionally, each of the interviewees expressed disbelief at the limited amount of reporting of these events and were surprised that the Hardy case was not well-known.

The most salient theme to emerge was that Hardy was not identified publically as a serial killer until his trial. This did not allow for any build up of publicity. One interviewee (AL) said:

If they had been looking for a man who had killed three young girls then it would have had a resonance and there would have been a build up from the search. But they didn't even know that he had killed the first girl until they arrested him for the second ... and the fact that the police didn't link them.

BC continued this theme and suggested: "I think that Trevor Joseph Hardy was not linked publically as a serial killer until after he was arrested so there was no real publicity about it". He then went on: "I do think the level of publicity was down to the fact that the police didn't want to link them and it was only after the third murder that it all came out". He also made comments about more recent serial killers and how they had been reported:

> Look at Harold Shipman. When it's known from the start you get serial killer syndrome but when it's just the coverage of an individual murder you don't. It all happened over about 18 months. If there had been a murder one month and then another then alarm bells would have been ringing . . . For quite a long time the murders weren't linked. I don't think they were linked until the trial. It was all due to the circumstances of when he was caught. It wasn't until he was arrested did they gather info on him for a second one . . . The main thing was that the case just appeared out of the woodwork.

DG said that: "It was more that there was no hunt for a serial killer at that time". BC even suggested that the police did not want it to be known that the cases were linked: "Certain police officers won't like the idea of having a serial killer on the loose as it would have led to fear and panic in the area". When asked how the case differed from recent high-profile trials, AL observed: "It wasn't a case of notoriety like the case of the Wests[1] that had been growing day by day. So that when the trial occurred there was a huge expectation".

The second theme was the issue of a north/south divide in the newspaper industry in the 1970s. AH remembers talking of the *News of the World* as having a "great week in the north". AL continued this theme when asked why the story had not featured more in the national press: "The reason was that in the 1970s things were very different than they are now. The case got

---

1.   Fred and Rose West tortured, raped or murdered at least 12 young women between 1967 and 1987, many at the couple's own home at 25 Cromwell Street in Gloucester, England.

lots of coverage in the north but not in the south. We had a big northern edition and it was very different than the southern paper". DG added: "Well in those days it was almost like two countries. Everything that happened north of Birmingham was for us and everything that happened south went into the London editions".

Social status was also a recurring theme in the interviews, although not all the sample agreed that it had had the same effect. Two interviewees thought that the area where the murders took place was "low life" (AH), or "fish and chippy" (AL). Others felt that due to the young age of the victims and the fact that they were out alone at night, it might be construed that they came from a lower social background. BC agreed it was an area of economic deprivation but said of the victims: "They weren't tarts or anything … anyway you couldn't get much lower than the Yorkshire Ripper". And DG, without mentioning the economic status of the area, appeared more surprised that the case had not attracted more attention because the victims were: "nice girls … the girls weren't prostitutes or anything. They were decent young women, girls on a night out, girls who just missed the bus".

The interviewees also thought that the question of whether Hardy was "mad or bad" had had an impact on how the case was covered. This issue appeared to be interwoven with the fact that, apparently, Hardy had no obvious motive. AH, for example, said: "The problem with the Hardy thing was that there was never a reason apart from the fact that he was barking mad. There was never an explanation", and then added, "I think that we find it easier to accept that certain people do monstrous things—can only do them because they are mad. I don't think we like to believe that there are people that are sane but evil". AL believed that: "Well, I think if there had been a clear motive, a motive other than his twisted little mind, then that may have generated more publicity". BC believed that: "He hasn't offered any insight. The prosecution don't know why he had done what he has done. The woman Beverley was brought into things but it was never spelled out why he didn't kill her and why he killed three other women. At the end of it all there were so many questions left unresolved and I think newspapers like to solve questions rather than leave them hanging in the air. And in this case they couldn't even speculate what the answers were". These themes were taken up more fully by DG:

I don't know what the psychological term for it is but he claimed that he had a disease that made him immune to the emotions of killing people. At the time it was said that if there had been a war on he would have been a war hero because he had no fear of death, either his own or other people's. He didn't think like other people … The judge at the trial said that they had to decide, and it was the first time that they had to do that, to decide whether he was mad or bad and it was clearly decided that he was bad.

The fact that Hardy was not labelled for his serial killing with a catchy nickname was also suggested as a reason why the case had not been covered more prominently. AL thought that a name: "Helps fire the public imagination but we didn't have a chance with Hardy until the court case. I can't remember what it was now … the beast of something. It was pretty lame". DG observed that: "I think one of the reasons was that no one christened him like the Moors Murders or the Black Panther.[2] Trevor Joseph Hardy wasn't given a name by the nationals. When people remember killers they don't refer to them by name. It's the Black Panther that someone will say rather than Neilson, that may seem very slight but in journalist terms it isn't".

All of the participants thought that the involvement of Hardy's girl-friend — Sheilagh Farrow — influenced coverage, and they believed that if she had given her version of events this would have increased exposure. In fact, getting her story was seen as one of the main objectives, and AH revealed that: "It was discussed with the editor that Sheilagh Farrow was the person we wanted to talk to and how she felt that she had given an alibi for him that enabled him to murder another girl. I tried to track her down for a week and failed to get her to talk". AL confirmed this view and noted that: "If we had known more about the girlfriend it would have lifted it. The whole thing with female offenders is that they are rare". So, too, BC added: "She [Sheilagh Farrow] would have been the story. If she had talked about her life with a serial killer — that would have been interesting". He continued: "I always thought that the biggest part of the story was the mindset of the live-in girlfriend. When she discovered she was living with a monster and the knowledge that she had given him a false alibi, which had enabled

---

2. Donald Neilson — who was sentenced to life imprisonment in 1976 — was dubbed by the press "The Black Panther".

him to kill again. Perhaps because she laid low and never came out of the woodwork is why it didn't get the impact".

So, Which Serial Killer Becomes the Celebrity?

The case of Trevor Hardy suggests the need for further investigation into the interaction between serial killing and its representation in the media. Above all, what the Hardy case demonstrates are absences—absences in literature, absences in knowledge and in current academic theorising. In particular, this case study suggests that recent theorising about serial killers needs to consider why some killers remain in the public consciousness, while others—like Hardy—fade into obscurity.

Hardy's absence from the national media would also seem to challenge Jewkes's characterisation of the news values that structure newsworthiness—even if the values that she describes were specifically related to "a new millennium", thus after Hardy started to kill. Nonetheless, what emerges from an analysis of the Hardy case is that the news agenda does not always conform to the criteria of newsworthiness that Jewkes and others have suggested might determine the level of interest in a case, and instead, what has news value would seem to be more fluid, complex and, at times, baffling—even to those employed in the industry. In other words, real-life determinations of what is newsworthy can sometimes be governed by local and idiosyncratic factors, which do not necessarily fit neatly into any preconceived pattern of what events are seen to have news value. Journalists working in Manchester in the 1970s recognised the newsworthiness of the crimes that Hardy had committed, with one even describing it is as "ticking all the boxes" to have become a major story. Yet this was not reflected in the news coverage.

What emerges from the paucity of the news coverage about Hardy are a number of other issues which need to be considered when investigating the newsworthiness of any particular serial killing. The most salient of these other issues that should be considered is the time-scale of when a number of murders are identified as being part of a series. In the Hardy case, the police—perhaps deliberately—ruled out any link between the murders of the second and third victims, at a time when the first victim was yet to be identified. One officer even told reporters that it, "looks like a one off job". In all of this we can see an almost perfect example of the police acting in what Hall and colleagues, in 1978, described as a "primary definer" of the news, and the media merely as a "secondary definer". As a result they simply reproduced an erroneous account from an expert and privileged source which served to downplay the newsworthiness of Hardy's crimes. Moreover, by the time that the murders did come to be linked, the case had become *sub judice*, and strict reporting restrictions were implemented as Hardy had already been charged with the murders of Wanda Skala and Sharon Mosoph. Any careless reporting could be deemed to prejudice a jury and lead to the trial being ruled unsafe. This timing was eloquently illustrated by one interviewee with the analogy of a long-jumper: "Look how far you go with a run up as opposed to a standing start". There had been no lengthy manhunt or speculation, no appeals for women to stay off the streets. Indeed, by the time Hardy was caught the press could report very little, and they were unable to create what another interviewee termed "serial killer syndrome".

This syndrome would seem to be self-propelling. As soon as the public is informed, interest gathers and the story picks up pace. The more demand from the public, the more the story is reported, and so on. This is particularly apparent in an age where public interest can be monitored easily by viewing figures and website analysis. This propulsion is also fuelled by the allocation of media resources. Once news teams have been deployed they invariably file a story. All of this can be illustrated through the recent example of serial killer, Steve Wright, who murdered five women in Ipswich, Suffolk, in 2006. The Wright case generated more than six weeks of media frenzy (see *Chapter 6*), with the increasing number of victims leading to, for example, the costly deployment of news "anchors" to Ipswich. Once in place they were able to cover each twist and turn of the investigation with more gravitas than regular reporters in the field, which, in turn, appeared to generate more public attention. It was also apparent very quickly that the murders in Ipswich were linked. As such, it was safe to report that the police were hunting a serial killer, and they in turn warned all women to stay indoors. Very quickly, the nation was gripped.

All of this is very different from the Hardy case, where the police denied any link until Hardy was charged with the crimes, and, as a result, Hardy has been allowed to disappear into obscurity. How many other British serial killers have been similarly overlooked by privileging "expert" opinion from state sources? More broadly, how has our understanding of "violence" come to be viewed merely through the prism of certain types of interpersonal crimes, but largely ignores deaths caused by large corporations or indeed by the state itself? Indeed, in this specific case we might question why the media did not want to break the police's account of Hardy's murders and in doing so create a "moral panic" about his activities. That there was none might suggest that "moral panics" are reserved for specific cases within specific social settings, or as Hall has described it, only "tactically exploited" when the need arises.

Gaps in more conventional theorising related to serial killers and the phenomenon of serial killing is also illuminated by the Hardy case. Trevor Joseph Hardy emerges as an extremely complex character, but, as with our observations about newsworthiness, when applying criminological theory his case, again, proves to be more of an exception to the rule. Hardy's killings could not be explained by Elliott Leyton's theory of "homicidal protest", and nor does the FBI's organized/disorganized dichotomy seem to fit. Hardy played a cat and mouse game with the police: he filed down his teeth to avoid detection, yet revisited the murder scene of one if his victims to leave her shoe. Was this a clue to help catch him? Or was he just taunting the detectives? Perhaps Hardy was following his crimes in the media? We now know, for example, from local newspaper analysis, that he had knowledge of at least one previous killer—Neville Heath—who was hanged in 1946, just a year after Hardy was born. Was Hardy inspired by these earlier killings? After all, Hardy bit the nipples off his victims, as Heath had done, and both pleaded diminished responsibility at their trials, even if they were both eventually found guilty.

In one sense Hardy might be a very early example of a serial killer who preys on those who use the "night-time economy" of old manufacturing towns and cities which, in our own time, have come to rebrand themselves as places that young people visit to eat, drink and spend—a trend which reflects an economic base that has moved from production to consumption. Writing in 2006, Simon Winlow and Steve Hall noted, for example, that this night-time economy was characterised by extreme anxiety, precariousness, atomisation, social division and hostile interpersonal violence, where "unpredictable stranger violence is becoming more common". Indeed, they conclude that "the night-time economy is now the primary site for interpersonal violence in Britain". Of course this phenomenon was not as prominent in the 1970s as it is today—although we should remember that two journalists described the area where the murders took place as "low life" and "fish and chippy". Perhaps, as a consequence, violence was seen to be unexceptional in an area which could be characterised in this way; also leading to a lesser police and media profile. As a result, violence—even serial killing—might have been viewed as normal within this marginalised social setting, thus Hardy and his victims were of little concern. In this way Hardy, his victims and how they were reported, might foreshadow a trend in serial murder that will become more prominent.

As with any case study, it is, of course, difficult to generalise more broadly from the findings of one particular example. Indeed, as my brief discussion of the Wright case suggests, I am not seeking to depart more broadly from Haggerty's interesting "provisional argument" about the relationship between serial killing and modernity, and of the crucial role of the mass media within that relationship. However, what the Hardy case reveals is that this relationship might be more complex and is dependent on a range of case-specific variables that might, or might not, engender the circumstances which would allow any particular serial killer to have "newsworthiness" and thus become "prime time".

The Serial Killer in the Academy

Jon Clements of the *Daily Mirror* telephoned. Seemingly a psychology graduate who is studying for a PhD in Criminology at the University of Bradford had been arrested and charged with the murders of three women. I'd never heard of Stephen Griffiths, but seemingly he had heard of me. Not only had he gone to the extent of buying some of my books but he had also given me four out of five stars on Amazon for my co-written book about the Ipswich serial murders! Can life get any more bizarre than this? My own PhD students were worried and, frankly, I started to get worried about them! What were they really up to? Was their interest in criminology merely a ruse to find out better techniques to kill or to evade the police? Jon and a number of other journalists wondered what I thought about all of this, so I wrote the following at the request of the *Sun*:

The arrest of a 40-year-old man on suspicion of murdering three sex workers from Bradford — Suzanne Blamires, Shelley Armitage and Susan Rushworth, the latter whom had not been seen since June 2009, comes just two weeks before the release of Michael Winterbottom's film "The Killer Inside Me". This serial killer thriller, based on the 1952 novel by Jim Thompson, stars Casey Affleck who plays the violent, sadistic protagonist whom we watch punching the face of one woman until it caves in and enjoying sado-masochistic sex with Joyce — a prostitute — whom he also later murders.

The central character in "The Killer Inside Me" is a sheriff in a small Texas town, although, as yet, we have little information about the 40-year-old arrested in Bradford. Even so, I was taken by the trailer for Winterbottom's film which suggested that "Some Kill for Love; Some Kill for Money; But Some Need No Motive", and these choices would indeed characterise a number of serial killers that I have met or worked with over the years, although others — like Peter Sutcliffe, the Yorkshire Ripper — claimed that he killed prostitutes because he heard voices telling him to do so, while others, like Steve Wright, has refused to discuss his motivation at all.

Most serial killers kill because they like the power that they can exercise over another person, and there is no better way of expressing that power than by taking that person's life.

Mention of Wright should remind us that sex workers have always been vulnerable to attack by serial killers — partly because prostitutes give access to complete strangers, and then travel with those strangers to dark places to perform sex acts in return for money. CCTV cameras have not helped deal with the problems posed by street prostitution — they have merely displaced those problems to even remoter places than the red light districts of our towns and cities and which has made it even harder for sex workers to look out for each other. Add to this the fact that most street prostitutes are overwhelmingly addicted to Class A drugs and you have an almost perfect deadly mix.

Hardly surprising then that the extent of the violence faced by sex workers is staggering. Between 1994 and 2004 sixty prostitutes were murdered in England and Wales, although there were convictions in only 16 cases. No wonder that serial killing and the sex industry have gone almost hand in hand.

The five murders committed by Wright in Ipswich was an opportunity to rethink our public policy related to prostitution so that, in the first instance, the police should have been encouraged to target and criminalise the men who use, exploit and live off the earnings of those who sell sexual services and, as they do in Sweden, punish the punters and the kerb crawlers. Second, Ipswich should also have made us consider — as they do in Australia and New Zealand — licensing brothels so as to develop a safer environment for sex workers and their clients and which, as a result of having to have a licence, has made them the subject of regular health checks and monitoring.

This is not to suggest that through licensing the provision of sexual services that prostitution is either inevitable or acceptable and some countries such as Germany, Greece and Austria have taken a more pragmatic approach and simply registered those who work within the sex industry and encouraged them to use a "managed zone" within a specified area of a city.

Third, events in Ipswich should have made us think hard about why some young people want to begin to sell sexual services, and to develop and maintain outreach services to help them deal with the addictions that have usually driven them into this sad and dangerous profession in the first place.

In fact aspects of all these approaches were at one point being actively considered in Government under the leadership of the former Home Secretary David Blunkett in a policy document called *Paying the Price*. But its proposals were eventually watered down and Katherine Raymond, one of Blunkett's advisors, explained in 2006 that this was through a combination of "political cowardice and public indifference".

More's the pity. But if now is the time of "new politics" under our new Coalition government shouldn't events in Bradford encourage us to re-think our approach towards prostitution? We missed that opportunity after Ipswich, but let's hope that the LibCons show more enterprise than their predecessors and that all of us too begin to show some responsibility and question why violence towards women is a suitable form of entertainment.

When he appeared at Bradford Magistrates' Court and was asked his name, Griffiths replied "Crossbow Cannibal". Clearly, he wanted to "emerge into public consciousness". Griffiths struck me as being on a journey not just in space and time, but also on another journey to express who he is, or at least wanted to be — his values, his interests, his desires. His was a journey of self-discovery that he still seems to be on. What more is there to say?

Griffiths has since been convicted of these murders and is serving a 'whole life' tariff. Currently located at HM Prison Wakefield, he is said to be on hunger strike and has made a number of suicide attempts.

More generally these inner, psychological journeys allow us to reveal — and sometimes to express — what excites and appals us and, all too often, what appals and excites a serial killer is the power and control that he can exert over women. Power and control that is expressed through murder but which is often denied to the serial killer in other spheres of his life, and where he might simply be thought of — if he is noticed at all — as an odd and eccentric face in the crowd. A nobody. Loser.

Some serial killers know all of this from an early age. Serial killers like John George Haigh — the "Acid Bath Murderer" — whose Plymouth Brethren parents were increasingly out of step with the world that they inhabited, and which left a mark on the young Haigh that he was at pains to hide for the rest of his life. A scholarship took him to the Queen Elizabeth Grammar School in Wakefield and, while he did his best to fit in to a school that had been founded in 1591 by a group of local worthies led by Thomas Saville, he was always a "scholarship boy", with "odd parents". So, as he grew older and moved to London, Haigh pretended to be someone else — at various stages a lawyer, a socialite, a stockbroker, an aristocrat — dreaming of a large house, fast cars and servants to take care of his every need.

Almost inevitably his lifestyle was financed by fraud, which resulted in various prison sentences when his scams were uncovered. During one spell at HM Prison Lincoln, Haigh conducted a number of biological experiments which involved dissolving the bodies of mice in acid that he had stolen from the prison tinsmith's shop. He would later use this same technique on his six human victims having misunderstood the legal term *corpus delicti* ("body of crime"). Put simply, Haigh wrongly believed that if no body was found he couldn't be charged with murder, although legally "*corpus*" refers to a figurative not a literal body of crime. He would have done better to have heeded his old school motto—*turpe nescire*—"It's a disgrace to be ignorant". Haigh was hanged in 1949.

And now yet another old "Savillian"—as old boys of the Queen Elizabeth Grammar School in Wakefield are called—is a British serial killer. Stephen Shaun Griffiths, charged in May 2010 with the murder of three prostitutes in Bradford is a former Goth (did he follow the band Corpus Delicti?) who studied psychology and was seemingly undertaking postgraduate research. Perhaps we'll discover that his thesis was about some aspect of serial killing—he was certainly obsessed with serial murder and serial murderers as his "wish list" on Amazon revealed. Perhaps that's why he lived in Thornton Road, in the red light area of Bradford where Peter Sutcliffe, the Yorkshire Ripper, killed four of his victims in the 1970s. He certainly disposed of the body of Susan Blamires in the River Aire, which was central to Sutcliffe's story too, although the police have yet to discover the bodies of Shelley Armitage and Susan Rushworth.

Does this imply that Griffiths used his criminological knowledge to ensure that he was an "organized" serial killer—careful and forensically aware—so as to ensure that nothing would be found to link him to their murders? He was certainly astute enough to realise that if he wanted to become infamous a catchy name associated with his activities would help. Griffiths wanted to be remembered; he wanted to stand out; he wanted to be a "somebody", even if his desperate attempt to appear demonic merely strikes as contrived. There's a PhD in that if you ask me.

CHAPTER SIX

The Righteous Slaughter of Some Shootings

Everybody—from GMTV to "Newsnight" and "Channel 4 News"—wanted me to discuss a motive with them. Not so much a *"whodunit?"*, more a *"why-dunnit?"*. It was almost as if discovering a motive for Derrick Bird's murderous activity in Whitehaven, Cumbria on 2 June 2010 would have given people an ending—a full stop to the punctuation of an awful tragedy which they felt that they had somehow been denied by Bird's eventual suicide.

Bird, a self-employed, divorced, local taxi driver, known as "Birdy", murdered 12 people, including his twin brother David, their family solicitor, Kevin Commons, and Darren Rewcastle, a work colleague—shooting them at point blank range in the face—injured eleven other victims and then took his own life, all in the space of 120 mad, bad and depressingly sad minutes. Family and friends were at a loss to understand what had driven Bird to this dreadful conclusion and almost universally described him as a quiet, sociable man whose simple lifestyle in the village of Rowrah was, according to the BBC News, "occasionally enlivened by a taste for foreign holidays". They meant Thailand.

And yet, as I teach my students, understanding murder—whether mass, serial or spree—normally involves three elements: first access, next opportunity and, only then, should we worry about motive. In other words, who has access to the murder victim(s) and how could they use this access to create the opportunity to take that victim's life? If you consider these two elements first you are much more likely to discover the killer than any amount of theorising as to why the victim might have been killed. Having done so, does motive matter at all?

After all, "motive" can be incredibly personal or banal, so either completely idiosyncratic and bizarre, or applied to each and every one of us so as to render it largely irrelevant to understanding why the tragedy has taken place. We never knew why Harold Shipman—the country's most prolific serial killer—killed at least 215 of his patients, even after a public inquiry into these murders, but we do know how he gained access to his patients and how he created opportunities to kill them over decades without being discovered.

In Bird's case it is also clear how he had access to his brother and to his second and third victims—the family solicitor and a work colleague—and the opportunity to kill them because he legally owned weapons. We also know that being a taxi driver gave him the background and knowledge to drive for some 45 miles on various highways and byways—killing as he went—until coming to an end near the village of Boot. Was there a psychological significance in this choice of location for him? Was this village—or the people who lived there—important to him in some way that we don't yet understand, or was it merely the actual, as well as the metaphoric, "end of the road"?

There are, of course, clues to motive in this case. We know that Bird had financial worries to the extent that he was afraid that unpaid taxes to the Inland Revenue—another regular feature in the life of some taxi drivers—might see him go to jail; we know that there had been a disagreement with his brother, perhaps over their mother's affairs, or their father's will; and, finally, we know that Bird had argued with his fellow taxi drivers, whom he thought were laughing at him behind his back and stealing fares from him.

And, in the course of at least two hours, I would suggest that there were three separate phases to what took place, with the first and last of those phases involving deliberate behaviour—the shooting of his brother, the solicitor and the taxi driver, and then finally committing suicide. In between we saw more random behaviour, as he drove from one village to the next. We also know that he shot several of his victims—including his twin brother—in the face.

Attacking someone's face seems to me to be very significant. In targeting the face, the perpetrator is despoiling the victim's appearance and in doing so deliberately attempting to obliterate their individuality. This invariably implies that the motives are personal and that the victim and perpetrator are in some way related to each other. Think about the phrase "losing face" and how significant that might be in a "face-to-face" society, where reputations are built up over generations and where everyone knows each other. If something goes wrong in this type of community you can't just become "another face in the crowd" but have to accept that everyone will know your business.

Bird targeted his twin brother's face. As he did so, it would have been like looking in a mirror and so a dreadful foretaste of how this tragedy would end.

So, if the first three murders were "personal", what motives might we consider would help to explain the next eight deaths, eleven shootings and then, finally, Bird's suicide?

Think back again to this idea of Whitehaven being a face-to-face society and the problems that beset Bird's life. Face-to-face societies are usually the best ones in which to live — they usually provide comfort and support. However, they can also be claustrophobic and suffocating. Beneath the surface, face-to-face societies often harbour discontents that might date back for generations, but which will often go unseen by the visitor passing through. Driving around the small towns and villages of this community and shooting randomly at those whom he encountered allowed Bird to extend his interfamilial quarrels and to impose on the community as a whole his solution to those quarrels.

This was about Bird exercising power and control in a community that he had, in all likelihood, been unable to control for some time. He then took his own life — not because he felt remorse for what he had done — but because this was a way to maintain his power and control over how these murders would be dealt with. Not for him a trial by the state on behalf of the victims and their families and the community as a whole, with a suitable punishment for his crimes handed down by a judge, but rather a self-imposed judgment that took him beyond the reach of the state — beyond the reach of the Inland Revenue, the police, prisons and the criminal justice system. First family, then community and then the state.

When Derrick Bird embarked on his killing spree he was in his own mind righting injustice as he saw it; reordering the world in a way that he would prefer; and playing God so as to settle — once and for all — who was right and who was wrong. As he would have seen it, his was a righteous slaughter. Pages 134-135 set out how I described events for the *Daily Mail* on 4 June 2010.

The scale of the deaths, the apparently quiet, ordinary personality of the killer and the beautiful setting of the Lake District have combined to make this one of most bewildering crimes of modern times.

Yet what cannot be denied is that there *are* chilling similarities between Derrick Bird's massacre and the murders at Hungerford by Michael Ryan and by Thomas Hamilton in Dunblane.

All three killing sprees took place in small, outwardly friendly communities with a strong spirit of neighbourliness.

So what provokes such seemingly random outbursts of violence?

In many respects, rural towns can be wonderful places to live, providing the kind of comforting support that is wholly absent from the anonymity of the inner city.

Yet the closeness of community can also be suffocating and claustrophobic.

It can act like a pressure cooker for some individuals, because almost everyone knows everyone else's business and feuds continue through the generations, fuelled by gossip and petty grievances.

There is no chance of hiding in a mass of humanity as there is in a city.

So a proud, insecure middle-aged man cannot bear to lose face. Unable to ignore a slight, he seethes inwardly with resentment until he explodes.

This is what seems to have happened with Derrick Bird, who, by all accounts, had a row with some of his fellow taxi drivers on Tuesday night.

Brooding on his loss of face among his colleagues, he appears to have lost all sense of proportion and gone on the rampage.

Bird's shooting spree ended up in a series of random killings as he travelled from town to town consumed by lethal rage.

Police officers gather close to the site near the village of Boot, where Bird's body was found

That might even have started in his twisted mind as something rational — a determination to take revenge against colleagues who he felt had undermined him.

One thing is certain: While he was at the peak of the murderous quest, the adrenalin would have been pumping through his body. He would have been on a monstrous high, feeling almost invincible, like Superman, as he discharged the weapon.

Again, in his twisted mind he was in control of the entire sequence of events. That control was exerted, just like in the cases of Michael Ryan and Thomas Hamilton, by dictating the moment of the end of the massacre by killing himself.

But it should be stressed that his suicide was not driven by remorse — it was still all about exerting his own power.

Yesterday's murders in the Lake District had chilling similarities to the 1987 Hungerford massacre.

And there is another disturbing aspect to his suicide. By some accounts, that came at the point when he decided to shoot his own twin brother.

It was a sadistic act of self-loathing. In effect, Bird would have been looking into the mirror as he pulled the trigger. It was a step that foreshadowed his own self-inflicted demise shortly afterwards.

What lessons can be learnt from this massacre? Obviously there are some procedural issues to resolve, such as the question of whether Bird had a legal firearms certificate.

Again, in small rural communities, it is much easier to obtain such a licence, because of the justified need to hunt vermin, than in inner city areas.

There may also be a need to examine whether the current laws on gun control are being enforced with sufficient rigour.

But on the psychological question as to whether it might have been possible to predict that Bird would turn into a mass killer, I think the answer must be no. As I often tell my criminology students, there can be a huge range of human emotions behind different murders: jealousy, passion, revenge, anger, deceit, or greed.

There is no scientific predictor for telling what might happen. It is only when a unique cocktail of these feelings comes together at a certain time, in a certain place, under certain circumstances, that death and carnage can result.

Vicious rage on its own, no matter how explosive, rarely leads to killing, no matter how fashionable it has become to talk about "letting all your feelings out". If it did, then we would be experiencing incidents like the Cumbrian massacre almost every week. Thankfully, the powerful restraints of civilisation still operate

And then Another One

Just a month later, I found myself driving down from Glasgow to a small town on the other side of the Scottish border. I had taken a few days leave to go up to Glasgow to promote my new book about Peter Tobin, which had been making the news in Scotland—partly because in the book I claim that Tobin is the notorious Glasgow serial killer from the 1960s called Bible John. That was not particularly newsworthy in England. Instead, the town of Rothbury in Northumbria had become the site of a story strangely familiar to Derrick Bird's and had, by the time of my journey, come to dominate the English media. I have to say that I also remember laughing at the geographic awareness of several of the London-based producers who had been encouraging me to just "pop over" to Northumbria, given that I was in Glasgow.

"*It's miles away*", I explained, adding, "*on the other side of the country*".

My explanation was usually greeted with a grunt of disapproval for Raoul Moat was big news.

Newly released from HM Prison Durham, Moat had gone to Samantha Stobbart's home—his ex-girlfriend's house—and shot her in the stomach, before also shooting and killing her new boyfriend, Chris Brown, whom he wrongly believed to be a police officer. He then sought out a real police officer to shoot, although thankfully PC David Rathband survived, albeit blinded and critically injured. For the next ten days Moat then played a game of cat and mouse with the Northumbria Police, who always seemed to be on the back foot from the moment that they failed to act on the security information that had been supplied to them by the prison. No intelligence-led policing was in evidence during the days that followed Moat's release, and some members of the public gradually came to see Moat as a form of anti-hero fighting injustice for the underclass. Moat, like Derrick Bird, was to eventually take his own life—in Moat's case in the town of Rothbury, to which I found myself driving on July 7 after my Glaswegian excursion.

I had half expected a "ring of steel" around Rothbury, with armed police stopping anyone driving into the town, and checking their cars for anything that could have been linked to Moat, or indeed looking for Moat himself. After all, Moat had been spotted around the town, and was known to be familiar with the area from camping holidays that he had previously undertaken. The police were pretty much convinced that Moat was in the local area and hiding out in the surrounding forest. In fact, I drove straight into the High Street, and parked up outside the Queen's Head pub, which was about 100 yards away from where Kay Burley was broadcasting live for "Sky News".

I sauntered unsteadily up to where Kay was standing (after all, it had been a long car journey) and greeted some familiar faces, such as their veteran reporter, David Crabtree. David and I had met in Ipswich during the Steve Wright investigation, and I had got to know him and his work well. In fact, my respect for "Sky News" had been cemented by all that they had done to report on the Wright investigation and, of course, I would also write a book about that case with another "Sky News" correspondent, Paul Harrison. Indeed the Tobin book had also been co-written with Paul. Secretly I was a bit miffed that Paul had managed to get out of the book promotion because he had had to cover the Queen's trip to Canada, which left me to do battle with the delights of a Sauchiehall Street audience in Waterstones all by myself.

After speaking to Kay Burley, I was due to walk and talk around Rothbury for a pre-recorded piece to be filmed with John Stapleton for GMTV, which was to be shown the following morning, by which time I would be back in the university. Sky's veteran news anchor, Jeremy Thompson, spotted me doing this and then joshed with Stapleton that, "You always steal our best interviewees".

I took the opportunity before meeting up with Stapleton to walk around Rothbury by myself, so as to get a sense of the place and what was happening. All around me armed officers were sweating in Kevlar and showing small children how their guns worked, before being filmed by the various TV crews that seemed to be patrolling the streets with them. The scene had a choreographed element to it. Small boys would rush up to the police officer, and jabber excitedly, "Show us your gun … please!", which would then allow our own version of *Robocop* to sigh, bend down, and point out the various elements to his weapon. Meanwhile, a TV crew would have quietly hovered into place, and then started to broadcast the reality of armed officers on our streets. Not so much Belfast at the height of The Troubles, more like "The Archers" meets "Midsomer Murders". Frankly, it was like the circus had come to town, but with everyone waiting for Moat—the ringmaster—to turn up.

I crossed over to the other side of the street from where "Sky News" was broadcasting and headed towards the Rothbury Parish Council Notice Board. An elderly woman, not unlike how I imagine Linda Snell might look, spotted me and let me know in no uncertain terms that, "You'll not find anything there". I smiled and then suggested to her that, "Your local community police team"—whose photographs dominated the notice board—"might actually be busy". Or, at least, I said, "I hope so". We passed the time of day quite pleasantly until she said that she had to get home as her daughter was coming over for tea.

By the time of my visit to Rothbury the police were in their "middle phase"—as I came to call it—of their operation. In this phase they were trying to reach out to Moat and establish some rapport with him, so that he would trust them enough to put down his weapons. Their problem was that Moat had been clearly articulating "future foreshortening". In other words, he had been describing how his life was, in effect, over, how everything had been taken away from him, so he had "nothing left to live for". Moat wasn't thinking in terms of weeks, months or years, but rather in minutes and hours. In these circumstances the person who describes himself in this way is always more likely to do something dramatic—such as shooting himself, or other people—so the police knew that they had to try to overcome these feelings. So, in one press conference after another, the police would advise Moat that he had to remember that he was a father, and that he "had a future"—both devices to try and get him to think about a life after this incident had ended.

The police had by and large stuck to this line and were, I think, making progress until they read out a letter from a member of the public who described Moat as a "nutter". Oh dear. A classic own goal that would have signalled the end of any rapport and trust that they had been able to build up with Moat.

A few days later I was criticised on Radio 4's "Feedback" by a member of the public for revealing too much about what was actually happening during these police conferences. I had been interviewed on "The World at One" by Martha Kearney and had described to her "future foreshortening" and how the police were obviously trying to overcome this in Moat. Perhaps it was a fair criticism, but to be honest I hadn't really felt any need to self-censor given that this type of observation was being made on the internet and was, in fact, no different from what I had already said on GMTV and "Sky News". Even if Moat had been listening to me—or watching me—was what I said really going to alter how he wanted this incident to end? I doubted it.

I remember liking Rothbury and, as a result, for the first time felt some connection with Moat, who until geography intervened, had been as different from me as night is to day. Moat was a classic "Cluster B personality type", a domestic violence perpetrator, and had just served a sentence for assaulting one of his children. Even so, at some point he had clearly fallen for Rothbury and I could see why. It was a town of cafes and the Co-op, where Alistair Turner Funeral Directors mingled with an ironmongers that had been established in 1898. The bakery advertised its "famous steak pies". And, just when you thought that it was going to be all things genteel, northern kitsch, Collie Dog Computers—with its collie dog logo—suggested at a hint of irony. Yes, I could understand why Moat liked coming here; it was undoubtedly a good place to live and, for him, a good place to die.

In the end he took his own life, as opposed to my fear that he would attempt "suicide by cop"—in other words provoking the police into shooting him—and something else that I had been openly discussing on the radio and TV, which perhaps might also have encouraged the police to exercise some restraint. Moat's suicide was obviously the third phase of the police operation, and this, too, is now the source of controversy and the subject of an investigation by the Independent Police Complaints Commission, given that a particular species of Tasers (which may or may not have been legal) were fired at Moat in the seconds before his death.

A Paranoid Narcissist with a Gun

Afterwards, messages posted on various internet sites mourned his suicide—"RIP—you're a legend", "Where can I buy a Moat T-Shirt?", "Why did the Police have to chase you rather than paedophiles?"—all of which suggest that Moat had become some kind of anti-hero to a significant group of people, rather than being seen for the paranoid, murdering narcissist that he was. In one way this was hardly surprising given that Moat was at pains to carefully construct a view of himself—leaving a 49-page letter with a friend that was intended to justify his actions, and then later telling the police that he would kill members of the public if he read anything that he believed to be disrespectful to him.

Moat had carefully managed his image so that his violence — shooting his former partner, killing her new boyfriend and then shooting and wounding a police officer — was minimised or justified. So, he suggested that he shot his former partner because she might be able to claim compensation and that he had aimed at her stomach so that she wouldn't want to wear a bikini and make herself attractive to other men. He claimed that he murdered Chris Brown — the new boyfriend — because he was a police officer — which he was not — and shot and wounded PC David Rathband because he was probably going to give a ticket to "a single mum without road tax".

In other words, Moat liked to present himself as some kind of superhero action figure — righting injustices and making the world a better place; challenging those in authority to get off the backs of the community. That's why he walked down Rothbury's High Street — just after Sue Sim, the Acting Chief Constable, suggested that he wouldn't do so. Moat was showing her that he was more powerful, and that she — a woman — couldn't tell him what he could, or couldn't do.

And, there must be many young men — perhaps some of whom have also spent a period of time behinds bars waiting for a "Dear John", or who have had run-ins with authority, or who don't want their girlfriends to have too much power — who found Moat's seemingly alpha-male, black and white, old-fashioned, no-nonsense approach attractive in an economic climate which has made jobs difficult to come by, and with fewer and fewer opportunities to legitimately make their way in the world.

For them Moat was cool masculinity. He was living the dream: Rambo; Robin Hood; The Incredible Hulk.

It's surely no surprise that Moat was a bouncer, for it is often the case that door security staff are on the fringes of the illicit economy and have strained relations with the police. Remember, too, that Moat was able to get access to firearms, guns, shelter, food and clothing — more likely as not supplied by a network of accomplices who owed him loyalty for favours done in the past.

Yet Moat is no hero — anti-hero or otherwise. His paranoia wouldn't allow him to take on board what the police kept telling him about Chris Brown, and his need to control everything meant that he could never accept that things change. His childlike need to be powerful meant he pumped his body with steroids, and then beat his partner and his child. But no matter—he still believed himself to be a good father and husband. That's what mattered most of all to Moat—what he believed, no matter what the reality. In the end he had his hair cut like Travis Bickle from "Taxi Driver". I'm reminded of a line that Bickle used in the movie—"All my life needed was a sense of some place to go". For Moat that place was a high-security prison, but rather than face that reality he exercised the ultimate form of power and control and took his own life. When Raoul Moat shot himself dead it was not through fear or cowardice. It was his final act of control. For power and control meant everything to this 37-year-old bodybuilder and former bouncer.

The media were asked not to report on Moat's true nature for fear he would retaliate by harming the public. Upset by perceived inaccuracies in previous reports, he left a message on a dictaphone threatening to kill someone every time he heard or read something he did not like. And Moat wouldn't have liked to hear the truth: that he was a paranoid narcissist, a man who lived by violence, who beat his partner and hit his child.

For me these events did not emerge out of the blue, but were, instead, the actions of a domestic violence abuser. Like all abusers, he tried to excuse and minimise his behaviour while blaming everyone else. In fact, it is tempting to see this whole episode as an extension of the domestic violence that Moat perpetrated on his former partner and their children and to that extent I think that Moat said two revealing things.

In his 49-page handwritten letter already mentioned above, he claimed that he shot his partner, Samantha, so she could claim compensation for her and their daughter. Nonsense of course, but here we have an almost perfect example of a "technique of neutralisation". In other words Moat was trying to underplay the fact he had shot his ex-girlfriend and provide a justification for his violence towards her. Then he said he shot her in the stomach to stop her wearing a bikini. Can there be any better example of his misogyny? Of his need to control a woman, perhaps even more so once she was no longer his? Interestingly, that touched a nerve. When I went on to Moat's Facebook page, I saw several entries—some of which were written by women — which beggared belief. To a lot of people, his ex-girlfriend had been unfaithful and "she deserved it".

In common with other paranoid narcissists, Raoul Moat carefully constructed a certain self-image. In his case, it was as a super alpha-male; a macho action hero. He was Rambo, a man who shot the policeman only because he was waiting in his patrol car ready to harass someone, "probably a single mother who couldn't afford her car tax". That image that he was at pains to construct touched on something deep in our society and, for me, there's no doubt the long-term significance of Raoul Moat will be the fact he attracted so much support on social-networking sites. Moat was not a hero or an anti-hero, but a dangerous murderer. Yet others saw him differently.

Moat has become a hero to some white, working-class males who no longer have a role in our society. Deprived of legitimate ways of constructing positive images and roles for themselves — through their labour — they need to find some other way of constructing images of themselves which they feel give them power and control. Why not become Robin Hood, Rambo or The Incredible Hulk? It's a fantasy of course, but one which Moat believed that he had been living. In that same dream he was a loving father and a good partner — no matter the evidence that stared him in the face. He may have believed that, but none of us should, and as for those people on Facebook, my heart goes out to them. For the key thing about Moat is that there was no rationality, no empathy. This was a man who lived by violence and understood that he would have to die by violence. It was all part of the image he'd created. But it was just an image. And those who have elevated and admired him would do well to remember that.

Similarities and Differences

It is tempting to try and see the common elements between these two shooting sprees and, also, how they might differ. Perhaps Moat followed the Bird case in the media as he sat in his cell at HM Prison Durham? There was certainly some speculation at the time that this might have been a "copy-cat" incident. So, too, to get an even more historical perspective, we might also like to contrast what happened in Whitehaven and Rothbury with the shooting sprees at Hungerford in 1987 and at Dunblane in 1996. Whitehaven, Rothbury, Hungerford and Dunblane — all small, genteel towns — the last kind of places in the country where you would expect a shooting spree to take place, but linked forever with Derrick Bird, Raoul Moat, Michael Ryan and Thomas Hamilton.

Michael Ryan was an unemployed labourer, who shot and killed 16 people — including his own mother — and wounded 15 others, on 19 August 1987, before finally shooting himself in the John O'Gaunt Community Technical College, where he had previously gone to school and spent a number of very unhappy years. Small for his age, isolated and often bullied, Ryan was seemingly fascinated by firearms and collected books and magazines about survival skills. A fan of the film "Rambo", he legally owned the two semi-automatic rifles and the handgun that he used to kill his victims. Thomas Hamilton also legally owned the two 9mm Browning HP pistols and the two Smith and Wesson .357 Magnum revolvers that he used to kill 16 children, and Gwen Taylor, their teacher, at Dunblane Primary School on 13 March 1996. When Hamilton entered the school at 0930 am, he was carrying 743 cartridges and then shot his gun 109 times before finally killing himself.

There are some obvious similarities between these four incidents — beyond their location in small, rural towns. First is the fact that, with the exception in Moat's case, the guns that were used by Ryan, Hamilton and Bird were legally held. As a result, Hungerford and Dunblane — the latter after a popular, grassroots campaign — led to legislative changes such as the Firearms (Amendment) Act 1988, which banned the ownership of semi-automatic rifles, and then the Firearms (Amendment) (No. 2) Act 1997, which banned .22 cartridge handguns. There have been no attempts in the wake of Whitehaven and Rothbury to ban all guns, with most people seeing these latter two incidents as unpredictable — although there are obviously still questions to be asked in relation to why the Northumbria Police did not act on the security intelligence that was passed to them by security staff at HM Prison Durham.

The incident involving Moat was also unusual in that it lasted for the longest period of time — some ten days — with Moat released from prison on Thursday, July 1, shooting his ex-partner and her new boyfriend in the early hours of Saturday, July 3, then PC David Rathband on July 4, before finally taking his own life on Saturday, July 10. In contrast, Derrick Bird's shooting spree lasted for some two hours, Thomas Hamilton's about the same length of time, and Ryan appears to have been active between 12:30 and 17:00 hours. Perhaps because of the length of time related to the incidents involving Ryan and, especially Moat, the police were eventually able to respond to what was happening and, for example, begin negotiations with both perpetrators. It is reported that Ryan's last words were: "Hungerford must be a bit of a mess ... I wish I had stayed in bed", and although we have, as yet, no definitive account of the negotiations between Moat and the police, a member of the public stated that he heard Moat say: "I haven't got a dad ... nobody cares for me".

Hamilton's shooting spree can be described as geographically static. In other words, he concentrated his activity on one particular location — Dunblane Primary School — which was clearly also psychologically significant for him. Part of this significance must be related to the fact that Hamilton — a former scoutmaster of the 4th/6th Stirling and 24th Stirlingshire troops — was concerned about local gossip that suggested that his activities with boys had a sexual undercurrent. Indeed, evidence emerged after the shootings which demonstrated that there had been police investigations into Hamilton's activities with children attending his "boys' clubs". So, like some monstrous Pied Piper of Hamelin, in targeting children in the local primary school he was not only silencing these boys (and some girls), but also demonstrating to the local community what he thought about the sources of this gossip and how that gossip had affected him. As with Bird, we might be tempted to see these respective incidents within the context of the control exercised by face-to-face societies and consider how those excluded and labeled by these societies attempt to maintain their sense of self and regain control.

With the exception of Ryan, three of the four perpetrators had been investigated by the police, or in Bird's case by the Inland Revenue. Bird was afraid of going to prison, and, of course, Moat had just been released from jail. Ryan, who only came to the police's attention when he renewed his shotgun licence, had a passion for weaponry, survivalism and combat, and to that extent had some interests in common with Moat. Hamilton came to police notice because of complaints that were made as a result of photographs that he had taken of boys in his charge without the permission of their parents, and the fact that on one occasion some boys had had to sleep in his van along with Hamilton after they had been out hillwalking.

Driving—being geographically transient—was much more apparent in the incidents involving Moat, Ryan and Bird. Bird was a taxi driver who clearly knew his way around the community; Moat drove from one location to another—keeping one step ahead of the police as he did so; and Ryan shot his first victim—Susan Godfrey—some seven miles to the west of Hungerford before driving back to the town. He had owned a number of fast cars and motorbikes. After returning to the town, Ryan then walked about the streets, shooting at people randomly. Being able to move from one location to another had a very instrumental purpose. It spread these shooting incidents over a much wider area, which, in turn, delayed the police response. However, while Bird seems to have deliberately wanted to extend what appears to have been an interfamilial dispute out into the community, Moat was at pains to present himself as a community activist. He wanted to be admired within the communities of the north east—and constructed his image carefully to do so—so did not randomly target members of the public. He also had some significant community support, which led to a series of arrests during this incident and after Moat had taken his own life. Ryan—who had clearly not really understood the message in "Rambo"—also randomly shot and killed those people whom he encountered and was, therefore, much less worried about his image than Moat appears to have been. Hamilton was happy to vent his spleen simply within the primary school.

All four perpetrators took their own lives. The great French sociologist, Emile Durkheim, suggested that we should not view suicide as an act of individual pathology, but rather as a reflection of the type of social structure and society in which that individual had lived. And while Durkheim's work on suicide has been much criticised, his division of suicide into egoistic, altruistic, anomic and fatalistic is helpful. An egoistic suicide, for example, comes as a result of the weakening of the bonds that would normally integrate the individual into society and prevent that individual becoming detached from the community. In short, the egoistic suicide occurs when the individual no longer feels that he belongs within the community where he has been living. In this respect there are clear links to the idea of future foreshortening, so that, as in Moat's case, he believed that he had "nothing left to live for". So, too, Hamilton felt rejected by the local community, and Bird was also anxious about gossip that was spreading within the Whitehaven area about his holidays abroad and other issues in his private life. Ryan had never really fitted into the community at all, while the more amiable Bird seems to have found it impossible to continue living in a community where he felt that work colleagues were stealing his fares and others were laughing behind his back about what he got up to in Thailand.

Earlier I described Moat — who seemingly asked for psychiatric help — as a classic Cluster B Personality Type. By this I mean I mean that his behaviour was dramatic, emotional and erratic. He would have in the past exhibited extreme "black and white" thinking — always imagining that he knew right from wrong — and his life would have been characterised by instability in his relationships, and an overwhelming need to have a positive self-image and identity. Throw in a need for admiration and attention-seeking behaviour and you have all the hallmarks of what is known as "borderline personality disorder". From what has been written about him, there would also appear to be elements of this borderline personality disorder in Ryan. To a lesser extent we can also see this in Hamilton, although it is difficult to escape the reality that much of the circumstances surrounding his case stemmed from his sexual interest in small boys. Put bluntly, he was a paedophile.

Only Bird remains difficult to label. After an event as dramatic as what happened in Whitehaven, there are always going to be those who would swear blind that "I always knew that something wasn't right about him". On the other hand, there are those who will claim that "he was just his normal self", or "I can't understand it — he was such an ordinary bloke". Both poles of opinion were in evidence after Bird took his own life, and, more likely as not, both sets of views were probably equally accurate and reflected differ-ent aspects of Bird's public persona. Some would remember an easygoing bloke, while others would telescope backwards and remember small, seem-ingly insignificant details at the time, but that later they felt could explain what had happened. And yet, if we were to consider all four cases, there is nothing uniquely pathological about any of these protagonists (even Moat) and any, or all, of these men, could easily have overcome the problems that beset their lives and have made a positive contribution to their communi-ties. In Bird's case, I am left wondering if simply a straw broke the camel's back—even if we will never know what that straw was. Here I'm not suggesting that somehow Bird "snapped", because clearly there was evidence of planning, but, rather, his shooting spree reflected his inability—as far as he was concerned—to cope in any other way.

Big Bang Lessons?

Is it possible to learn anything from these awful events that might prevent similar shootings in the future? Well, I suppose the first thing to note is that there are considerable gaps between these incidents. Hungerford and Dunblane were separated by nine years and Whitehaven occurred 14 years after Hamilton entered Dunblane Primary School. In other words these incidents are rare in our culture. By way of comparison, the journalist Dave Cullen, in his book about the school shootings in Columbine, Colorado in April 1999, quotes a Federal Bureau of Investigation (FBI)report that documents that there had been 37 shooting incidents at schools between 1974 and 2000, involving 40 attackers. This figure obviously excludes shootings that take place in the United States outside of schools, such as at the workplace, or more widely in the community and which can be used to give some idea of the frequency of these events in cultures with different gun control laws from our own.

Here, we might note that only a month separated Whitehaven from events leading up to Moat taking his own life in Rothbury, but as I have outlined above, a number of factors make this series of incidents different from what happened at Hungerford, Dunblane and Whitehaven. For example, I have drawn attention to how events that culminated in Rothbury were drawn out and prolonged, rather than immediate and decisive as they were in the other three incidents. I have also suggested that it is possible to see Moat's actions not necessarily as a shooting spree, but rather within the broader context of his domestic violence. And while Ryan, Hamilton and Bird seemed to have issues with the communities in which they lived, Moat was much more eager to present himself as a friend of his community.

We might also note that all four perpetrators were men—and, moreover, men who had legal access to guns. The exception here in this latter respect is

Moat. In one sense we should take comfort in the fact that these incidents are so rare, as this suggests that we have got our gun laws just about right, and nor can I see any particular reason as to how we could have predicted that three of these men would take the actions that they did (we await evidence in relation to how the police responded to the security information passed to them by HM Prison Durham). And, at a time when there has been an astonishing explosion of the global supply and availability of cheap weapons that can be purchased on the internet—it has been estimated that there are, for example, 125 million Kalashnikovs circulating in the world at any given time and which (|before it ceasde trading) could be purchased at Kalashnikov USA—the relative absence of people like Moat from our culture is worth celebrating.

Of greater concern must be whether or not Moat's was a "copycat" incident and thus inspired by what had happened at Whitehaven. There is no specific reason to believe this—beyond the fact that Whitehaven had occurred only a month previously and was very widely reported—but, nonetheless, questions must remain as to whether or not Moat saw in himself the same circumstances that had led Bird to start shooting. In this respect it may be that how events of this kind are reported will need to come under greater scrutiny. In much the same way that suicides are carefully reported so as not to romanticise or glamorise the taking of a life, so, too, it might be that a code of practice will have to be developed which would equally prevent this type of incident being romanticised. However, would this work? While the broadcast and print media would no doubt—perhaps grudgingly—abide by whatever such a code of practice might dictate, this would still leave the internet free to speculate, congratulate and glamorise in exactly the same way that various sites did about Moat. The proof of the pudding will surely be how long it is before we have another shooting spree of the types that occurred in Hungerford, Dunblane and Whitehaven. Let's hope that such an event, if it occurs, will be many years in the future.

CHAPTER SEVEN
The Offender Profiler

I have constructed what are known as "offender profiles" in four "live" cases for the police — all in the late 1980s and early 1990s, and at a time when I was still working directly with serious and violent offenders. However, I can't pretend that constructing these profiles was a very successful experience. While in each of these incidences the offender was actually caught, I'm still not at all convinced that my profile had any part to play in their detection. In fact, in at least two of these cases, I was also spectacularly wrong, and suggested behaviours that simply did not fit with the reality of the perpetrator. And that, after all, is at the heart of the "first wave" of American profiling — the belief that you can tell something about the offender's characteristics, based on how the offence was committed, what happened to the victim and how the body may have been left. I became convinced that the fault for these errors wasn't so much mine — although clearly I had to accept responsibility for my suggestions — but rather what we had, even by then, come to imagine was "offender profiling".

Of late, the discipline of offender profiling has developed and in doing so become much more scientifically robust — thanks largely to people like David Canter, Julian Boon and Laurence Allison — and I tend to see a difference between this "second wave" of offender profiling and their approach to what they do with how profiling is still practiced in North America. Above all, the British approach to offender profiling has been keen to emphasise its academic roots and scientific robustness, so most British profilers now regularly publish their work in peer-reviewed journals, which most obviously allows their methods to be discussed and encourages debate about how profiling might continue to make a contribution to catching offenders.

I thought about my own profiling experiences when I was reading a recent and best-selling book on the subject. *Inside the Mind of BTK: The True Story*

Behind the Thirty-Year Hunt for the Notorious Wichita Serial Killer—was written by John Douglas, one of the originators of "offender profiling" in the United States, and is largely concerned with his part in the apprehension of a notorious American serial killer called Dennis Rader, who was dubbed by the press the "BTK". Douglas is well-placed to write a book of this type. As an employee of the Federal Bureau of Investigation (FBI) in the USA he was one of a number of agents who gave prominence both to the phenomenon of serial murder and offender profiling as a means of apprehending this type of murderer.

Sometimes I read books for pleasure—just simply as entertainment. Of late I have become a big fan of the Stieg Larsson trilogy, and can easily forgive him for some of his trite characterisations about serial killers. I read books by, or about Charles Dickens all the time and Dickens remains one of my literary heroes. After all, he could claim to be the original penal reformer and public criminologist—walking the streets at night to observe what was going on, visiting prisons and police stations, and talking to offenders both inside and out of jail. As far as I am concerned, along with *The Ballad of Reading Gaol*, *Little Dorrit* remains the best example of prison writing that can be found in the English language. I suggest this because Dickens in particular gave prisoners a "voice" (clearly Wilde wrote *The Ballad of Reading Gaol* having served a prison sentence), at a time when prisoners were only described in the abstract, or their voices used by the state to preach gallows redemption to the masses. This is especially apparent in his *American Notes*, where Dickens describes his visit to the Eastern Penitentiary in Philadelphia and uses a methodology to do so that is close to ethnography and what we might now call "new journalism"—mixing interview and observation, and a desire to immerse himself in the world that he is seeking to describe.

However, on this occasion I read what Douglas had written in a more critical way and tried to deconstruct the taken-for-granted assumptions about offender profiling that Douglas uses to explain the apprehension of Rader. I also hoped to see what was not being described by him, both in terms of offender profiling and alternative discourses which might better explain the phenomenon of serial killing and reduce its incidence.

Let's start by outlining the working methods that Douglas claims that he employs when working as an offender profiler. So that you can follow my argument, I will identify specific pages in the book where I quote Douglas, and his co-author, Johnny Dodd.

Profiling the Profiler: His Working Methods

John Douglas — dubbed the "legendary FBI profiler" by his publisher, makes it quite clear in his writing that "climbing inside the heads of monsters is my speciality", and that he is "convinced that those of us with a police background ha[ve] the ability to understand the mind of an incarcerated felon far better than any psychologist or psychiatrist". Douglas expands that "street smarts" are vital in such work (it should be noted that being streetwise is not the sole preserve of the police) and thereby deliberately broadens the gulf between academics and law enforcement. He also claims to use this speciality as the means by which he constructs an offender profile. He suggests, for example, that he "takes that expression frozen on the face of a murder victim and works backwards. I have to place myself inside the head of both the offender and the victim at the time of the crime". Douglas even goes so far as to compare himself with the fictional six-year-old boy, Cole Sear, who saw the dead in the 1999 psychological thriller *The Sixth Sense*, even if: "I not only saw dead people — although, actually, they were corpses — but also people killing people. When I plunged myself into a case, I became someone else. I became the killer". To this extent, Douglas helps to portray himself and other behavioural profilers as cursed-heroes; men who are compelled to do such noble work despite the unpleasant aspects it entails. Indeed, Douglas stretches this metaphor to the extreme by making constant reference to his near-death experience, brought about, he believes, by the stress of his vocation. He describes an extreme scene when he was sitting at night by a plot in an FBI cemetery that had been earmarked for his body (when his former employers believed he was not going to survive the coma into which his body had retreated) and he realises that a killer could be nearby visiting the grave of a victim.

Throughout *Inside the Mind of BTK,* references are constantly made to the disturbing dreams Douglas has about acts of murder, and the litany of disturbed nights he endures, to the point that he becomes less like a rational investigator and more like a shaman who is guided by visions, wild imagi-nation and hallucinations. So, while on the trail of Dennis Rader, a serial killer in Wichita, Kansas who claimed the lives of ten people between 1974 and 1991, prior to his arrest and conviction in 2005, Douglas advises that he went to Wichita "to wallow in Dennis Rader, to open up his sick head and dive into his swamplike mind".

Leaving the hyperbole of the "true crime" genre to one side—although here it should also be noted that Douglas was the model for the fictional Federal Bureau of Investigation (FBI) Agent Jack Crawford in the novels of Thomas Harris, such as *Red Dragon* (1981) and *Silence of the Lambs* (1988), many other offender profilers (from different backgrounds) have also written true crime accounts of their work in the United Kingdom (for example, Paul Britton's *The Jigsaw Man* and *Picking up the Pieces;* David Canter's *Criminal Shadows: Inside the Mind of the Serial Killer* and *Mapping Murder. Walking in Killers Footsteps;* Laurence Allison and Marie Eyre's *Killer in the Shadows;* my own books with Paul Harrison called *Hunting Evil and The Lost British Serial Killer*). What should be made of Douglas's claims, not only in relation to Dennis Rader, but also of his "submerged" approach to offender profiling more generally, and how this may help to understand the phenomenon of serial killing? If Douglas's claim that his explanations about how the mind of a serial killer works can be harnessed to help to prevent others from falling victim to violent crime, then an exploration of the validity of this claim is a worthwhile exercise.

And, as described, we should not ignore that Douglas, in partnership with a number of FBI colleagues, effectively invented modern profiling (see above) and that this "medical-psychological" tradition of analysing serial killing from the perspective of the serial killer and his motivation—based on interviews undertaken by Douglas and others in the 1970s and 1980s, largely dominates contemporary theorising about the subject, as well as having captured the public's imagination of their understanding about serial killing. This critique of the origins and development of offender profiling seeks to assess its strengths and weaknesses by considering the BTK case that Douglas uses in his most recent book. In doing so we suggest that a "structural" approach to understanding the phenomenon of serial killing is more likely to produce the result that Douglas envisaged — in other words, fewer people falling victim to violent crime.

Originating Offender Profiles

Offender profiling takes as its central premise that the characteristics of an offender can be deduced by a carefully-considered examination of the offence. As Peter Ainsworth of the University of Manchester put it:

> Offender profiling generally refers to the process of using all the available information about a crime, a crime scene, and a victim, in order to compose a profile of the (as yet) unknown perpetrator.

While it is difficult to be precise about the actual origins of offender profiling, this premise was, to all intents and purposes, established in the 1970s within, and by, the FBI's Behavioral Support Unit (BSU) — now known as the Investigative Support Unit (ISU) — which became famous through Thomas Harris's books, and subsequent movie adaptions. However, it should be acknowledged that what might now be called "offender profiles" were constructed in 1956 by James Brussel in relation to the case of the "Con Edison" bomber in New York, and that Brussel subsequently wrote about his experiences in his 1968 autobiography *Casebook of a Crime Psychiatrist*. So, too, Dr Robert Brittain — Consultant Forensic Psychiatrist at the Douglas Inch Clinic in Glasgow prior to his death in 1971 — who had a clinical interest in sadistic psychopathic killers, was asked by Glasgow CID to offer an opinion about the type of person they were seeking in the so-called "Bible John" murder case in the late 1960s. His subsequent paper, "The Sadistic Murderer " (1970), remains the classic introduction to the subject, and can also be viewed as a profile.

However, it is Brussel's work which had the greatest influence on the FBI, so, for example, Howard Teten (who was a protégé of Brussel) helped establish the bureau's Behavioral Science Unit in 1972. Interestingly, Douglas was, in turn, a protégé of Teten. As *The New Yorker* columnist and author Malcolm Gladwell has recently written, "In the close-knit fraternity of profilers, [this] is like being analysed by the analyst who was analysed by Freud". It is no surprise therefore that *Inside the Mind of BTK* closely follows the narrative style and pace of Brussel's *Casebook of a Crime Psychiatrist*. Leaving these literary allusions aside, what the FBI wanted to do at a practical level was to find a way of using the wealth of forensic information that they were able to generate from crime scenes and see if, from that evidence, they could suggest something of the type of offender who had committed the offence. So, in part using their collective experience of investigating multiple murder and sexual assaults, and crucially through carrying out extensive interviews with 36 convicted serial killers, they began to assert that the personality of an offender — in cases of serial rape or murder — could be gleaned from a consideration of the following five areas: the crime scene; the nature of the attacks themselves; forensic evidence; a medical examination of the victim; and victim characteristics.

A little is known about the 36 interviews that Douglas and his colleagues conducted, and in his most recent book, for example, he describes the fact that their interview protocol involved "thousands of questions" and ran to 57 pages in length. It is also known that many of these questions were aimed at providing some basic information about the killer's motivation, victim selection, and the impact that the murders might have had on the killer. So, too, it is known that Douglas and other profilers working within the FBI set out to answer whether or not their interviewees were "born to kill", or whether, for example, some childhood trauma had influenced their behaviour. The fruits of these interviews eventually led to the publication of Ressler, Burgess and Douglas's *Sexual Homicide: Patterns and Motives* in 1988.

Douglas provides a glimpse of how one of these interviews was conducted in 1981 when he visited Attica Correctional Facility in New York with Robert Ressler to interview David Berkowitz — also known as "The Son of Sam". Berkowitz is an American serial killer and arsonist who murdered six people and wounded seven others in New York from July 1976 until his arrest in August 1977. Douglas explains that he and Ressler had gone to Attica to "pry information out of the head of one of the nation's most notorious serial killers". He continues:

We'd arrived unannounced, on a fishing expedition of sorts, hoping to convince David Berkowtiz, aka Son of Sam, to help us with our criminal profiling study, which involved a fifty-seven-page interview questionnaire. We wanted answers to such questions as *What was his motive? Was there a trigger that set him off on his murderous spree? What was his early childhood like? How did he select his victims? Did he ever visit the grave sites of his victims? How closely did he follow the press coverage of his crimes?* His answers would help us better understand the killers we were hunting (emphasis in original).

Seemingly, Berkowtiz was brought to see Douglas and Ressler who were waiting for him in a tiny interrogation room, although as the following exchange reveals it is clear that Berkowtiz had no idea who Douglas or Ressler were, or what they wanted:

"Who are you guys?" he asked the moment he spotted us seated at the far end of the only piece of furniture in the room—a linoleum-covered table. As planned, the guards had quickly exited before Berkowitz had a chance to tell us to take a hike. "We're FBI agents, David" I told him. "We'd like to talk to you. We're hoping you might be able to help us ... It's like I always say," I explained, "if you want to learn how to paint, you don't read about it in a book. You go straight to the artist. And that's what you are, David. You're the artist ... you're famous. You're huge. You had all of New York scared shitless. In a hundred years, no one will remember my name. But everybody will still know who the Son of Sam was.

This flattery seems to have worked, for Douglas suggests that Berkowitz became "putty in our hands" and over the course of the next five hours "he walked us through every dark, twisted corner of his sad life, sharing details he'd never told anyone".

Talking with Serial Killers

Douglas does not tell the reader what these details might have been, so there is no way of validating this claim, and nor is it revealed if Berkowtiz actually completed the 57-page questionnaire that formed the basis of Douglas and Ressler's research. Indeed, they seem to have simply chatted for a number of hours. However, there are more worrying issues that this account reveals, if this is indeed an accurate depiction of the interview. Ignoring the (absence of) the ethics of the origin and conduct of the interview—although it should be remembered that Douglas claims that those with a police background are better able to understand a convicted offender than psychologists or psychiatrists—consider how credulous Douglas and Ressler seem to have been when they interviewed Berkowitz.

After all, Berkowtiz—at the time of this interview (three years into a 365 year sentence), might have had a variety of reasons for agreeing to be interviewed, after he realised that was, in fact, why he had been taken to the interrogation room, rather than simply falling for Douglas's flattery. Should it not also be considered whether serial killers necessarily tell an interviewer the truth? Might they attempt to confuse, or alternatively be over-eager in the hope of getting some sort of favour such as parole, a better work detail, or simply a more favourable cell allocation? That Douglas and his colleagues interviewed serial killers who were caught may suggest something about their offending, which may differentiate them from those offenders who remain at large who may have used different approaches. In all of this we might detect the forensic equivalent of a responder-bias. More than this, I have consistently suggested that in my own work with serial killers and other serial offenders in the United Kingdom I encountered two distinct groups: those that spoke and those—the majority—who were "silent and uncommunicative".

Those serial killers who were prepared to talk to me had invariably developed a very robust, and self-serving view as to why they had repeatedly killed. Time after time, their views and insights were more often than not socially constructed to suit the nature and circumstances of their arrest, conviction and imprisonment. All too often their explanations were either: (i) rooted in the forlorn hope that, for example, there might come a day when release was possible through parole; (ii) proffered to engineer a more favourable prison transfer; or (iii) sometimes to maintain a conception of "self" more in keeping with their own sense of who they were, and to what they thought they were entitled. Others simply wanted to talk so as to break up the monotony of the prison routine.

I would further argue that when I investigated their explanations for their offending in any depth they could have been applied more generally to most people in society. After all, who has not had a beloved parent, grandparent, uncle or aunt die? Who did not feel lonely, bullied, or excluded as a child?

Who has not been saddened by the end of a close and loving relationship with another person? Who would not like to be given a little more credit for one's achievements, and a little less criticism for one's failings? Would these everyday prosaic life-events be enough to push us into "killing for company", as the true crime author, Brian Masters, claimed in respect of the British serial killer, Dennis Nilsen? Are these justifications enough to account for the phenomenon of serial killing? While some British serial killers, such as Robert Black, who abducted, sexually assaulted and killed at least three girls in the 1980s, undoubtedly had appalling childhoods filled with abandonment and abuse, is this justification enough to explain reliably the aetiology of their crimes, especially when so many others have had similar experiences, but have not gone on to kill and kill again?

These observations about the explanations that serial killers give for their motivation stem from my experience of working with them after they had been caught and imprisoned. However, even in the immediate aftermath of arrest—long before their trial and conviction, those serial killers who are prepared to talk regularly construct a picture that is often far removed from the reality of events. Peter Sutcliffe, for example, after his arrest for a series of seven attempted murders and 13 murders of women in Yorkshire in the 1970s, gave a variety of interviews to detectives working on the case. He appeared forthcoming, but as Michael Bilton, the leading expert on the murders has commented, "It is now wholly evident that he was grossly deceitful and manipulative". Specifically, Sutcliffe—better known as the Yorkshire Ripper, sought to hide any sexual motive for his crimes, and, instead, wanted to paint a picture of himself as simply mad and presenting with auditory hallucinations, which would thus influence every aspect of his trial and his sentence.

So, too, Fred West, who, before taking his own life, left 111 pages of autobiography. However, as David Canter explains, anyone hoping to discover clues in this autobiography as to why West killed 12 people would be disappointed for "the journal ignores all of this". Canter's observation would come as no surprise to John Bennett, the detective in charge of the West investigation. After his arrest, West's interviews with the police amounted to 145 tape-recordings that translated into 6,189 pages of transcript. Nonetheless, since his retirement Bennett has commented that, "West's interviews were worthless except to confirm that nothing that he said could be relied upon as anything near the truth". Indeed, Gordon Burn — one of West's most perceptive biographers simply dismisses him as a "bullshitting liar", who claimed, for example, to have travelled the world with the Scottish pop singer Lulu. West, on occasion, claimed he had murdered up to 30 people, but this was never established. Gordon Burn explains that West would talk "palaver while apparently talking the truth. Laying out and simultaneously covering up".

Killers Who Will Not Talk

The second group that I have encountered was the mirror opposite of the first. In short, people in that group never talked at all about the motivation that drove them to murder, and they kept their secrets well-guarded. For example, just after his conviction in April 2001 for the murder of 15 of his patients, the West Yorkshire Police decided to reinterview Harold Shipman — Britain's most prolific serial killer, about the deaths of other patients whom he had attended whilst practising in Todmorden. The videotape is very revealing, as the following transcript suggests:

Police Officer: No replies are going to be given to any questions during the course of this interview and any subsequent interviews. I think it is fair to say for the purposes of the tape that we are happy that we are interviewing Harold Shipman.

(Officer gets up and walks round the table to place a picture in front of the face of Shipman, who has turned to face the wall.)

Police Officer: To start with, if I can try to jog your memory by showing you a photograph ... that's Elizabeth Pearce. Of the three ladies there it's the elderly lady dressed in black. For the benefit of the tape Dr Shipman's eyes are closed.

(Officer returns to desk and picks up two photographs.)

Police Officer: Unfortunately we don't have a photograph of Mr Lingard. To try and jog your memory here is a photograph of Eagle Street and there is a photograph of where Mr Lingard lived. Just for the benefit of the tape, Dr Shipman's eyes are closed and he didn't look at all.

(Officer returns to desk and returns with another photograph which he places again in front of the face of Shipman.)

Police Officer: Just to try and jog your memory, Dr Shipman, I have here a photograph of Lily Crossley. Just for the benefit of the tape Dr Shipman's eyes are closed and he didn't look at all.

This final note from the police officer exactly sums up this second group of silent and uncommunicative serial killers—"just for the benefit of the tape Dr Shipman's eyes are closed and he didn't look at all". Not only did he not look, but he also never spoke. Shipman never discussed why he killed 215 (and possibly 260) elderly people either in Todmorden or Hyde, and ultimately—like Fred West, he chose to commit suicide in his cell at HM Prison Wakefield in January 2004, rather than reveal the circumstances that led him to murder.

So, to apply Gordon Burn's phrase about Fred West more generally, there is one group of serial killers who "lay out", and another who "cover up"; some who talk endlessly—although not necessarily to any purpose—and others who refuse to, or indeed cannot, talk at all.

Organized and Disorganized

These criticisms notwithstanding, the FBI used the interviews that Douglas and his colleagues conducted to theorise that offenders could be characterised as either "organized" or "disorganized", and that these distinctions would be related to the personal characteristics of the offender. An "organized" offender, for example, is one who uses a great deal of logic and planning, such as wearing gloves, bringing a rope or handcuffs to incapacitate the victim, and classically is very much in control of the crime scene, and as such, few, if any, clues are left. It is also suggested that "organized" offenders have a specific personality type. They will typically be intelligent, sexually active and competent, and are likely to have a partner. They will have skilled or semi-skilled jobs, and to all intents and purposes will appear "normal". However, this mask of normality hides an anti-social personality. It is also suggested that "organized" offenders follow reports of their crimes in the news, and that they are often propelled to commit crime as a result of anger and frustration in their personal lives.

On the other hand "disorganized" offenders do not plan their offending. Their crimes are sudden and opportunistic (not the same as "random") and the offender will use whatever comes to hand to help him or her commit the offence. So, for example, a man might tie up his victim using her scarf or underwear; he will attack by using weapons he finds in the home or the vicinity of the offence. There is little attempt to conceal evidence, and often the victim's body is simply abandoned, rather than hidden. More than this, the "disorganized" offender is said to live alone, or at home, e.g. with his parents, and usually offends within his local area. He will be socially and sexually immature, and will often have a history of mental illness. Finally, it is suggested that this type of offender commits the crimes involved whilst frightened or confused.

In other words, and as Douglas, Burgess and Ressler would later describe in 1992 in their *Crime Classification Manual*—a handbook of offender profiling issued by the FBI, "The crime scene is presumed to reflect the murderer's behaviour and personality in much the same way as furnishings reveal the homeowner's character". Thus, offender profiling could be used to predict the characteristics of the, as yet, unknown offending subject based on information that was available at the crime scene, and would be a boon to the police in terms of identifying and prioritising suspects.

There has been a great deal of criticism about this "homological assumption" at the heart of offender profiling, and indeed about other issues related to profiling's origins, development and application. For example, the American academics, Copson and Marshall, have gone as far as to suggest that many profiles are so idiosyncratic as to be indivisible from the identity of the profiler, and the Canadian scholar, Kim Rossmo, argues that offender profiling has no scientific validity whatsoever, is largely intuitive and has never been subject to any rigorous academic scrutiny. He further suggests that their central finding—"organized" or "disorganized"—should, instead, be seen as a continuum, rather than two distinct categories.

But is this criticism justified when we consider Douglas and his work in relation to Dennis Rader—whom he interviewed for the latter part of his most recent book, and about whom he was consulted on three different occasions by the Kansas police at various stages of their investigation into the ten murders?

Bind, Torture and Kill

Rader, who identified himself at the time in a series of taunting notes that he sent to the police by the three words: "bind, torture and kill", or more popularly as "BTK", struck first in January 1974 when he killed the Otero family in their home; 38-year-old Joseph, his wife, Julie, their son, Joey, and their 11-year-old daughter, Josephine, who was found hanging from a water pipe in the basement of the house with a large quantity of semen on her leg and the floor nearby. The as-yet unidentified Rader would strike again in April the following year when he stabbed 24-year old Kathryn Bright (Kathryn's brother, Kevin, escaped the attack despite being shot twice), and in March 1977 he bound and strangled Shirley Vian. Over the next four years he committed at least four more murders, although the police investigation into these crimes made little progress. Then in October 1984 two detectives from Wichita visited Douglas at FBI Headquarters in Quantico, having previously taken his advice about the murders in the autumn of 1979, although it is this second meeting that opens *Inside the Mind of BTK*.

"Let's go to the conference room", I told [the Wichita detectives]. "Several of my colleagues are waiting for you there. I want you to walk us through the case". After the Wichita detectives had walked Douglas, Roy Hazlewood — author of the true crime best-sellers *Dark Dreams* and *The Evil That Men Do* and Ron Walker through the case, the three FBI agents "climbed into the head" of the BTK and offered their opinion as to the type of person who was committing these crimes. As Douglas explains:

> We were going to toss out ideas about what sort of person might be responsible for those seven unsolved murders in Kansas, how police might track him down, and ways they could get him to crack once they had a possible suspect ... in many ways, our goal here felt similar to what musicians do when they get together and jam[.] The objective of the session was to keep moving forward until we ran out of juice, until we were tapped out. It was up to the two detectives from Wichita to take notes, jotting down elements they found helpful.

We don't know which elements the Wichita detectives did actually find helpful, but, on the other hand, we do have a very detailed note about the sum total of advice that Douglas, Hazlewood and Walker provided.

The advice that they gave — based on the account provided by Douglas in *Inside the Mind of BTK*, which takes up 13 pages of narrative — is worth assessing, especially in relation to what might be the motivating factors behind the seven (as then) murders, based on their analysis of the crime scenes left by BTK, his victim selection, how he dealt with his victims, and also some of the basic biographical details that Douglas and his colleagues suggested would fit the type of person committing these murders.

Douglas "kicked off the session" by suggesting that BTK was mid- to late-thirties, divorced, lower middle class and living in rented accommodation. Hazlewood thought that he would be middle-class and "articulate". Walker suggested that as BTK had never engaged in any sexual penetration, he would be sexually inadequate and immature, and Hazlewood thought that BTK would be a "sexual bondage practitioner" and "heavily into masturbation". As a result, suggested Hazlewood, "women who have had sex with this guy would describe him as aloof, uninvolved, the type who is more interested in her servicing him than the other way around". Douglas, too, believed that BTK would have "racked up a bit of sexual experience", and that his partners would be either "many years younger, very naïve, or much older and depend on him as their meal ticket". According to Walker, he would be a "lone-wolf type of personality" although he could function in social settings, but only "on the surface" — a conclusion with which Douglas agreed, and which, for him, suggested that he wouldn't stay at any one job for any length of time because he wouldn't like people to have power over him. As such, he would not be a "team player", and Hazlewood thought that he would be a "now person" who wanted instant gratification. His IQ would be somewhere between 105 and 145. All three thought that he might have some connections to the military (unsurprising given recent previous military drafts for Korea and Vietnam), and Douglas suggested that he would drive a "nondescript type of car — perhaps a sedan". They also all thought that he would collect detective stories and be interested in law enforcement. Finally, Douglas suggested that, "This guy isn't mental …but he is crazy like a fox".

It is of interest to note that the results of this brainstorming session were produced at a period in the case when detectives were in possession of three letters from BTK to the media (one of which was a poem), a letter he sent to a potential victim who inadvertently evaded him, and a recording of his voice made when he called 911 informing the police where to find the body of his seventh murdered victim.

So, after six hours, the FBI handed the Wichita detectives a blueprint for their investigation, and as Malcolm Gladwell has put it, what they had to do was:

> Look for an American male with a possible connection to the military. His IQ will be above 105. He will like to masturbate, and will be aloof and selfish in bed. He will drive a decent car. He will be a "now" person. He won't be comfortable with women. But he may have women friends. He will be a lone-wolf. But he will be able to function in social settings ... he will be either, never married, divorced or married, and if he is married his wife will be younger or older. He may or may not live in a rental, and might be lower class, upper lower class, lower middle class or middle class. And he will be crazy like a fox, as opposed to being mental.

Gladwell employs irony to make his point that these characterisations were both so general as to fit millions of suspects and in themselves contradictory, and, therefore, unlikely to be of much help to the police. But, in any event, Dennis Rader was actually a pillar of his local community; a happily married family man with two children, the President of his local Lutherian Church, a Boy Scouts leader, and a reliable employee of the Sedgwick County animal services division.

At the End of it All

These criticisms might be too ungenerous to Douglas, although we should also note that Rader was not, in fact, caught as a result of any profile constructed by the FBI. Two attempts had been made by murder squad detectives to solve the case by re-evaluating the entire case file in the late seventies (the Hotdog squad) and in the mid eighties (the Ghostbusters). Both squads used behavioural profiling to no avail.

In 2004, spurred on by hearing that a local author was about to write a book about the BTK case, Rader began communicating more than ever with detectives. In March alone he sent eleven communications, packages, poems, dolls, and sketches to the detectives hunting him, with contents ranging from crime scene souvenirs to false confessions to other killings. In his correspondence with detectives, BTK asked if a floppy disk could ever be used to trace the machine in which it was used, and upon believing the lie that detectives fed to him (via a personal advert in the *Wichita Eagle* newspaper) when they said it was a "safe" method of communication, he sent his last correspondence to them on 15 February 2005. The package contained (among other things) a purple 1.44mb Memorex floppy disk, which, unknown to BTK, also contained metadata embedded in a deleted Microsoft Word document that was still on the disk. The metadata contained the words "Christ Lutheran Church", and the document was marked as last modified by "Dennis". A search of the church website showed Dennis Rader as president of the congregation council.

Nor should we necessarily discount the help that profiling has provided to the police in other cases — both in the United States of America and also in Europe. And it should be remembered that there have been developments that have pushed profiling in different directions from the early days that Douglas describes in *Inside the Mind of BTK*. Yet, all that having been said, does theorising of this type — based as it is on "climbing into the heads of monsters", actually deliver a better understanding of the phenomenon of serial killing, and, as a result, ensure that fewer people fall victim to violent crime? Or, are there other approaches that might have greater success?

The Canadian social anthropologist, Elliot Leyton, has been at the forefront of attempts to outline a "structural" analysis of the phenomenon of serial killing. For, as he argues in *Hunting Humans*, the "individual discourse" of the medico-psychological tradition about serial killers fails to meet the challenge of causation by ignoring cultural and historical specificity. After all, dangerous and deranged individuals are a constant feature over time, and between cultures. Yet, given that this is so, how are we then to explain why Britain had no serial killers during the 1920s and 1930s, while Germany had 12? Indeed, why did the late 1970s and early to mid 1980s produce so many British serial killers? For Leyton, focusing on North America, the answer to these questions of cultural and historical specificity is to argue that serial killing cannot just be understood as the result of a greater or lesser number of dangerous personalities existing in society at any one time, but rather has to be seen as the product of the socio-economic system which cannot reward the efforts of all, and thus may dangerously marginalise certain people. By no means is this solely a problem for capitalist societies, as communist countries that produce marginalised groups have also provided examples of serial murderers.

Leyton goes further and argues that serial killing should be viewed as a form of "homicidal protest" —which in essence suggests that some people will react to challenges to their position in the economic and social structure by killing those in the challenging group. In other words, to truly understand why serial killers kill we need to investigate the very nature of the social structure that has created these people whom we label as serial killers and then provides them with readily identifiable groups of victims.

And, as is implicit in this analysis, it also suggests that the responsibility for serial killing, therefore, does not lie so much with the individual serial killer, but can be equally found within the social and economic structure of their culture, which may not reward the efforts of all, and in particular may marginalise large sections of society. It, therefore, should come as no surprise that the victims of British serial killers have been exclusively confined to certain marginalised groups in our culture—the elderly, gay men, prostitutes, immigrants, babies and infants, and young people moving home and finding their feet elsewhere in the country, and that women make up a significant number in all but one of these categories. It is people from within these marginalised groups who are the focus of the murderous efforts of serial killers and if we really wanted to deliver on Douglas's objective of reducing the numbers of people who fall victim to violent crime, then we would be just as well concentrating on eradicating homophobia, prejudice against sex workers, and supporting young people and the elderly in our communities, rather than climbing into the heads of serial killers.

CHAPTER EIGHT

Explaining "Ordinary" Murder and Murder Investigations

So far in this book I have been concerned with spree, mass or serial killers. The names and circumstances in which these individuals came to kill are well-known and have been widely reported—even if their victims are hardly remembered at all. I have also considered how some serial killers come to "disappear" from public view. Yet there has been surprisingly little rigorous academic attention paid to the phenomenon of "everyday", "common place" murder, to the extent that Dr Fiona Brookman of the University of Glamorgan has gone as far as to claim that the broader subject of homicide has suffered from "academic neglect" in this country.

As a consequence, questions related to explaining what motivates one human being to kill another human being are rarely considered in criminology or psychology, despite the widespread fascination that this type of question generates more popularly. Even defining "murder" is fraught with difficulties. And—a theme I have discussed when considering Raoul Moat and Derrick Bird—what would an attempt to answer the question of motivation look like? Should we consider the wider social structure in which the murder has taken place, and into which the murderer has been socialised?

In other words, is there a relationship between murder and, for example, poverty, gender, or race? Or, do these "macro" issues become less important in answering this question of motivation when we consider the "micro" level of the dynamics of the crime itself? Are murderers "pathological"—different, in some way, from you and me, or are the roots of violence and murder far more widespread and common than we care to acknowledge?

Nor have we really considered how the police use the media during murder investigations, and how that relationship might come under strain if the murder is high-profile and the police are seen as failing to catch the perpetrator. So, within this chapter I am going to present case studies of some "everyday" murders, plus findings from in-depth interviews I conducted with four senior investigating officers (SIOs), at Birmingham City University, all of whom were in charge of high-profile murder investigations which lasted for significant periods of time, and which generated sustained and intense national broadcast and print media interest. These four SIOs are Albert Kirby, John Bennett, Chris Stevenson and Roy Lambert, who were respectively in overall charge of, or at least partly in charge of, the investigations into the murder of James Bulger in 1993, the murders committed by Fred and Rose West prior to their arrest in 1994, the murders of Holly Wells and Jessica Chapman in Soham in 2002 and the five murders committed by Steve Wright in Ipswich in 2006.

It is doubtful whether there exists a single, "grand" theory of murder. So while my focus here is firmly rooted in what is known as "individual positivism"—seeking to explain the crime of murder as primarily generated by forces within the individual murderer as a result of a psychological predisposition to kill—the complex interplay between the "faulty individual" and the "faulty social circumstances" that permits murder should also be remembered. The complexity of this interplay is an important point to bear in mind, for murder is a diverse phenomenon—which again makes the idea of one grand, explanatory theory illogical. For example, murder is not just committed by people, but also by large, multinational corporations and even governments, to the extent that taking a life is not always universally condemned, or even classified as unlawful. To illuminate this point further we need to consider what we mean when we define and label an act as "murder", and also consider who has the power to avoid having this label applied to their behaviour.

Defining Murder

The classic definition of murder has been attributed to Sir Edward Coke and the term is embedded in the Offences Against the Person Act 1861 which also provides for associated offences. Coke stated that:

Murder is when a man of sound memory, and of the age of discretion, unlawfully killest within any county of the realm any creature in rerum natura under the King's peace, with malice aforethought, either expressed by the party or implied by law, so as the party wounded or hurt etc. die of the wound or hurt etc. within a year and a day after the same.

The only substantive change to this definition in England and Wales has been to remove the "year and a day" rule in 1996; the idea of "malice aforethought" — or *mens rea* (the guilty mind) — remains central within the legal definition of murder. Murder is thus the intentional killing of one human being by another or other human beings and is thus different from what is called "homicide". In very general terms, in England and Wales, homicide is used generically to describe the killing of a human being by another person regardless of motive, or whether the act was lawful or unlawful. Examples of lawful deaths, for example, might include deaths caused as a result of acts of war; when a prisoner is executed by a state that retains the death penalty; or when a boxer kills his opponent. Killings which are unlawful are described as murder, manslaughter or infanticide (terms which suggest that there are different levels of culpability) and it is the first of these unlawful killings which is the focus of this chapter.

In short, I am not dealing with serial killers and the phenomenon of spree or mass murder, but with interpersonal murders — those routine, all too often domestic and commonplace murders that generate local newspaper headlines or, if the victim is especially newsworthy and there was some form of sexual element to the murder, national attention. Thus, the specific type of murder that we are considering does not reflect the overall extent of murder in any given year and I am only going to consider statistics from England and Wales, given that there are different criminal justice jurisdictions in Scotland and in Northern Ireland.

How Much Murder?

According to the *Home Office Homicide Index* — which covers the offences of murder, manslaughter or infanticide — there were 651 such deaths in 2008–2009, which represented a decrease in the number of homicides by

14 per cent over the previous recording period. Indeed, this was the lowest number of homicides recorded since 1998–1999, when 642 such offences were recorded. Unsurprisingly, this led to a number of favourable newspaper headlines with, for example, Alan Travis in *The Guardian* (on 21 January 2010) noting that, "Murders drop to lowest level for 20 years in England and Wales". Here, however, we should note my observations in *Chapter 1* that this will be an underestimate of the overall level of murder.

Even so, interrogating these figures more closely allows us to build up a picture of the type of interpersonal murder that I want to describe. More than two-thirds of murder victims were male (71 per cent) and the most common method of killing both men and women was by a sharp instrument. In short, they were stabbed by a knife, or by a broken bottle. Indeed, despite the widespread publicity that gun crime attracts, there were only 39 shooting victims in 2008–2009, which, again, compared favourably with the previous reporting period when there had been 53 victims. The second most common method used to murder men was by hitting or kicking (28 per cent), and for women, strangulation or asphyxiation (18 per cent).

Female victims were more likely to have been killed by someone whom they knew, such as their partner, ex-partner or lover, with around three-quarters (76 per cent) knowing the main suspect. Only half of male victims knew the main suspect in the murder inquiry. Overall, the risk of being a victim of homicide was 12 murders per year per million of the general population — in line with the homicide rate of most Western European countries — but children under one year old were the most at-risk group of being murdered at the rate of 27 murders per year per million of the general population and children more generally are extremely vulnerable — see Case Study (1) below.

Case Study (1)

"'It sounds ridiculous, but he was a doting father,' says John Mayhew of his former employee David Cass. This weekend, Cass smothered to death his children, three-year-old Ellie and one-year-old Isobel, before killing himself ... Cass, whose children's bodies were found in a caravan in Southampton on Sunday, parked in the garage where he had worked for four years. He had separated from the children's mother, Kerry Hughes, four months earlier and appears to have smothered the girls, before telephoning Hughes to tell her what he had done". (*The Guardian*, 24 September 2008)

There were 50 victims under 16 years of age in 2008–2009, and over half were killed by their parents (56 per cent), such as in the cases of Ellie and Isobel Cass. A further 14 per cent of victims under the age of 16 years knew the main suspect. Again, despite the widespread publicity that cases of this kind generate, there were only two offences during this reporting period where someone under the age of 16 years was killed by a stranger.

The *Home Office Homicide Index* also attempts to collect information about the circumstances in which these murders took place, although as of 24 November 2009, these circumstances were not known in 26 per cent of the cases which had been recorded (a figure that will inevitably reduce as the police continue with their investigations). Over half (53 per cent) of the murders recorded were the result of a quarrel, a revenge attack, or a loss of temper, with just seven per cent — or 45 offences — occurring during the commission of other crimes, such as robberies or burglaries.

Theories and Explanations

I have already indicated that there can be no single, or "grand theory" of murder but, rather, that there is a complex interplay between the "faulty individual" and the "faulty social circumstances" that permits murder. However, we can pursue further the question of what it is that might be "faulty" about the individual by considering the contributions of how to explain murder from three different branches of psychology: psychoanalytical psychology; evolutionary psychology; and, finally, social learning and cognitive psychology. No attempt is made to consider purely sociological or biological explanations for murder — such as the discredited XYY theory (which suggested that murderers had an extra Y chromosome and were thus "super males"); the part played by the male hormone testosterone, or low levels of serotonin; or the link between violent crime and the brain or the central nervous system.

Throughout what I am going to say it is helpful to bear in mind suggestions that there is a difference between "instrumental" and "expressive" violence. What I mean by this is that instrumental violence would be used to achieve a specific, recognised objective, such as, for example, facilitating a robbery. In other words, this form of violence is rational because it allows the perpetrator to make some type of gain. On the other hand, the objective of expressive violence is to inflict harm and is "a less rational expression of personality or identity". Expressive violence is about anger, often in response to an insult. However, we should not presume that there is always (or perhaps ever) a clear distinction between these two different forms of violence. Often, the boundaries are blurred and fluid—see Case Study (2) below.

Case Study (2)

A teenager who killed the school-leaver Jimmy Mizen during a frenzied scuffle in a south London bakery was given a life sentence and ordered to serve a minimum of 14 years yesterday after an Old Bailey jury found him guilty of murder. Jake Fahri, 19, was said to have gone beserk after challenging Mizen and his brother in the shop and throwing a heavy glass dish of sausages at him. The dish shattered after hitting Mizen on the chin and a shard of glass cut vital blood vessels in his neck.

Mizen, who had celebrated his 16th birthday the day before, died within minutes in the arms of his brother in the bakery's storeroom, in a welter of blood, while Fahri sauntered smiling from the shop. The case is believed to be the first in which a glass dish has been classed as a murder weapon. Fahri, who pleaded not guilty, had claimed that he had been acting in self-defence.

Mr Justice Calvert-Smith told him: "A trivial incident over absolutely nothing in a High Street bakery ended three minutes later with the death of a blameless young man."

The court was told that Fahri, who had a history of difficulties controlling his temper, had not wanted to lose face after picking a row with the two brothers as they stood in front of him in the queue at the shop, where they had gone to buy sausage rolls. Fahri demanded that they should get out of his way and became angry when Mizen's older brother Harry suggested he should say, 'Please.'

He promised to wait for them outside the shop and stormed back in after seeing the Mizens telephoning their older brother for help. The brothers bundled him out of the shop and he then returned a third time, wielding a metal framed advertising sign and kicking through the shop's glass door. As the 6ft 2 inch tall, 14 stone Jimmy Mizen, wrested the sign away, Fahri, 5ft 7ins, picked up the dish from the counter and hurled it at him.

Crispin Aylett QC, prosecuting, said: 'A trivial incident, brought about by the defendant's rudeness, escalated into something horrific. The defendant reached for any and every available weapon with which to attack the Mizen brothers. The whole incident lasted no more than three minutes — three minutes of absolute madness on the part of this defendant'.

Fahri, who lived close to the Mizen family and had attacked Harry Mizen twice previously, showed no emotion as he was sentenced, but as he was taken to the cells he called out, 'I will be all right, mum, I'll be all right' to his weeping mother in the public gallery.

Detective Chief Inspector Cliff Lyons said: 'Jake Fahri is an aggressive young man who throughout his life continually demonstrated an inability to control his emotions and restrain his temper. As we have all come to know Jimmy was the exact opposite of Fahri; a peaceful, courteous person with only the best intentions". (*The Guardian*, 27 March 2009)

There are a number of issues to consider in this report about the murder of Jimmy Mizen, especially as it touches on several of the themes which have already been discussed, and others which will be discussed below. For example, we know that Fahri was convicted of murder and, therefore, had to be given a life sentence by Mr Justice Calvert-Smith. We know that his "tariff" has been set at 14 years, and we can infer that work will need to be done with him in prison about his temper control before he would be considered safe to be released back into the community. It is also clear that Jimmy and Harry Mizen knew Fahri previously—we are informed that Fahri had attacked Harry on two earlier occasions, and that this murder was cleared up very quickly by the police. Finally, we know that while the weapon that Fahri used was unusual—a glass dish, it fits into the general pattern of how murders are committed, in that most male victims are stabbed. However, should we see Fahri's violence as instrumental or as expressive? Was his attack on Jimmy and his brother rational and done so as to achieve a specific objective, or should it, instead, be seen as expressing aspects of Fahri's personality and identity? Perhaps there are elements of both instrumental and expressive violence in Fahri's attack? I want to return to the murder of Jimmy Mizen and also to the murders of Ellie and Isobel Cass shortly. But, for the moment, let's see if we can explain these ordinary murders by considering some psychological theory.

Psychoanalytical Psychology[1]

The foundation of psychoanalytical and clinical psychology is the work of Sigmund Freud (1859–1939), and his suggestion that the workings of the mind affect personality and behaviour—including criminal behaviour. Criminal behaviour is viewed as the product of some mental conflict, which can often be traced back to problems in childhood. Freud suggested that there were three core aspects of the human psyche: the id; the ego; and the superego. The id contains the unconscious, primitive biological drives for survival, such as aggression and sex and is said to work on a "pleasure principle". In other words, it seeks to avoid pain but both satisfy and enjoy these primitive drives, without regard to how others might suffer, or the negative consequences that might flow from following these primitive urges. The id is also the site

---

1. Not to be confused with psychoanalysis. Psychoanalytical psychology and psychoanalysis are related, the former having grown out of the latter. However, by and large, psychoanalysis is what happens within psychoanalytical psychology, and Freud described the latter as "a collection of psychological information obtained [via psychoanalysis] which is gradually being accumulated into a new scientific discipline".

of the "death instinct"—a willingness to self-destruct. The ego is the real "self" that also controls the drives of the id by responding to the needs of others, and conforming to what is expected of an individual as a result of social convention. The superego, which, like the ego, develops throughout childhood, is that part of the personality which has internalised the moral and ethical rules of society, largely by the child being socialised by his parents or carers. Freud—who had quite a bit to say about violence—suggested that criminal behaviour was either the result of mental disturbance, or the product of the offender's weak conscience.

A modern application of Freud's psychoanalytical approach can be found in James Gilligan's (2000) *Violence: Reflections on our Deadliest Epidemic*, based on his interviews with violent men in his capacity as a prison psychiatrist. For Gilligan the internal mental conflict that is the key to understanding why some men use lethal violence, is shame and loss of self-esteem. He suggests that violent men have often themselves been the objects of violence in the past—especially in their childhood—and that, as a consequence, they experience feelings of embarrassment, powerlessness, and worthlessness. So, in a situation where they feel that their self-worth is being challenged, and in which they also reason that there is no other way to diminish that sense of shame—Gilligan also suggests that violent men lack the emotional infrastructure that serves to inhibit violent impulses through, for example, guilt or empathy—they will use violence to rebuild their wounded self-esteem.

This takes us back to instrumental and expressive violence and also to the murder of Jimmy Mizen. The "trivial incident over absolutely nothing", as it was described by Mr Justice Calvert-Smith, was, perhaps, for Fahri, something much more symbolic. From the newspaper report it would seem that the Mizen brothers had stood in front of Fahri in the queue in the baker's shop and that, when he had complained that the brothers should get out of his way, he was told that he should say, "Please". Did this trigger feelings of shame to the extent that the physically smaller Fahri believed that the only way that he could re-establish his own sense of self-worth was to use violence? He certainly seems to have wanted to continue with the incident—returning to the shop on two occasions—and, thus, does not seem to have been able to rebuild that sense of self-worth in any other way, which perhaps also indicates that he lacked empathy, guilt, or indeed fear for his own safety.

It also suggests that while this murder may not have been premeditated there were a number of opportunities for Fahri to have walked away from the baker's shop, which would have allowed the conflict to have come to a more peaceable conclusion. Here, too, we might remember the importance of "micro" rather "macro" explanations of murder. What seems to have mattered were not great sociological or cultural questions of age, gender, race or poverty, but rather the dynamics of the incident in the shop itself. None of what has been described is meant to excuse Fahri's behaviour, nor should we ignore the fact that this analysis is difficult to test in any empirical way.

Indeed, one of the major criticisms of psychoanalytical approaches is that they are difficult to prove. We cannot directly observe the id, the ego or superego, nor can we actually prove (or disprove) that they exist—despite attempts to do so through, for example, psychoanalysis, ink blot tests or dream analysis. How then can we be certain that they play any role at all in shaping an individual's behaviour? We might also criticise psychoanalytic psychology for being overly deterministic. In other words, everything is explained by internal conflicts and tensions within the individual's psyche thus, for example, environmental factors are overlooked. However, especially with Gilligan's work, there are interesting ideas that work well with attempts to understand how social situations can influence human behaviour. This is a theme which is taken up within the discussion of social and cognitive psychology below and, in particular, where I discuss the work of the criminologist Jack Katz. So, too, we should not ignore the fact that HM Prison Grendon, which uniquely operates on psychotherapeutic principles within a series of therapeutic communities housing very violent offenders, is the only prison in the country that is able to demonstrate a treatment effect. In other words, their psychodynamic approach to working with violent offenders reduces the incidence of their future reoffending.

Evolutionary Psychology

The basic premise of evolutionary psychology is bound up with biological assumptions that human existence is primarily determined by genetic adaptation and inheritance. In other words, human behaviour has ancient biological origins and the behaviour of humans has thus undergone a process of natural selection to ensure that the adaptive "selfish genes" which ensure reproductive success are passed on from one generation to the next. "Proximate" accounts within evolutionary psychology suggest immediate causes or factors as to why an individual might respond to a given situation, while "ultimate" accounts look much more historically into our evolutionary past for an explanation. So, would murder be an adaptive or a maladaptive strategy to ensure that one's genes are passed on from one generation to another? Would killing parents or one's children make sense from an evolutionary psychological perspective?

In *The Murderer Next Door* (2005), David Buss uses an evolutionary psychological approach to explain that murder is evolutionarily functional and, as such, a normal trait in human beings which is inherently logical, especially as it is a behaviour that is advantageous to reproduction. At the most obvious level, for example, the killer survives and is still able to reproduce, while his victim perishes, effectively ending his genetic line. So, too, the killer—should he wish—would be able to have sex with his victim's mate, and will also, through the murder, have scared other would-be killers by his behaviour. In turn, Buss suggests, this will make him more attractive to even more potential mates, given that he will be able to provide protection from other predatory men. Indeed, so great are the advantages of murder that Buss questions why there are so few.

A less enthusiastic, but still evolutionary approach can be found in Martin Daly and Margo Wilson's *Homicide* (1988). They suggest that murders are usually the result of young men trying to gain dominance over other young men—and here we could also reconsider the murder of Jimmy Mizen from this perspective—or women trying to gain independence from proprietary partners. As such, murder is not pathological but rather a strategy for survival in situations where resources or breeding opportunities are scarce. In keeping with the idea that murder is a strategy for ensuring the survival and continuance of the killer's genes, Daly and Wilson suggest that homicide will occur less often between individuals who are genetically related and point out that, whilst most murders take place within families, such killings occur between spouses, who are, of course, not genetically related. They also theorise that children are more likely to be killed by step-parents rather than biological parents, who do not have a genetic relationship to these dependent children but who may be seen by the step-parent as a drain on resources in the household.

Unfortunately for Daly and Wilson, evidence from this country does not support this theory. For example, just over 90 per cent of children who are murdered are killed by a biological parent and only eight per cent by a step-parent. Here, too, we should remember the murders of Ellie and Isobel Cass (see Case Study 1 above) and not only question why they were killed by their biological father, but also why he then chose to commit suicide. This hardly makes sense from an evolutionary perspective, whether considered from a proximate or ultimate account. David Cass — the "doting father" — effectively ended his own genetic inheritance, and it is difficult to explain this act either from the "here and now" of the murder itself, or through attempting to decipher his behaviour as an evolutionary adaptation, more historically. So, too, Buss's theory that murder makes genetic sense is rather undermined by his own observation that there should be more rather than fewer murders. If murder was an adaptive, as opposed to a maladaptive evolutionary strategy, then it would be much more common than it is, which further suggests that if humans have progressed biologically without resorting to murder in great numbers then we should view murder as a pathological not a normal, trait in human behaviour.

Social Learning and Cognitive Psychology

Social and cognitive psychology is concerned with how behaviour is affected by social situations and focuses on the immediate, interpersonal dynamics of those situations that produce violence. As such, the focus is not so much on the individual and his personality but rather on how external factors affect human behaviour. Particular attention is paid to how people process information and why they might perceive some situations as ones in which they will have to use violence. A T Beck (1999), for example, suggests that, in fact, aggressors — through a process of "cognitive distortion" — perceive themselves to be the victims in a violent situation and so have to fight to re-establish their sense of worth and self-esteem. Of course not all individuals would react to the same situation in the same way, so it is also necessary to differentiate between situational instigators that may motivate aggressive behaviour and the more lasting structural components of a child's background that moulds and socialises a child to respond in a violent way. In relation to this latter issue, social learning theory suggests that the acquisition of any particular behaviour by a child—in this case, violent behaviour—occurs through learning by direct experience (the child has been the object of violence), or through observation (that is to say, through watching violence being used on siblings or parents, or on television).

Social learning theory is most closely associated with Albert Bandura (1973) and his work on aggression. Bandura suggested that we have to think about three crucial aspects to understanding aggression: the acquisition of aggressive behaviour; the process of instigation of the aggression; and, finally, the conditions that maintain the aggression. We have already discussed the first of these aspects—how aggressive behaviour is acquired—but have not yet discussed how aggressive behaviour might be instigated or maintained. By "instigated" Bandura means to suggest that an aggressive encounter was often the product of certain environmental conditions which had previously produced violence. So, too, violence might be "maintained" because this type of behaviour has been positively reinforced in the past and the aggressor has gained some sense of pride or achievement from behaving in this way.

Like Bandura, Jack in *The Seductions of Crime: The Moral and Sensual Attractions of Doing Evil* (1988) has been concerned with analysing the situational and "foreground" factors of violence, and he pays particular attention to the emotional or psychological state of the murderer at the time of the murder. In other words, what it feels and means to kill and what is achieved as a consequence. Katz describes different emotional levels that are involved in the "typical murder", such that the killer commits an "impassioned attack", or a "righteously enraged slaughter" of a victim who has humiliated the attacker. Thus, through this slaughter the killer can defend his sense of "good" against "evil" by transforming his humiliation into a rage that will prove fatal. In this way, what Katz argues has links to the work of Gilligan and Beck, in that all three emphasise that instead of violence being senseless it has meaning and value for the attacker. Once again, we might want to re-interpret the murder of Jimmy Mizen through the lens of these hypotheses.

Did Fahri see himself as the victim in this social encounter with Jimmy and Harry Mizen? Did he transform his humiliation into rage? What was it that Fahri hoped to achieve through his use of violence?

Of course, we will never really learn the answers to these questions, but what is most important to bear in mind is that there can be no single explanation or grand theory as to what happened in this specific murder, or, more generally, when we consider the phenomenon of murder as a whole. Rather, what we have is a complex set of incident-specific factors which are played out against a background of more general circumstances—some of which are more likely to produce violence than others.

Police-Media Relations During a Murder Investigation

Given the complexity that I have just described, how is the conduct of a murder investigation communicated by the police through the media to the public, and what role do the media play within a murder investigation? Can the media be harnessed as an "investigative resource" in a murder inquiry, or are police-media relations more pragmatic with the senior investigating officer (SIO)—who is in overall charge of a murder investigation—simply balancing a number of goals so as to achieve what might be described as "effective media handling".

We should note that the *Murder Investigation Manual* (MIM)—which is not in the public domain—does provide guidance as to how SIOs should deal with the media. But how practical is this advice in the light of the various technological changes that have occurred in relation to how the media now gather and then communicate information to a wider audience, and at a time when reporting is characterised as being "driven by impact"? How do SIOs ensure effective media "handling" during a murder investigation—especially if that murder is "high-profile" in an era of blogs, web-based news and 24-hour news channels? Are they able to control the "pack of feral beasts" that Tony Blair, the former Prime Minister, complained of when he left Downing Street?

And, while these seem like new questions which need to be answered, Dr Rob Mawby of Leicester University reminds us that the work of Steve

Chibnall in the 1970s — which examined the relationship between the police and crime reporters in London — still has relevance, and that his conclusion that the police-media relationship was reciprocal, but asymmetric in favour of the police, is the beginning of an answer. But what particular pressures might be placed on this reciprocity at the time of a high-profile murder investigation? Does the asymmetry still favour the police when they are investigating murders that are not solved in a few days, or do the media then begin to project an image of the police and policing which challenges the assumption that they are a functioning prerequisite of the state?

It is impossible to be precise about the duration of the media interest that each of the cases mentioned in this chapter generated at the time (and which I was a part of in relation to the Wright investigation), but if we consider when the victim(s) were first reported as missing and then when a suspect was arrested and charged (and which limits what can be reported), some indication of the length of time that the media covered these cases can be inferred. So, for example, James Bulger went missing on 12 February 1993 and the main suspects were arrested on 20 February 1993. Of course this was not the end of the media's interest in this case, but in terms of our specific interests in this chapter, of the four cases described here, the initial police investigation undertaken into James Bulger's disappearance and murder was of the shortest duration. The West investigation can be seen as continuing at least throughout February 1994 and until Fred and Rose West were charged at the end of June 1994; Holly Wells and Jessica Chapman went missing in Soham on 4 August 2002 and there were no arrests in the case until August 17; and, finally, in Ipswich, the initial police investigation began on 30 October 2006 when Tania Nicol was reported as missing, and continued until Steve Wright's arrest and formal charge on 21 December 2006.

During interview, a number of different themes were generated which were common to all four SIOs. In particular, all described the "pressure" that came with the levels of media interest that these cases generated. A measure of that interest is conveyed by Bennett who described, for example, how "the numbers [of journalists] increased from ten to fifteen individuals to ten to fifteen news crews of national media, Sky TV and every other outlet that you can think of in the UK". Lambert acknowledged that the levels of media interest in the Ipswich case — which lasted for some six weeks — brought with it "more pressure than normal on the people involved with the investigation", and Stevenson described being "anxious" about the investigation when "the whole world is watching". This level of interest also ensured that those journalists and broadcasters who covered the cases were nationally — sometimes internationally — based, rather than local journalists with whom the police had had regular contact.

What has been described thus far should not be taken to imply that all four shared similar views. This was far from the case. John Bennett and Albert Kirby, for example, were almost mirror opposites of each other in their approaches to, and attitudes about, the media. However a broad strategy did emerge which was common to all four, although this was implemented with varying degrees of success and partly predicated upon the SIO's own personal skills and qualities and occupational history and experience. It is this broad strategy which is the focus of this chapter. This strategy has two components and was best described by Lambert, who claimed to have learned from the experiences of Kirby, Bennett and Stevenson and who stated that, "You need to service the needs of the media, but keep them at arm's length". As is obvious, there is a tension between these two components — a tension which, if not sufficiently managed, might weaken, or indeed break, the overall strategy. We describe all of this in more detail below.

Servicing Needs at Arm's Length

Lambert, who was SIO for one of the five murder investigations in Ipswich in 2006, recognised the need to "establish a good professional relationship between the media and the police", and had arrived at that conclusion as a result of studying what had happened at Soham four years earlier. Indeed, he stated that the strategy that was adopted in Ipswich had "evolved" through learning "lessons and remembering some of those things that caused people problems [in previous cases]". As such, what he describes might be seen not only as the evolution of good practice about how to handle police-media relations in a high-profile murder investigation, but also as the blueprint for an approach about how such cases will be handled in the future. As already mentioned, it was Lambert who characterised this collection of good practice by saying, "You need to service the needs of the media but keep them at arm's length".

However, this statement was made in response to a question about the fact that Suffolk Constabulary had initially allowed the media to use the police canteen in their headquarters in Martlesham, which was also being used by the police personnel who were responsible for conducting the investigation. Lambert believed that this decision had been taken for purely pragmatic reasons—"We have all this media here and we have to service them. We've got to give them somewhere to sit, the phones, have cups of tea, and whatever, and I think that took precedence over the needs of the investigation". Nonetheless, by servicing these needs in this way, the investigation suffered "leaks, the press were probing our offices, people found where they shouldn't have been, walking on our campus, where all the incident rooms were".

Thus Lambert's "at arm's length" was merely meant to suggest that the police should have had a physical separation from the media in relation to a specific issue that had occurred in Ipswich (and, in due course, other catering facilities were established which kept the police and the media apart). However, Lambert's description can be used more broadly to describe the overall approach which had, by 2006, evolved since the early 1990s, although there was clearly evidence of good practice present in earlier cases. Nonetheless, by the time of the Ipswich case it would seem that the approach adopted had become more fully developed. I use this idea of servicing the media's needs at arm's length both in relation to other issues that Lambert describes, and also more generally with what was discussed by Kirby, Bennett and Stevenson about how they had handled their investigations.

Quite apart from ensuring that the media had access to such practicalities as tea and telephones, servicing the media's other needs involved: appointing a police spokesperson who could answer questions about the investigation; "giving them something" that could be reported; and facilitating an ongoing dialogue to establish, and then maintain, good relations. All of these issues were constantly negotiated and re-negotiated throughout the duration of the murder investigation, and demanded considerable skill—and time—to be exercised by the SIO almost on an hourly basis.

Even appointing the spokesperson was not a simple process, and there was some debate between the interviewees as to whether this person should be the SIO, or another senior police officer who was "well briefed". There was more agreement between the four interviewees about the importance of getting the right spokesperson appointed because, as Bennett described it, "facing the media was a tortuous event that I didn't particularly enjoy". Even so, he felt that, "If there was important information to be said where there were going to be questions about the investigation then I would have to front it". Bennett's use of the phrase "have to" clearly implies coercion, or at least reluctance and he also revealed that he had had a deputy with whom he had wanted to share this responsibility. However, that deputy "did not feel comfortable with confronting the media at all because he felt that he might say something that might damage the enquiry in an unguarded moment". Again, we should note Bennett's use of the word "confronting" and what this implies about how his own relationship with the media might have been characterised. His approach can be contrasted most immediately with that of Kirby and Stevenson.

Kirby, for example, stated that he "appreciated the value of the media and [had] no fear as to what value the media can offer in any major crime enquiry". Nor does this appear to be a post-hoc rationalisation but rather is an approach that he brought with him into the Bulger investigation. As a consequence, he immediately wanted to "brief them properly and not allow them to publish stuff which is inaccurate or that might cause harm to the family or damage to the force". He also invested his time in establishing good relations with a number of local journalists and suggested that "you've got to know them and work with them". Stevenson also understood the importance of working with the media and described how his predecessor in the Soham investigation was "beginning to come over on television looking really haggard" and, therefore, how this had started to have an impact on how the investigation was perceived by the public, which, in turn, he saw reflected in how the investigation was being reported. Thus, when he took over from this colleague he recognised that "we clearly need[ed] to turn these negative headlines around" and had a freelance press officer call a meeting with all the media covering the case. He describes this meeting as "pens and papers down, cameras off, we're going to have a little chat, engaging with them and bringing them back round". So, too, Lambert believed that "there should be a talking head, but it doesn't have to be the detective in charge, as long as it is someone good with the media, looks good and comes across well. That's the most important thing". This idea of "looking good" of course contrasts with the "really haggard" appearance of Stevenson's colleague in Soham.

However, as is clear form what Lambert describes, here again we have a distance—an "arm's length"—while servicing the media's needs. A police spokesperson was appointed in Ipswich but, unlike the other cases described here, not the SIO in charge of any of the murder investigations. This spokesperson was Detective Chief Superintendent Stewart Gull, who had spent most of his career within the Suffolk Constabulary and had the distinction of being the only Suffolk officer to have served in every rank prior to his promotion, some six months before the murders, when he had taken up his new role as Head of Crime Management. And, despite Lambert's belief that Gull was "good with the media", as events progressed in Ipswich, Gull was dismissively labelled as a "country copper" and asked if he personally, and Suffolk Constabulary more generally, were "up to the job" in bringing the killer to justice, with the local force being described as "overwhelmed" and "beleaguered" (see reports in *Daily Telegraph*, 14 December 2006; *Guardian*, 13 December 2006; *Independent*, 13 December 2006). However, Gull was undoubtedly well-briefed about each individual murder investigation, and we can only speculate if having an SIO as spokesperson would have prevented the more negative headlines that characterised some aspects of how the investigation was reported.

The idea of "giving them something", or as Bennett described it "feed [ing] them with information" to report was the second aspect of the approach aimed at servicing the media's needs. As might be expected, Kirby who wanted to "know them and work with them" was most adept at describing all of this. Thus, for example, he described discussing with the media what they were looking for and that they effectively gave him "a shopping list". So "the press office then would arrange meetings for underwater search teams, search units, family liaison officers, another control room, all these type of things". Kirby explained that he was trying to "make their job easier and more informed" and in doing so "you're on a winner", because by doing all of this "we can control it, and control it very effectively". He suggested that he knew "what they were after [and] we gave them everything that they wanted". At one stage he characterised this as a way to "cheat the press" adding "in inverted commas". On a practical level this meant for Lambert that there had to be an "individual press officer for each investigation [and] the media office was manned from 0600 until 2300 so that we got into a routine of trying to service them every day. We had a deliberate ploy of giving them something if we could—new or different every day". So, too, Stevenson recognised that the failure to "give them something" was what had initially gone wrong in Soham and that, as a consequence, to use Bennett's phrase, they could not "control it very effectively":

> Nobody called out a press officer, as the Inspector in the Control Room is author-ised to do. No press release was issued at 0500 and no one put an entry on the press line which would have been more accurate to say that Cambridgeshire Police have spent the night looking for two 10 year-old girls who have been missing from Sunday evening from Soham and the brief details. We did not call out the on-call press officer, so the first that [the force's press team] knew about it was driving to work, listening to the local radio and they pick up this breaking story. By the time that they arrive in the office at headquarters on Monday morning at 0730 the phones are ringing their heads off, because the media immediately recognised that this was big story and of course it hit the nationals by Monday afternoon, and they were completely overwhelmed. They never recovered from that.

The idea of "giving them something" might be seen as one of the ways that the police actively shape the news, through what has been described as "supermarket journalism". In other words, generalist news reporters accept police-prepared packages—"backgrounders"—which might include state-ments, textual information, and images. This could be interpreted as the police attempting to be transparent, but so, too, it has the potential to gen-erate "an unquestioned police-centric version of crime news". However, the danger for the SIO if he did not feed the media with information—or "give them something"—was, as Bennett put it: "they'd manufacture it or exag-gerate it or go outside and blame you for not giving them any information".

Even more difficult for the SIO was when the media began to use their own resources to investigate what might have happened and attempt to discover who might be responsible for the murder(s). So, for example, Kirby described turning up to interview one suspect and when "detectives came out of the house the street was floodlit with lanterns, searchlights, flashing cameras—it caused immediate problems for us". Lambert also described how it was the media that were "driving" one line of enquiry about a potential suspect—"a fat man in a blue BMW"—and how an interview given by a local man named Tom Stephens to the *Sunday Mirror* led directly to his arrest (although he was never charged). So, too, Stevenson complained that one newspaper "knew what was going on, they had twigged it, and they were surveying the surveillance team and they had outed Huntley". Stevenson claimed that this compromised the surveillance of Huntley—who was later arrested, charged and convicted of the two murders.

The final aspect of servicing the media's needs was to establish and then maintain an ongoing dialogue with the media and not allow, as Stevenson characterised it, to "let things go flat". This might involve a great deal of the SIO's time because, as Stevenson maintained, "The key thing is engaging with [the media] and being prepared to do off the record briefings ... I think the more you build up a rapport with the journalist and appreciate that they have a job to do, dialogue will encourage success". Both Lambert and Kirby described how they would "sit down with the media", "ask them what they needed", "brief them"—both on, and off, the record. Again, Bennett is the least enthusiastic about this approach and, for example, described the pool facility that had been established in Gloucester as of "no use whatsoever. It was pointless because the media just sharked each other up ... This was about creating something to sell newspapers or get viewers to watch. The competitiveness within [the media] is incredible". He further described the media as "a machine to make money—it is not there to give the news", and finally characterised them as "irresponsible. That's the bottom line to it". As evidence for his distrust in maintaining a dialogue with the media Bennett explained:

> We put alarms on Cromwell Street [the site of the police's investigation] when we were not using it anymore. We made it quite clear that it was a crime scene and it could not be intruded upon. ITV broke into the building, having employed people to disarm the alarms and photographed it inside downstairs before the trial. Now you could say that our alarm system wasn't good enough, but it was a state of the art alarm system. But for every state of the art alarm system there are state of the art people who can remove these things. And if you start involving people from special forces that's what they do.

Bennett was even reduced to employing a scanning device in his office to ensure that his conversations weren't being bugged, and so scarred has he been with what happened during the West investigation that, even now, he refuses to deal with the media—"I won't ever give interviews to the media about anybody's investigation". On the other hand, Kirby is a regular media commentator during major police investigations and was present, for example, for much of the Ipswich investigation. He suggested that "when I go to these scenes I find the press officer and introduce myself. I say could you give the SIO my compliments and let them know that I am here and what my role is?"

Servicing the media's needs is more often than not done so as to control how an investigation is reported. And, while Bennett is clearly the most suspicious of the advantages of this part of the approach, all four SIOs wanted to keep the media at a distance from the actual investigation itself. This "arm's length" component had a number of dimensions. Most immediately there were practicalities that had to be considered, and we have already described how, at Ipswich, the media had to be given separate catering facilities which were removed from police headquarters. So, too, Bennett suggested that when journalists came into Gloucester Police Station to be briefed on the first floor at the media reporting centre, "very quickly we found that there were reporters looking for toilets on the third and fourth floors, and there were people wandering around the building". Bennett described this as journalists going "on walkabouts", and so the police had to establish a system to book people in and out of the building. Similar arrangements were made in Ipswich and Lambert remembers that "we had to have the barrier down on the front of the campus with police officers checking".

However, keeping the media at arm's length also involved having the SIO structure their expectations though regular briefings both off, and on, the record, and by keeping the media busy so that they did not start to begin to investigate the murder(s) themselves. This was what Kirby described as "cheat[ing] the press", by acknowledging the pressures that the media were under to produce a story and at what times that pressure became more intense. For example, he explained:

They've got to get the material out haven't they to either the papers or news bulletins. They've got to do it. The pressures are there and if you turn around at 0930 and

say 'Sorry I can't tell you' and they've got a slot to fill in the lunchtime news, they
will do it one way or another.

Lambert, too, recognised that "a slight remove is quite useful" but, in a
memorable phrase, maintained that the SIO had to "keep [his or her] eye
on the squirrel—on what you know, rather than what you or others think".
The particular danger for all four investigations was leaks—sometimes from
within the investigation team itself—and Lambert acknowledged that leaks
did take place at Ipswich, partly because "the media were paying people
for interviews". So, too, Bennett remains angry that people close to the
investigation, who had signed confidentiality agreements, "betrayed them
because of money".

Indeed, all four SIOs acknowledged that the media's access to money and
other types of resources, such as helicopters, or to specialists such as media
barristers, posed them distinct problems. Bennett remembers a "Sunday
tabloid newspaper reporter open a briefcase with ten thousand pounds in
it and give it to a witness", and so, too, Kirby acknowledged that, "You will
find journalists go round the back door. They were trying to find officers
in the force that would speak to them and you know what policemen are
like—you put a television camera and a microphone and they can't shut
their mouths". Here Kirby is not alleging that officers were paid for these
interviews and so, too, Lambert was at pains to point out that he did not
know if money changed hands for the leaks that emerged during the Ipswich
investigation. Bennett was also forthcoming that prior to the trial of Rose
West, the media: "spent thousands of pounds bringing barristers to Winchester Crown Court to tell Mr Justice Mantell why they were not going to
[divulge sources] and then [things] were suddenly complicated because they
had to—we had forced them into a situation". He continued:

> If I can tell a jury that Ann Marie West had received a contract of £25,000 to write
> a book, had been taken to a hotel, what have you, the defence have got to come up
> with something ... we've put everything on the table and the jury sees it for what
> its worth.

Keeping the Media Onside in a Murder Investigation

Murder investigations which take place with the "whole world watching" clearly place additional strain on the police and, in particular, would appear to threaten their ability to shape the reporting of how that investigation is being undertaken. This was most clearly felt by Bennett. However, it should be noted that the media interest in the West investigation was sustained for the longest period of time of the four cases being discussed here, and that as far as media handling is concerned, lessons were clearly learned. All four SIOs were acutely aware of the need to manage the media's coverage more than they would have done so ordinarily. In part, this would seem to be a consequence of the greater resources that are available to the media when a murder captures national, as opposed to local, headlines. As a consequence, national—and in some cases international—journalists cover the case, thus the SIO is asked to deal with journalists and broadcasters with whom he has no previous experience of working. Money also allows the media to use their own, and other, resources to conduct their own investigations. As such, they do not need to rely on pre-prepared police packages, as tempting as these might be. In this way, the balance of power in shaping the news would seem to move from the police to the media and thus, at first sight, Chibnall's conclusion that there is an asymmetrical relationship which favours the police rather than the media, appears to break down.

However, even in those investigations which lasted for a number of weeks—sometimes months—it is clear that SIOs were aware of the various ways that they could keep the media "on side", although the approach of "servic[ing] the needs of the media but keep them at arm's length" was only fully formed—or at least articulated—by the time of the Ipswich investigation. The most obvious development of the police-media relations by this stage was that the police spokesperson was not the SIO of any of the murder investigations, but was simply chosen because he looked "good" on the media. This was only partially successful and even in this investigation there were leaks and tensions between the media and the police, and it is abundantly clear that the ongoing nature of the relationship between the police and the media during a high-profile murder investigation is characterised by suspicion and negotiation. Nonetheless, by adopting these elements of good practice the balance of power appears to return to the police. Indeed, from the SIO's perspective, it is also clear that they want to keep the media positive about the conduct of their investigation and that when the relationship breaks down — as it clearly did for Bennett — considerable difficulties emerge. These difficulties go beyond how the investigation gets reported and would, *in extremis,* seem to challenge the competency of the police and their value as a functional prerequisite of social order.

POSTSCRIPT

Still Looking for Laura?

The media are often accused of saturating a particular community that is experiencing problems and then, when those problems have disappeared, they will disappear too, leaving that community to get on as best as it can. This same criticism is also applied to individuals. After all, the media, we are constantly reminded, have a very short attention span. At the heart of this criticism is the idea that the community, or the individual feels abandoned, so actually wants the media interest to continue even after they are no longer "newsworthy". I'm not certain that any of this has much to commend it and I wonder if Rothbury is disappointed, or really rather relieved, that the scores of journalists, cameramen and photographers have all packed up their trucks and shutter cases and gone home?

I also wonder about what has happened to Laura Stainforth. What went on after her return from France and the subsequent conviction and imprisonment of Williams for five years in June 2009 at Grimsby Crown Court? When he was sentenced it was revealed by Judge David Tremberg that Williams had told Laura that he was 19 years old and had sent to her photographs of a man "with a muscular body". Williams, a father of three, is 50 years old, fat, balding and bespectacled. Not Brad Pitt then. The judge also described him as a "sexual predator" who had deliberately targeted a "naïve, young girl", and a spokesperson for the Crown Prosecution Service added, for good measure, that he was "every parent's worst nightmare". Williams will be on the Sex Offenders' Register for life.

Details about Laura remain more difficult to come by and, because of her age, there were also reporting restrictions placed on journalists at the time of the court case. Indeed, because Williams pleaded guilty, this also served to keep information to a minimum. My hope that we might find out a little more about the circumstances behind what happened when the case came to court was, therefore, not fully realised, although clearly the lies that Williams told about his age and the photographs that he sent to Laura provide some context for understanding what had happened. As he passed sentence on Williams, Judge Tremberg suggested that Laura had felt "used" and that she was now "withdrawn, the effect on her and her relationship with her family has been substantial. She feels isolated and unhappy".

Some 12 months later, I was keen to know if this was still the case, or whether Laura has just got on with her life and reconnected to her family and friends. I wasn't so much interested in what had happened in the past, but rather was more concerned about Laura's present and her future.

But is my interest in what has happened to Laura ethical? If a year ago she was described as "withdrawn", "isolated and unhappy", would my interest in her merely exacerbate those feelings, or might she actually welcome the opportunity to talk about her life on her return home? Perhaps this is simply a form of self-justification and merely another example of a middle-aged man "using" Laura? I certainly hope not, and given that I had commented about her at the time of her abduction, I do feel that wanting to find out about what has happened to Laura since that time is legitimate. After all, my interest in Laura was not just about her and her circumstances, but also how her case was symptomatic of the other 66,000 young people below the age of 16 years who run away for at least a night, some of whom end up slapped, beaten up and otherwise hit and hurt. These are matters that I have regularly written and talked about and have tried to draw to public attention.

Of course, these interests may be legitimate, but nonetheless, they still might also cause harm.

And what about my experiment in public criminology? Has it proved worthwhile by, at the very least, allowing some reason into the heat of the public discussion about crime and punishment? I think that you will have to judge that for yourselves based on what I have written. My hope is that what I have discussed might even encourage a few more of my peers to take up public criminology too. That would be fantastic. But there are limits, and while I will continue to engage with the media, I know that initiating—rather than responding to—approaches by the media, or by members of the public who have been at the centre of media interest, would be, even for me, a step too far. That thought brings me back to Laura.

I couldn't really resolve the ethical questions that were involved in making contact with Laura, so I was left with what can only be described as a "messy compromise". In other words, even though it was relatively easy to get access to Laura's family's address, I chose not to write directly to them asking to interview Laura, but, instead, telephoned Humberside Police Headquarters and spoke to the police media liaison officer who had worked on the case. I explained what I was doing and what I was interested in, and then asked that if I sent a letter to the police, whether they could pass that on to Laura and her family. This was agreed, although I was given no indication as to whether I would receive any response. Several months later I'm still waiting for a reply.

What would I have asked Laura if she had replied and agreed to be interviewed? In my letter I said that I wanted to know if she was now happy and had settled back into her life in Cleethorpes. I would certainly have asked those two questions, but thereafter I'm not certain what else we might have discussed. Sometimes interviews are determined, not by pre-set questions but, instead, having to respond to the person who is doing the answering. Had Laura been open, chatty, happy and confident, perhaps I would have asked her about events in France and what she thought of Williams and his sentence and was she worried about his release in 2011? On the other hand, if she had still been unhappy, isolated and withdrawn, I know I wouldn't have gone anywhere near these subjects. And, in not doing so, how would I have felt about that non-ending being the ending of the book? Disappointed? Frustrated? Perhaps I would have felt relieved. All in all, perhaps it's just as well that Laura and her family didn't reply.

That might not satisfy everyone, but it is the best ending I can offer.

A GUIDE TO FURTHER READING AND OTHER REFERENCES

Introduction

The various debates about public criminology are well explained in Ian Loader and Richard Sparks (2011) *Public Criminology?* (London: Routledge), even if I disagree with much of what they argue. I mention that the phrase "public criminology" was borrowed from "public sociology" — see Michael Burawoy (2005) "2004 Americam Sociological Association Presidential Address: For Public Sociology", *British Journal of Sociology*, 56(2), 259–90. References for Dr Rob Mawby's work can be found in the guide for *Chapter 8*, and an account of Martina Feilzer's work as a columnist is contained within M. Feilzer (2009) "The Importance of Telling a Good Story: An Experiment in Public Criminology", *Howard Journal*, 48(5), 472–84.

Chapter 1

There are a variety of popular and academic books related to children and childhood. I relied on Libby Brooks (2006) *The Story of Childhood: Growing Up in Modern Britain* (London: Bloomsbury); Chris Jenks (1996) *Childhood* (London: Routledge); Jenny Kitzinger (1997) "Who are you Kidding? Children, Power and the Struggle against Sexual Abuse", pp. 165–89, in: A. James and A. Prout (eds), *Constructing and Reconstructing Childhood* (London: Falmer); Frank Furedi (2001) *Paranoid Parenting: Abandon Your Anxieties and Become a Good Parent* (Harmondsworth: Penguin); and Phillipe Aries (1962) *Centuries of Childhood* (London: Jonathan Cape).

Issues relating to children running away from home — or being "thrown away" — are to be found in the work of the leading British charity, The Children's Society. See, in particular, C. Newman (1989) *Young Runaways: Findings from Britain's First Safe House* (London: The Children's Society); The Children's Society (1999) *Still Running: Children on the Streets in the UK* (London: The Children's Society); G. Rees (2001) *Working with Young*

Runaways: Learning from Practice (London: The Children's Society); and G. Rees and J. Lee (2005) *Still Running II: Findings from the Second National Survey of Young Runaways* (London: The Children's Society).

For a general introduction to measuring crime and how crime statistics are constructed see C. Coleman and J. Moynihan (1996) *Understanding Crime Data* (Buckingham and Philadelphia, Penn.: Open University Press; and M. Maguire (2007) "Crime Data and Statistics", pp. 241–301, in: M. Maguire, R. Morgan and R. Reiner (eds), *The Oxford Handbook of Criminology* (Oxford: OUP). There is a variety of interesting books about the nature of evil. See, for example, M. Midgley (1984) *Wickedness: A Philosophical Essay* (London: Routledge); and, more recently, T. Eagleton (2010) *On Evil* (New Haven: Yale University Press).

Chapter 2

My own academic work related to serial killing can be found most readily in *The Journal of Forensic Psychiatry and Psychology* and in particular, K. Soothill and D. Wilson (2005) "Theorising the Puzzle that is Harold Shipman", *Journal of Forensic Psychiatry and Psychology*, 16(4), 658–98. This article deals with the background to the Shipman case and attempts to apply Elliott Leyton's "homicidal protest" thesis to the murders that Shipman committed. I broadened the argument at the heart of this article in an academic and theoretical book called *Serial Killers: Hunting Britons and their Victims, 1960–2006* (Winchester: Waterside Press), and many of the examples provided in this work are recounted here. A more popular approach can be found in *Hunting Evil: Inside the Ipswich Serial Murders* (London: Sphere), which I co-authored with Paul Harrison and which attempts to view these murders from the perspective of those who were killed, as opposed to the motivation of the offender, Steve Wright. I also wrote *A History of British Serial Killing* (London: Sphere), which, again, can be used to guide further reading, although it should be noted that, with the exception of Martin Fido's (2001) *A History of British Serial Killing* (London: Carlton Books), there are very few true crime overviews of British serial killing. Both my own work and that of Fido can be used to research specific British serial killers who have been mentioned in this and subsequent chapters.

The idea that serial killers are a "house divided" is to be found in Ian Brady (2001) *The Gates of Janus: Serial Killing and its Analysis by the "Moors Murderer"* (Los Angeles: Feral House).

A number of true crime books relating to Jack the Ripper are mentioned in this chapter. However, for those who are new to the subject, Stewart Evans and Keith Skinner (2000) *The Ultimate Jack the Ripper Sourcebook* (London: Robinson), remains in my view the best introduction, given that readers can actually consult primary sources for themselves.

There are several American academic books dealing with defining serial killing and readers may wish to consult the work of Stephen Holmes and James de Burger (1988) *Serial Murder* (Newbury Park, Ca.: Sage); and Ronald Holmes and Stephen Holmes (1994) *Profiling Violent Crimes* (Thousand Oaks, Ca.: Sage). Also of use is James Fox and Jack Levin (2005) *Extreme Killing: Understanding Serial and Mass Murder* (Thousand Oaks, California: Sage). This is, clearly, a very popular area of American academic research and those who are interested in pursuing this more thoroughly should consult the bibliography that I produced in *Serial Killers: Hunting Britons and their Victims, 1960–2006.*

Issues relating to the development of forensic science can be gleaned from the biography of Sir Bernard Spilsbury written by Colin Evans (2007) *The Father of Forensics: The Groundbreaking Cases of Sir Bernard Spilsbury, and the Beginnings of Modern CSI* (Cambridge: Icon Books). Keith Simpson's (1980) *Forty Years of Murder* (London: Grafton Books) is also instructive.

Chapter 3

Those who are interested in the various arguments surrounding cop culture should start by reading Robert Reiner (2000) *The Politics of the Police* (Hemel Hempstead: Harvester Wheatsheaf), and compare his thesis with a more "appreciative" understanding of this culture in P. A. J. Waddington (1999) *Policing Citizens* (London: UCL Press). A general introduction to this whole debate can be found in D. Wilson, J. Ashton and D. Sharp (2001)

What Everyone in Britain Should Know About the Police (Oxford: Oxford University Press), and, more recently, in N. Howe, D. Wilson and D. Kemp (2010) "Police Disclosures: A Critical Analysis of Some Recent Police Autobiographies", *Howard Journal*, 49(3), 203–14. The report by the Think Tank Reform, by D. Bassett, A. Haldenby, L. Thrives and E. Truss (2009) *A New Force*, can be downloaded from the website http://www.reform.co.uk Alison Halford's blog cean be found on her website http://www.alisonhalford.co.uk

Chapter 4

I have written about the penal reform functions of prison films and TV programmes in D. Wilson and S. O'Sullivan (2004) *Images of Incarceration: Representations of Prison in Film and Television Drama* (Winchester: Waterside Press), where we debate the various merits and debits of "Bad Girls" and "Porridge". The references contained within this book can also be used as a guide to further reading. So, too, I have written more academically with Dr Nic Groombridge (2009) about "Banged Up" in "I'm Makin a TV Programme Here!: Reality TV's Banged Up and Public Criminology", *Howard Journal*, 49(1), 1–17. The division of prisoner autobiographies into "cons" and "straights" accounts was first outlined by the late Steve Morgan (1999) in "Prison Lives: Critical Issues in Reading Prisoner Autobiography", *Howard Journal*, 38(3), 328–40. The memoirs for David Blunkett are (2006) *The Blunkett Tapes: My Life in the Bear Pit* (London: Bloomsbury).

Chapter 5

Given the subject matter of *Chapter 5*, those books mentioned in the guide for *Chapter 2* are still relevant. However, I also used within this chapter, Nick Davies (1993) *Murder on Ward Four: The Story of Bev Allitt, and the Most Terrifying Crime Since the Moors Murders* (London: Chatto and Windus) — although it should be noted that this book is now very difficult to source. Much easier to get access to is C. Clothier (1994) *Allitt Inquiry: Independent Inquiry Relating to Deaths and Injuries on the Children's Ward at Grantham and Kesteven General Hospital During the Period February to April 1991* (London: The Stationery Office). I also mention within the text that serial killing can be viewed as a form of "homicidal protest". This idea is contained within Elliot Leyton (1986) *Hunting Humans: The Rise of the Modern Multiple Murderer* (Toronto: McClelland and Stewart). Readers might also like to consult C. Grover and K. Soothill (1999) "British Serial Killing: Towards a Structural Explanation", *The British Criminology Conferences: Selected Proceedings*, Volume 2. Available at: http://wwwlboro.ac.uk/departments/ss/bccsp/vol02/08GROVEHTM

The case of Trevor Hardy is discussed in G. Garrett and A. Nott (2001) *Cause of Death: Memoirs of a Home Office Pathologist* (London: Constable and Robinson), and his appeal in the judgement of Mr Justice Teare (2008) *Regina* v. *Trevor Joseph Hardy*, 12 June, Royal Courts of Justice, London. The concept of newsworthiness is to be found in Y. Jewkes (2004) *Crime and Media* (London: Sage).

I have also cited the work of Kevin Haggerty, Simon Winlow, Steve Hall and Michael Bilton — the latter having written about Peter Sutcliffe. See K. Haggerty (2009) "Modern Serial Killers", *Crime, Media and Culture*, 5(2), 168–87; S. Winlow and S. Hall (2006) *Violent Night: Urban Leisure and Contemporary Culture* (Oxford: Berg); and, M. Bilton (2003) *Wicked Beyond Belief: The Hunt for the Yorkshire Ripper* (London: HarperCollins). Readers would also do well to consult Lawrence Byford (1981) *The Yorkshire Ripper Case: Review of the Police Investigation of the Case — Report to the Secretary of State for the Home Office* (London: Home Office).

The serial killer, George Haigh, was rather brilliantly described by Molly Lefebure (1958) — who worked as secretary for the Home Office pathologist, Keith Simpson — in *Murder with a Difference: Studies of Haigh and Christie* (London: Heinemann).

Within this chapter, I describe the FBI's "organized/disorganized" categories. Readers might like to consult the FBI's own crime classification manual, edited by J. E. Douglas, A.W. Burgess, A .G. Burgess and R. K. Ressler (1997) *Crime Classification Manual: A Standard System for Investigating and Classifying Violent Crimes* (New York: Simon and Schuster). In my view the best introduction to the subject of offender profiling remains Peter Ainsworth (2001) *Offender Profiling and Crime Analysis* (Cullompton, Devon: Willan).

At the heart of profiling is the premise that the characteristics of an offender can be deduced by a careful, considered examination of the offence. In particular, the crime scene is regarded as reflecting the murderer's behaviour and personality. So the key here is to understand that from the offence characteristics — how the crime was committed, why the victim was chosen and dealt with etc., we can tell something of what type of person the offender is — i.e. by noting the offender's characteristics. This premise presumes that an offender will always behave in the same way — regardless of the context in which he or she offends. A good, critical examination of the validity of this premise can be found in Alison Laurence (ed.) (2005) *The Forensic Psychologist's Casebook: Psychological Profiling and Criminal Investigation* (Cullompton, Devon: Willan), which also has the advantage of introducing the reader to a more psychological approach to profiling and suggests the variety of ways in which psychologists help with police investigations.

Chapter 6

Within *Chapter 6*, I use a number of criminological and/or forensic psychological ideas and theories. The theory that there are "techniques of neutralisation" which allow offenders to disengage from a dominant culture that would normally prevent them from committing crime — and thus also to offset any guilt that they might feel as a consequence of offending — was first outlined by Gresham Sykes and David Matza (1957) "Techniques of Neutralization", *American Sociological Review*, 22. Matza's (1964) *Delinquency and Drift* (New York: Wiley), and (1969) *Becoming Deviant*, (New Jersey: Prentice-Hall) are also relevant. Jack Katz (1988) *The Seductions of Crime* (New York: Basic Books) makes good use of the differences between instrumental and expressive violence, and I describe the significance of someone attacking the face in *The Lost British Serial Killer: Closing the Case on Peter Tobin and Bible John* (London: Sphere) which was published in 2010. There are several good introductory textbooks to forensic psychology. I particularly like Peter Ainsworth (2000) *Psychology and Crime: Myths and Reality* (Harlow: Longman); so, too, Clive Hollin (2007) "Criminological Psychology", pp. 45–77, in: M. Maguire, R. Morgan and R. Reiner (eds), *The Oxford Handbook of*

Criminology (Oxford: OUP), is of use. I also mention Dave Cullen (2009) *Columbine* (London: Old Street Publishing). For further guidance about the various theories related to murder see below, although here it should be noted that I built up the pictures of Michael Ryan in Hungerford and Thomas Hamilton in Dunblane from newspaper accounts.

Chapter 7

I have previously mentioned the FBI and its approach to offender profiling, so, too, have I drawn attention to Peter Ainsworth's work (see above). He also provides a good introduction to offender profiling more generally in Ainsworth (2001) *Offender Profiling and Crime Analysis* (Cullompton, Devon: Willan). An accessible, critical examination of the validity of offender profiling can be found in Alison Laurence (ed.) (2005) *The Forensic Psychologist's Casebook: Psychological Profiling and Criminal Investigation* (Cullompton, Devon: Willan). I also mention Malcolm Gladwell (2007) "Dangerous Minds: Criminal Profiling Made Easy", *The New Yorker*, 12 November, 1–8. Robert Brittain (1970) "The Sadistic Murderer", can be found in *Medicine, Science and the Law*, 10, 198–207.

I have previously written about Charles Dickens in (2009) "Testing a Civilization: Charles Dickens and the American Penitentiary System", *Howard Journal*, 48(3), 280–96.

I use a number of true crime books within this chapter that readers might also like to consult. These are: Gordon Burn (1998) *Happy Like Murderers: The True Story of Fred and Rosemary West* (London: Faber and Faber); David Canter (1995) *Criminal Shadows: Inside the Mind of the Serial Killer* (London: HarperCollins); David Canter (2003) *Mapping Murder: Walking in Killers' Footsteps* (London: Virgin Books); J. Bennett and D. Gardner (2005) *The Cromwell Street Murders: The Detective's Story* (Thrupp, Stroud: Sutton Publishing); Brian Masters (1986) *Killing for Company: The Case of Dennis Nilsen* (London: Coronet Books); and the text of Harold Shipman's police interview can be found in a number of places including Carole Peters (2005) *Harold Shipman: Mind Set on Murder* (London: Carlton Books).

Chapter 8

The best starting point for any discussion about murder is Fiona Brookman (2005) *Understanding Homicide* (London: Sage), which has quickly established itself as the standard student introduction to this subject. Also worth consulting is S. D'Cruze, S. Walklate and S. Pegg (2006) *Murder* (Cullompton, Devon: Willan), and I quote from this work in several places throughout this chapter. I also found Peter Morrall's (2006) *Murder and Society* (London: John Wiley) of use.

I mention a number of specific books. These are: A. Bandura (1973) *Aggression: A Social Learning Analysis* (Englewood Cliffs, NJ.: Prentice-Hall); A.T. Beck (1999) *Prisoners of Hate: The Cognitive Basis of Anger, Hostility and Violence* (New York: HarperCollins); D. Buss (2005) *The Murderer Next Door: Why the Mind is Designed to Kill* (New York: Penguin); M. Daly and M. Wilson (1988) *Homicide* (New York: De Gruyter); J. Gilligan (2000) *Violence: Reflections on Our Deadliest Epidemic* (London: Jessica Kingsley); J. Katz (1988) *The Seductions of Crime: The Moral and Sensual Attractions of Doing Evil* (New York: Basic Books).

A good introduction to the life of Sigmund Freud and his work is Anthony Storr's (1989) *Freud* (Oxford: Oxford University Press), which also guides the reader to other more specialised readings. I mention the work of HMP Grendon—the only prison in Europe to operate wholly as a therapeutic community—in this chapter, and for those who are interested in this prison they should consult E. Genders and E. Player (1995) *Grendon: A Study of a Therapeutic Prison* (Oxford: Oxford University Press). Grendon's success—as measured by reconviction rates—can be found in P. Marshall (1997) "A Reconviction Study of HMP Grendon Therapeutic Community" (Research Findings No. 53) (London: Home Office Research and Statistics Directorate); and R. Taylor (2000) "A Seven-Year Reconviction Study of HMP Grendon Therapeutic Community" (Research Findings No. 115) (London: Home Office Research, Development and Statistics Directorate).

Quotes used by the four senior investigating officers (SIOs) come from interviews conducted with colleagues, Diane Kemp and Nick Howe, at Birmingham City University in 2009–2010. Within this section of the chapter, I mention the work of Rob Mawby and Steve Chibnall. Readers should consult: R. Mawby (1999) "Visibility, Transparency and Police Media Relations", *Policing and Society*, 9, 263–86; R. Mawby (2007) "Criminal Investigation and the Media", in: T. Newburn, T. Williamson and A. Wright (eds), *Handbook of Criminal Investigation* (Cullompton, Devon: Willan); R. Mawby (2010) "Police Corporate Communications, Crime Reporting and the Shaping of Policing News", *Policing and Society*, 20, 1, 124–39; S. Chibnall (1975) "The Crime Reporter: A Study in the Production of Commercial Knowledge", *Sociology*, 9(1), 49–66; S. Chibnall (1975) "The Police and the Press", pp. 67–81, in: J. Brown and G. Howes (eds), *The Police and the Community* (Farnborough: Saxon House); S. Chibnall (1977) *Law and Order News* (London: Tavistock); S. Chibnall (1979) "The Metropolitan Police and the News Media", pp. 135–49, in: S. Holdaway (ed.), *The British Police* (London: Edward Arnold); S. Chibnall (1981) "The Production of Knowledge by Crime Reporters", pp. 75–97, in: S. Cohen and J. Young (eds), *The Manufacture of News: Deviance, Social Problems and the Mass Media* (London: Constable).

INDEX

A

abnormality 58
abuse *xxiv*, *30*, *41*, *141*
academia/academics *xix*, *xxiii*, *33*,
    34, *151*
  academic neglect *167*
  on TV *31*
  snooty *33*
access *131*
accountability *xxiv*
  local accountability *80*
achievement *157*
"Acid Bath Murderer" *129*
action *73*, *75*, *84*, *140*, *142*
Adams, Gemma *45*
addiction *111*
adrenalin *134*
adults
  selfish adults *43*
aggression *174*, *179*
Ainsworth, Peter *153*
Aitkenhead, Decca *104*
alcohol *69*
Alderton, Anneli *45*
alibi *116*, *118*, *122*
Allison, Laurence *149*, *152*
Allitt, Beverley *110*
alpha-male *140*
  super alpha-male *142*
Amazon *126*, *130*

anger *135*, *160*, *172*
anti-social behaviour order (ASBO)
    xv
anxiety *125*, *182*
Archer, Jeffrey *88*
"Archers, The" *137*
Armitage, Shelley *127*, *130*
arrogance *42*
Ashbrook, Robin *106*
Ashworth, Dawn *48*
asphyxiation *170*
assault *95*, *139*
Association of Chief Police Officers
    (ACPO) *68*, *85*
atomisation *125*
attacks
  nature of *154*
attention-seeking *146*
Attica Correctional Facility (USA)
    154
Audit Commission *80*

B

backgrounders *186*
"Bad Girls" *92*
Ballad of Reading Gaol, The *150*
Bandura, Albert *179*
"Banged Up" *97*
Bangkok Hilton *92*
banking crisis *xxii*
Barlinnie Gaol *88*
  Barlinnie Special Unit *xviii*
Barrett, David *39*

BBC *95*
  BBC News *131*
  BBC Online *37, 45, 50*
  BBC Oxford *32*
  BBC Radio 4 *38*
Beck *178*
behaviour *174*
Bellfield, Levi *56*
benchmarking *105*
benefits *40*
Bennett, John *157, 168*
Berkowitz, David *154*
Bible John *136, 153*
big story *186*
Bilton, Michael *113, 157*
"bind, torture and kill" *161*
biology
  biological assumptions *176*
  biological parents as murderers *178*
Bird, Derrick *131, 132, 133, 134, 136,*
   143, 167
Birmingham City University *xxi,*
   33, 168
Birmingham Post *xviii*
black and white *140, 146*
Black Panther *122*
black people *73*
Black, Robert *61, 157*
Blair, Tony *180*
blame *141*
Blamires, Susan *127, 130*
blogging *xvii, 180*
blueprint for an investigation *163*
Blunkett, David *98, 102, 104, 106,*
   128

bobbies on the beat *80*
bondage
  sexual bondage *162*
bonds *145*
Boon, Julian *149*
Boot village *132*
"born to kill" *154*
Boyle, Jimmy *88*
Bradford *xxii, 127, 128*
  Bradford Magistrates' Court *129*
  Bradford University *126*
Brady, Ian *54, 61*
Braidwood Inquiry *83*
Brennan, Detective Superintendent
   Andy *41*
bribery *78*
Bright, Kathryn *161*
British National Party (BNP) *41*
Brittain, Robert *153*
Britton, Paul *152*
broadsheet *xvi*
"Bronson" *90*
Bronson, Charles *87, 88*
Brookman, Fiona *167*
brothel
  licensed brothels *128*
Brown, Chris *136, 140*
Brumfitt, Paul *53*
Brunel University *105*
Brussel, James *153*
brutality *95*
bugging *76, 188*
Bulger, James *168, 181, 184*
bullying *94, 95, 99, 143, 156*
burglary *37, 80, 114, 171*

domestic burglary *80*

Burn, Gordon *158, 159*

Buss, David *177*

Byford, Sir Lawrence *61*

C

callousness *42*

Calvert-Smith, Mr Justice *172, 175*

Canter, David *149, 152, 157*

Carrabine, Eamonn *91*

Carr, Maxine *118*

Casciani, Dominic *37*

Casebook of a Crime Psychiatrist 153, 154

Cass, David *170*

cat and mouse *125, 136*

Caulfield, Mr Justice *117*

causes of crime *67*

CCTV *25, 127*

celebrity *112, 118*

  celebrity criminals *87*

  celebrity killers *123*

Central London Teenage Project *29*

challenging authority *140*

change *74*

  changing behaviour *98*

Channel 4 *56, 61, 62, 78*

Channel 5 *97, 102, 106*

chaotic lives *107*

Chapman, Jessica *168, 181*

chase (vicarious pleasures of the chase) *31*

Chibnall, Steve *181*

Chief Constables *82*

childhood *28*

  Good Childhood Inquiry *43*

children *25, 39*

  ambivalence about *28*

  child killers *xv*

  Children's Society *29, 35, 43*

circle

  Circles of Support and Accountability *xvi, xx*

  Circles UK *xxi*

civic

  civic society *64*

  civic spaces *105*

civilisation

  restraints of civilisation *135*

class *40*

claustrophobia *133*

Cleethorpes *25, 44*

Clements, Jon *126*

Clennell, Paula *45*

clues *159*

Coalition *xxii*

COBRA *76*

cocktail of feelings *135*

Coke, Sir Edward *168*

Columbine *147*

combat *144*

comment

  "no comment" *52*

commodities *58*

common-sense *74, 80*

Commons, Kevin *131*

communication *xviii*

community

community interventions *104*

community safety *xxiv*

"Con Air" *92*

"Con Edison" bomber *153*

confidentiality agreement *189*

conjecture *50*

cons' accounts *89*

conscience *175*

conservatism

conceptual conservatism *74*

control *133, 141, 144, 159*

Cook, Frank *88*

cop culture *84*

copycat crimes *142, 148*

Cornwell, Patricia *60*

corpus delicti *129*

corruption *78, 96*

courtroom *xx*

cowardice *141*

Crabtree, David *137*

crime

crime and punishment *xvi, xix, xxi*

Crime Classification Manual *160*

crime fighters *82, 84*

crime figures *25, 39*

crime scene *xx, 153, 154, 159, 160, 162, 187*

alarms at *188*

media intrusions at *188*

Crime Squad *xviii*

crime statistics *36*

crime-trends *36, 39*

detection of *36*

glamorising crime *148*

knife crime *37*

measuring crime *36*

recorded crime *36*

criminal

Criminal Cases Review Commission (CCRC) *45*

criminal justice system *xvi, 133*

criminal lifestyle *89*

criminals *67*

Criminal Shadows: Inside the Mind of the Serial Killer *152*

dangerous criminals *95*

criminologists *xvi, xviii, xxii, 37, 105, 111*

criminology *xxii, 67, 130, 135, 167*

criminology conferences *xxi*

public criminology *102, 105*

Cromwell Street *187*

Crossbow Cannibal *129*

cross-examination *49, 51*

Crossley, Lily *159*

Crowther, Brian *119*

Cullen, Dave *147*

cult-TV *92*

culture *56, 57, 64, 67*

cop culture *70, 72*

culture of difference *82*

"them" and "us" *64*

"Cutting Edge" *62*

cynicism *73*

D

Daily Mail *xvii, 97*

Daily Mirror *119, 126*

Daily Telegraph *39, 103, 105*

Daly, Martin *177*

damage *41, 58*

danger *142, 165*

   dangerous dogs *41*

   dangerous strangers *111*

Dark Dreams *161*

"Dear John" *140*

death row *xvi, xx*

deceit *135, 157*

   police deception *164*

decency *91, 92, 94*

dehumanisation *91*

Delagrange, Amelie *56, 57*

demons *130*

   demonisation *43*

depravity *41*

depression *30*

deprivation

   economic deprivation *121*

detection *51, 60, 149*

   detection rate *79*

   detective stories *162*

determinism *67*

Devil *42*

Dewsbury *40*

   Moorside Estate *40*

Dexter *59*

diaries *xxiii*

Dickens, Charles *150*

difference *88*

diminished responsibility *117, 125*

disappearance *25, 40*

discontent *133*

discretion *72*

disjunction *58*

disorganized offenders *159*

displacement *127*

distortion

   cognitive distortion *178*

DNA *45, 47, 48, 49, 50, 63*

documentaries *xvi*

Dodd, Johnny *151*

domestic violence *37, 139, 147*

Donovan, Michael *40*

doubt *52*

   reasonable doubt *51*

Douglas Inch Clinic *153*

Douglas, John *150, 151*

Dover *25*

Dowler, Milly *56*

drama

   dramatic approximation *95*

   dramatic depersonalisation *91*

dream analysis *176*

Driver, Beverley *114*

drugs *42, 69, 95*

   drug addiction *95*

   drug mule *91*

   easy access to *54*

Dunblane *53, 134, 143, 147*

   Dunblane Primary School *143, 144*

Durham Prison *136, 142, 143*

Durkheim, Emile *145*

dysfunction *114*

Dziekanski, Robert *83*

E

Eastern Penitentiary (USA) *150*

economy

illicit economy *140*

Edinburgh University

student radio *34*

effectiveness *79*

ego *174*

elephant in the sitting-room *64*

embarrassment *175*

emotional infrastructure *175*

empathy *42, 175*

employment

unemployment *67*

engagement *xix*

engagement with the media *xv*

English Prisons Today *xviii*

entertainment *93, 98*

eroticism *58*

error *50*

escalation *173*

Essex

Essex Police *68*

Essex University *68*

ethics *xix, 46, 55, 58, 78, 99, 155, 175*

ethnography *150*

Europe *25, 164*

European Court of Human Rights *76*

Evening Times *103*

evidence *xix*

evil *39, 41, 42, 94, 117, 179*

Evil That Men Do, The *161*

sane but evil *121*

exclusion *144*

ex-offenders *98, 102, 105*

experimental programmes *104*

expert *51*

eye

deadness in the eye *41*

Eyre, Marie *152*

F

Facebook *141, 142*

"face-to-face" society *132, 133, 144*

Fahri, Jake *172*

failings *157*

fairness *xi, 36, 94*

fame *88*

family

lone parent families *30*

low-income families *30*

stepfamilies *30*

fantasy *142*

Farrow, Sheilagh *122*

fascination *58*

fault

faulty individuals *168, 171*

faulty social circumstances *168, 171*

fear *141, 175*

Federal Bureau of Investigation
       (FBI) *113, 150, 152, 160*

Behavioural Science Unit *153*

"Feedback" *138*

Feilzer, Martina *xvii*

fiefdoms *82*

film and TV dramas *92*

firearms *37, 39, 131, 135, 140, 143*

Firearms (Amendment) Act 1988 *143*

Firearms (Amendment) (No. 2) Act 1997
  143

fire-starting *xvi*

firing the public imagination *122*

"fish and chippy" *121*

fitting up *78*

folie à deux *110*

footprint for criminologists *xi*

Ford, D C Richard *52*

forensics

  forensic awareness *130*

  forensic evidence *60, 154*

  forensic science *xvi, 47, 49, 154*

*Forget You Had a Daughter: Doing
  Time in the Bangkok Hilton*
  89

France *25, 35, 39*

fraud *129*

Fred and Rose West *168, 189*

freedom

  A Sense of Freedom *88*

  Freedom of Information Act *61*

free will *67, 68*

frenzied scuffle *172*

Freud, Sigmund *154, 174*

From the Inside *89*

front line *75*

frustration *160*

"future foreshortening" *138, 145*

G

gallows redemption *150*

gangs *39*

Garrett, Geoffrey *114*

Gates of Janus, The *54*

gay people *29, 74*

gender *167*

genetic adaptation *176*

Gilligan, James *175*

Gladwell, Malcolm *153, 163*

Glamorgan University *167*

globalisation *58*

Gloucester *187*

  Gloucester Police Station *188*

GMTV *131, 137, 139*

God

  playing God *133*

Goddard, Dave *119*

Godfrey, Susan *145*

going native *xix*

good *179*

  good practice *182, 183, 191*

  "good press" *60*

Google *xx*

Grantham Hosptial *110*

gratification *115*

  instant gratification *162*

Greater Manchester *68*

greed *135*

Gregory, Sandra *89, 91*

Grendon Prison *xiv, 53, 176*

Griffiths, Stephen *126, 129, 130*

Grimsby *25*

Groombridge, Nic *xvi, xvii*

grooming *26*

Guardian *xvii, 70, 87, 102, 103, 170*

guilt *175*

Gull, Detective Chief Superintend-
    ent Stewart *62, 63, 185*
guns *140, 143, 170*
    access to *147*
    Few Kind Words and a Loaded Gun, A *88*
    gun control *135, 147*
    gun crime *39*
    shotgun licence *144*

H

Haggerty, Kevin *111*
Haigh, John George *129*
Halford, Alison *75*
Hall, Steve *125*
hallucinations *157*
Hamilton, Thomas *53, 134, 135, 143*
hanging *xv, 130*
Hannibal Lector *42, 57, 59*
happiness
    unhappiness *28, 30*
Hardy, Trevor *110, 112, 114, 123*
harm *184*
    inflicting harm *172*
Harrison, Paul *46, 137, 152*
Harris, Thomas *153*
Hart, Alan *119*
"haves" and "have nots" *64*
Hazlewood, Roy *161*
health
    Health Act 2006 *101*
Heath, Neville *116, 125*
Henwood, Detective Superintend-
    ent Andy *63*

hero
    anti-hero *136, 139*
    cursed-heroes *151*
    superhero *140*
Hindley, Myra *109, 110*
historical figures *xvi*
hitting *170*
HM Prison Larkhall *92*
HM Prison Service *68*
holiday camps *97*
Home Office *37, 38, 74, 83, 169*
    Home Office Homicide Index *169, 171*
homicide
    Home Office Homicide Index *169, 171*
Home Secretary *37, 82, 98, 99, 103,*
    104, 117, 128
homicide *167, 169*
    homicidal protest *125*
    Homicide (the book) *177*
homoeroticism *91*
homophobia *xxiii, 165*
hostage-taking *90*
hostility *118*
    hostile interpersonal violence *125*
hot spots *xxii*
Howard Journal of Criminal Justice
    xv, xvii
Howard League *xiv*
Howard, Michael *117*
Howe, Nick *xvii*
Hulk (The Incredible Hulk) *140,*
    142
Hull Prison *117*
human emotions *135*
humanisation *105*

humanity *92*

Hungerford *134, 135, 143, 145, 147*

Hunt, Detective Inspector Gene *78*

hunting

    Hunting Evil and The Lost British Serial
        Killer 152

hunting

    Hunting Evil: Inside the Ipswich Serial
        Murders 46

hunting

    Hunting Humans 164

Huntley, Ian *118, 187*

hurt *xxiv*

Hyde *54, 159*

hysteria *28*

I

id *174*

identity *25, 35, 146, 172, 174*

    identification *47*

idiosyncracy *xix, 123*

image *140, 142, 145*

    images of pain, torture, etc. *58*

immigrants *165*

impact *xxi*

incarceration

    inappropriate incarceration *95*

incompetence *95, 118*

indecent exposure *114*

independence *70*

Independent Police Complaints
    Commission (IPCC) *139*

individuality *132*

infanticide *169*

influence *xxiii*

    influencing the public debate *xiv*

Ingram, David *25*

inheritance *176*

injustice *140*

ink blot test *176*

Innocence Betrayed: Paedophilia, the
    Media and Society xx

innovation *74*

Inside the Mind of BTK, etc. 161

instability

    relationships of *146*

intelligence *143*

    intelligence-led policing *136*

internet *35, 138, 139, 148*

    anonymity *35*

    downloading pornographic images *40*

    internet chatroom *25*

    online communities *28*

    online reports *25*

interpersonal dynamics *178*

interviews *33*

Ipswich *xxii, 36, 62, 124, 126, 128, 137,*
    181, 188, 189, 190

    Ipswich Crown Court *54*

Ireland, Colin *61, 110*

isolation *73*

ITV *187*

ivory towers *xvi*

J

Jack Crawford *152*

Jackson, Craig *xvii*

Jack the Ripper *57, 59, 64*

    Ripperologists *59, 65*

    Ripper walks *59*

    worst Briton ever *60*

James, Erwin *88*

James, James *102*

jealousy *135*

Jeffreys, Alec *48*

Jewkes, Yvonne *112*

"Jigsaw Man, The" *152*

John O'Gaunt Community Technical College *143*

journalism

    investigative journalism *xx*

    "new journalism" *150*

    supermarket journalism *xx*

journalists *46*

    international journalists *190*

    investigative journalists *186, 188*

    journalists going "walkabout" *188*

Jo Whiley Programme *26*

jury *49, 52*

justice *xi, 49*

justification *140, 141, 157*

K

Kansas (USA) *161*

Katz, Jack *176*

Kearney, Martha *138*

Kelly, Ian *48*

kicking *170*

kidnap *41*

Killer in the Shadows *152*

"killing for company" *157*

Kirby, Albert *168*

L

labelling *xi, xxiii, 42, 53, 56, 113, 122, 144, 146*

lads' mags *91*

Lake District *134, 135*

Lambert, Roy *168*

Langdale, Timothy QC *50*

language of the media *62*

Lapland New Forest *41*

Lard Yao Prison, Thailand *91*

Larsson, Stieg *150*

Lau, Peter *50*

law enforcement *151, 162*

Lawrence, Stephen *74*

leaks *38, 189, 190*

Leatham, Andrew *119*

leaving home *xxiii*

Leech, Mark *88*

Leeds *113*

Leeds University *57*

left-leaning principles *xvii*

legends *139, 151*

Leicestershire Police *47*

Leicester University *xx, 48, 180*

Lemaitre, Sergeant Pierre *84*

lesbians *29, 95*

Levy, Peter *33, 35*

LexisNexis *102*

Leyton, Elliott *110, 125, 164*

life imprisonment *114, 117, 173*
   whole life term *52, 117*
limits on reporting *181*
Lincoln Prison *129*
Little Dorritt *150*
live broadcasting *31*
Liverpool Daily Echo *103*
lives less ordinary *26*
Loader, Ian *xviii*
loneliness *28*
"looking good" *185*
Look North *35*
losers *129*
"losing face" *132*
Love, Andy *90*
"low life" *121*
loyalty *140*

M

machismo *73, 74, 75, 84*
Macpherson Inquiry *74*
"macro" issues *167*
madness *173*
   mad or bad *121, 122, 157*
making things "better" *xxiv*
malice aforethought *169*
Manchester Evening News *113, 114,*
   118, 119
Manchester University *153*
manhunt *124*
manipulation *157*
Mann, Lynda *47*
manslaughter *117, 169*

Mantell, Mr Justice *189*
manual *xviii, xix*
Manzoor, Safraz *56*
Mapping Murder: Walking in Killers
   Footsteps *152*
marginalisation *126, 165*
Martlesham *183*
massacre *135*
mass murderers *53*
Masters, Brian *157*
masturbation *162*
Matthews, Karen *40*
Matthews, Shannon *40, 43*
Mawby, Rob *xx, 180*
McCann, Kate and Gerry *39*
McCombe, Mr Justice *41, 43*
McDonnell, Marsha *56*
McTeer, Janet *63*
media *xv, xx, xxi, xxiii, 148*
   access to money *189*
   allocation of media resources *124*
   "a machine to make money" *187*
   arm's length relationship with the police
      183, 185, 188
   as an investigative resource *180*
   asymmetrical relationship *190*
   balance of power *190, 191*
   briefing the media *187*
   buying witness accounts *189*
   cheating the press *185, 188*
   complicity *33*
   controlling media situations *185*
   crime reporting *111*
   effective media handling *180*
   "giving them something" *185*

"good with the media" *185*

intimacy *33*

keeping the media onside *190*

managing the media *xx*

media barristers *189*

media dialogue *187*

media frenzy *124*

media goatee *34*

media investigations *186, 188, 190*

media needs *181, 185*

media pressures *181*

    pressure to produce a story *188*

media reporting centre *188*

media skills *34*

media studies *35*

"media tart" *xix*

negotiations with the media *190*

off the record *187*

old media *xvii*

"pack of feral beasts" *180*

paying for interviews *189*

police-media relations *180*

police use of the media *167*

pool facility *187*

ready-made for prime time *118*

rise of the mass media *111*

role in investigations *180*

surveying the surveillance team *187*

suspicion of the media *190*

value of the media *184*

Meehan, Craig *40*

mental health *95*

    mental disturbance *175*

    mental illness *42, 103*

mentors *97, 102, 104, 105, 107*

Merseyside Police *75*

message *93*

Metropolitan Police Service *75, 80*

"Midsomer Murders" *137*

minimising behaviour *140, 141*

miscarriages of justice *45*

misogyny *141*

missing *25, 29, 30, 63*

mission *73*

Mizen, Jimmy *172, 173, 175, 177, 179*

Moat, Raoul *136, 139, 142, 143, 167*

mobility *60*

modernity *126*

    modernity's self-image *111*

monsters

    "climbing inside the heads of monsters"
        151, 164

Moore, Peter *53, 110*

Moors Murderers *54, 118*

morality *74, 99, 111, 175*

    moral panic *125*

Morrall, Peter *57*

Mosoph, Sharon *116, 117, 124*

motivation *67, 152, 154, 157, 167*

motive *121, 127, 131, 133, 155*

    sexual motive *157*

murder *41, 80, 95, 167, 169*

    diverse phenomenon *168*

    former "year and a day" rule *169*

    Murderer Next Door, The 177

    murder investigations *190*

    ordinary murder *167*

    "typical murder" *179*

    unsolved murders *111*

murder

Murder Investigation Manual (MIM) 180

myths 80, 87

N

naming and shaming *xv*

Narborough 47

narcissism 139, 141

narrative 31, 38, 40, 63, 89, 100, 111

   serial killers 47

near-death experience 151

neglect 30

neighbourliness 134

neutralisation 141

New Bridge *xv*

"news" 29, 38, 44

news 31

   24-hour news channels 180

   breaking news 62

   news agenda 36

   newsroom culture 111

   news values 112, 123

   newsworthiness 111, 112, 113, 114, 118,
      123

   offenders following the news 160

   police-centric crime news 186

   web-based news 180

"Newsnight" *xvi*

Newsnight 131

News of the World 119, 120

newspapers

   newspaper reports 25

   selling newspapers 56

New Statesman 103

New York 153, 155

New Yorker 153

Nicholls, Annette 45

Nicholson, Andrew 106

nicknames 122

Nicol, Tania 45, 51, 63, 181

night-time economy 125

Nilsen, Dennis 47, 53, 61, 110, 157

No More Victims *xvi*

Non-governmental Organization
     (NGO) *xviii, xix*

"non lethal force" 85

no-nonsense 74, 140

normality 53, 58

   appearing normal 159

   normal location (in prison) 88, 91

   normal relationships 114

Norris, Colin 54

Northumbria Police 136, 143

O

O'Brien, Stanley 114

obscurity 123, 125

Observer, The 102

Offences Against the Person Act
    1861 168

offender profiling 113, 149

   handbook 160

   North America 149

   "second wave" 149

   "submerged" approach 152

offenders

   disorganized/disorganized offenders 160

family and friends *131*
Old Bailey *172*
Oldham Magistrates' Court *117*
"one-stop" criminological shop *xix*
on the radar *63*
opportunity *xix, 131*
   opportunistic crimes *160*
organized offenders *60, 130, 159*
Osmond, Louise *62*
Otero family *161*
own goal *138*
Oxford Prison *92*
"Oz" *92*

P

paedophiles *xx, 26, 27, 139, 146*
Palmer, Roy *51*
paperwork *73, 74, 80*
paranoia *139, 140*
Parker, Norman *88*
parole *97, 99, 115, 156*
passion *135*
pathology *40, 114*
   individual pathology *145*
Peace, David *78*
Pearce, Elizabeth *158*
Peckham, Audrey *89*
peer-review *xxi, 33*
personality *154, 159, 172, 174*
   anti-social personality *159*
   borderline personality disorder *146*
   Cluster B personality type *139, 146*
   dangerous personalities *165*

lone-wolf *162*
pessimism *73*
Peterhead Prison *xiv*
Philadelphia *150*
Picking up the Pieces *152*
Piles, Stephen *105*
Pitchfork, Colin *48*
planning *160*
pleasure *57, 92, 93*
   pleasure principle *174*
policing
   Police Authorities *82*
   policing strategy *80*
   tripartite model of policing *82*
policy *xix*
   policy-makers *xxi*
politicians *xxi*
"Porridge" *92, 95, 96*
Portugal *40*
positivism
   individual positivism *168*
poverty *67, 167*
power *127, 133, 135, 140, 141, 162*
   powerlessness *175*
pragmatism *73, 74, 75, 84*
precariousness *125*
prejudice *50, 73, 124*
   against sex workers *165*
press
   press conferences *138*
   press officers *xx, 184, 186*
primary definers *124*
primitive urges *174*
prison
   holiday camps *xv*

prison conditions *89*

prison landings, etc. *96*

prison officers *102*

prison regimes *xiv*

Prisons Video *xv*

prison writing *150*

use of prison *xxii*

prisoners

alien other *92*

"Prisoner Cell Block H" *93*

Pritchard, Paul *84*

problem-solving *73*

prostitution *xxiii, 36, 42, 52, 53, 61,*
74, 113, 121, 127, 130, 165

protecting society *73*

psychiatry *151, 156*

psychology *98, 99, 126, 130, 151, 156,*
167, 171

clinical psychology *174*

cognitive psychology *178*

evolutionary psychology *176*

"medical-psychological" tradition *152*

psychoanalytical psychology *174*

psychological predisposition *168*

psychometric evaluation *45, 46*

psychopaths *42*

psycho-therapy *53*

public

public criminology *xiv, xv, xviii, xxiii, 91*

Charles Dickens *150*

public debate *xv*

public discourse *xxi*

public interest *112*

monitoring *124*

public opinion *xi*

public persona *146*

public policy *xv, xix*

publicity *40*

build up of publicity *119*

local publicity *118*

public service pretensions *104*

Q

quarrelling *171*

R

racism *78, 95, 167*

Rader, Dennis *150, 152, 160, 163, 164*

Radio 4 *138*

rage *135, 179*

Rambo *140, 142*

Rampton, James *105*

random

random behaviour *132*

random crimes *160*

rape *25, 36, 41, 47, 102*

serial rape *154*

rapport *138, 187*

Rathband, David *136, 140, 143*

reality *96*

reason *xvi*

light of reason *42*

recorded crime *79*

Red Dragon *57, 152*

red-hot nature of the public discourse *xvi*

red light districts *127, 130*

"Red Riding" *78*

re-fashioning *31*

reform *80, 82, 85, 91, 94, 97, 105, 107, 150*

  penal reform *xiv, 105*

Reiner, Robert *72, 111*

relationships *94, 157*

remorse *118, 133*

rent a quote *xix*

research *xiv, 29, 74, 75*

respect

  disrespect *140*

Ressler, Robert *154*

restorative justice *104*

revenge *135, 171*

Rewcastle, Darren *131*

"ring of steel" *136*

riot *96*

River Aire *130*

robbery *37, 171, 172*

Robin Hood *140, 142*

Rochdale Canal *116*

roof-top protests *96*

Rothbury *136, 138, 139, 142, 147*

Rowrah *131*

Royal Canadian Mounted Police *83*

Royal Courts of Justice *45, 117*

Rudge, Matt *57*

running away *28, 29*

Rushworth, Susan *127, 130*

Ryan, Michael *134, 135, 143*

S

sadism *118, 153*

safety *65*

satisfaction *57*

Scarborough Prison *97, 100, 102*

"scared straight" *104*

schadenfreude *58*

science *48, 49, 149*

Scotland *79, 136*

Scotsman, The *103*

Scott-Lee, Sir Paul QPM *69, 70*

screws

  predatory screw *94*

"Se7en" *59*

secondary definers *124*

security staff *140*

Seductions of Crime, etc, The *179*

Segregation Unit *88, 89*

selectivity *111*

"self" *175*

self

  self-defence *172*

  self-destruction *175*

  self-discovery *129*

  self-esteem *175, 178*

  self-harm *30, 95*

  self-image *142, 146*

  "selfish genes" *177*

  self-loathing *135*

  self-perpetuating oligarchy *85*

  self-propelling stories *124*

  self-serving charm *42*

  self-serving views *156*

  sense of self *144*

Self, Will *88*

selling newspapers *187*

sensuality *58*

serial killers *xiv, xv, xx, xxii, 36, 42, 45,
52, 53, 56, 64, 109, 113, 114,
118, 129, 150, 154*

  as celebrities *56*

  definition *53*

  Glasgow serial killer *136*

  "homicidal protest" *165*

  "My Dad the Serial Killer" *56, 62*

  psychology of *64*

  ready-made for prime time *111*

  "serial killer specifics" *47*

  serial killer syndrome *120, 124*

serial killers

  *Serial Killers: Hunting Britons and Their
Victims, 1960-2006 xxii, 113*

serial rape *154*

serious offences *149*

sex *58, 174*

  sex discrimination *76*

  sexism *78*

  sex offenders *xiv, xv*

  sexual assault *48*

  sex workers *127*

sex

  Sexual Homicide: Patterns and Motives 154

shaman *152*

shame *175*

Sharp, Doug *xvii*

Sheedy, Kate *56*

Sheffield *61*

Shipman, Harold *47, 54, 110, 120,
132*

silence *158*

shooting *131, 140, 143, 170*

  random shooting *133*

show of force *84*

silence *159*

Silence of the Lambs, The *57, 152*

silencing *70*

  silencing potential witnesses *144*

silver bullet *58*

Sim, Sue *140*

Skala, Wanda *115, 117, 124*

Sky TV *181*

  Sky News *31, 46, 62, 114, 137*

slaughter *179*

  righteous slaughter *131, 133*

slobs *xv*

slopping-out *96*

Smith and Wesson *143*

Smith, Jacqui *37*

Smith, Noel "Razor" *88*

social

  social convention *175*

  social division *125*

  social learning *171, 178, 179*

  social-networking *142*

  social situations *178*

  social structure *145*

  social surveys *37*

socio-economics *165*

sodomy *41*

Soham *118, 168, 181, 184, 186*

solidarity *73, 75, 85*

solitary confinement *96*

somebody

  wanting to be a somebody *130*

"Son of Sam" *154*

Southampton *171*

Sparks, Richard *xviii*

special units *88, 89*

speculation *124*

spokespersons *183, 185, 190*

spree killers *53, 131, 133, 134*

stabbing *170*

Stainforth, Laura *25, 28, 32, 39*

Stapleton, John *137*

status *112*

    social status *121*

staying away *29*

Stephens, Tom *187*

step-parents *177*

stereotyping *73*

Stevenson, Chris *168*

Stewart, Janet *115*

stigma *40*

Stobbart, Samantha *136*

straight's account *89, 92*

stranger violence *126*

Strangeways (Manchester Prison) *114*

strangulation *47, 115, 116, 170*

"street smarts" *151*

success

    measuring success *xvi*

suffocation

    in small societies *133*

Suffolk Constabulary *52, 183, 185*

suicide *30, 95, 96, 131, 135, 136, 143, 145, 148, 159, 178*

    egoistic, etc. suicide *145*

    "suicide by cop" *139*

    suicide in all but name *69*

Sunday Mirror *187*

Sunday People *119*

Sun, The *105, 127*

superego *174*

Superman *55, 135*

support *107*

survivalism *144*

suspicion *73*

Sutcliffe, Peter *54, 61, 110, 113, 127, 130, 157*

T

tabloids *189*

    tabloid staples *xv*

tactical exploitation *125*

talking heads *184*

targeting the face *132*

tariff *173*

tarts *121*

Taser-gun *74, 83, 139*

"Taxi Driver". *141*

Taylor, Laurie *xvii*

Teare, Mr Justice *117*

techniques *xix*

temper *173*

    loss of temper *171*

tensions *190*

Teten, Howard *153*

Thatcher, Margaret *79, 83*

theft

    car theft *80*

"The Murderer in Our Midst" *56*

therapy *53*
   therapeutic communities *176*
thin blue line *65, 70*
thinking
   "Thinking Allowed" *xvii*
   think tank *xxi*
Thompson, Jeremy *137*
threats *xix*
throwaways *29*
ticking all the boxes *123*
timescale *143*
Times, The *103, 113*
   Times Higher Education *xvi*
Tobin, Peter *xxii, 136, 137*
Todd, Michael QPM *68, 76, 83*
   Achilles Heel *76*
Todmorden *158, 159*
Tolputt, Harriet *114*
Tom Ripley *59*
tools *105*
Too Young to Die? *xvi*
training
   presenting training *xviii*
Travis, Alan *170*
Travis Bickle *141*
Treadwell, James *xvii*
treatment *176*
Tribune *xvii*
triggers for offending *155*
trite characterisation *150*
truancy *67*
true crime genre *xxiii, 152*
trust *138*
truth *49, 158*
Tulloch, John *105*

twisting *31*
Twitter *xvii*

U

underclass *40, 136*
unguarded moments *184*
United States of America *xx, 150, 164*
   policing *79*
"us" and "them"
   prison in *96*

V

values *64*
Vancouver *83*
vandalism *80*
Vian, Shirley *161*
victims *xix, 37, 39, 45, 59, 60, 80, 111, 113, 121, 124, 125, 131, 149, 153, 167, 177*
   babies and infants as *165*
   characteristics *154*
   elderly victims *42, 54, 165*
   families and friends of *63, 117*
   gay men as *165*
   medical examination *154*
   murder, of *170*
   nice girls *121*
   "offenders as victims" *47*
   readily identifiable groups *165*
   through the eyes of the victims *62*

victim selection *154, 155, 162*

young people moving home *165*

viewing figures *124, 187*

violence *37, 39, 58, 80, 94, 102, 112, 125, 127, 134, 140, 149, 153, 167, 175, 178, 179*

domestic violence *141*

expressive violence *172*

instrumental violence *172*

lethal violence *175*

Violence: Reflections on our Deadliest Epidemic *175*

voice *95, 150*

denied in childhood *34*

voiceover (VO) *63*

voices *xix, 127*

vulnerability *64*

W

Wakefield Prison *159*

Walker, Ron *161*

weapons *39, 132, 135, 138*

global supply of cheap weapons *148*

sharp instrument *170*

website analysis *124*

Wells, Holly *168, 181*

werewolf *57, 58*

werewolf culture *58*

Western Mail *103*

West, Fred and Rose *47, 109, 110, 120, 157, 159, 181*

West Midlands Police *69*

West Sussex *25*

West Yorkshire *78*

West Yorkshire Police *41*

Whitechapel *59*

"Whitechapel" *59, 70*

Whitehaven *131, 133, 142, 146, 147*

whole world watching *182, 190*

Wichita *152, 161*

wickedness *41*

Williams, Robert Andrew *25*

Williams-Thomas, Mark *xvii*

Wilson, Margo *177*

Winchester Crown Court *189*

Winlow, Simon *125*

Wintercomfort *89*

Wise, Gordon *46*

women *75, 88, 93, 94, 140, 165*

Woman in Custody, A *89*

Woodhill Prison *87*

"World at One, The" *38, 138*

worthlessness *175*

Wright, Peter QC *51*

Wright, Steve *45, 49, 54, 62, 65, 124, 127, 137, 168, 181*

writing styles *xviii*

Wyner, Ruth *89*

Y

yobs *xv*

Yorkshire Ripper *54, 61, 78, 109, 113, 121, 127, 130, 157*

young prisoners *99*

youth offending team *105*

Lightning Source UK Ltd.
Milton Keynes UK
UKOW051052280313

208320UK00002B/4/P